THE ORIENTAL ANNUAL, OR SCENES IN INDIA

THE ORIENTAL ANNUAL, OR SCENES IN INDIA

BY THE

REV. HOBART CAUNTER, B.D.

WITH

TWENTY-TWO ENGRAVINGS

FROM DRAWINGS

BY

WILLIAM DANIELL, R.A.

GYAN

Published by

GYAN

Gyan Publishing House
5, Ansari Road
Daryaganj, New Delhi-110002
Phone: 011-47034999, 9811692060
E-mail: books@gyanbooks.com

Distribution Network
gyanbooks.com
India, USA, Canada, UK, Australia, France

ISBN : 978-81-212-3855-7 (**PB**)
First Published, 1836

2nd Impression 2020

Printed at: Gyan Press, Delhi.

The book at your disposal is the edition of an old book originally published long back. The Text quality of this book may not be at par as compared to our other books but many readers approached us to reprint this important book so that it could satiate their hunger. We request all the readers of this book to help us to improve its quality by providing the necessary text of those pages which are not properly visible. Your valuable support in this case will be highly appreciated and acknowledged and our future readers will be benefitted immensely.

THE

ORIENTAL ANNUAL,

OR

Scenes in India;

COMPRISING

TWENTY-TWO ENGRAVINGS

FROM ORIGINAL DRAWINGS

BY WILLIAM DANIELL, R.A.

AND

A DESCRIPTIVE ACCOUNT

BY THE REV. HOBART CAUNTER, B.D.

LONDON:

PUBLISHED FOR THE PROPRIETOR, BY

EDWARD CHURTON, 26, HOLLES STREET.

1836.

The Oriental Annual 1836

The Adjutant.

From a Drawing by W. Daniell R.A.

THIS VOLUME IS,

BY GRACIOUS PERMISSION,

DEDICATED TO THEIR ROYAL HIGHNESSES

THE DUCHESS OF KENT AND THE PRINCESS VICTORIA.

PREFACE.

THE first series of the ORIENTAL ANNUAL is now completed. The signal success of the first two volumes has encouraged the proprietor to incur a further expense in rendering the engravings still more worthy of public patronage.

Upon this head it will be sufficient to say that five of the subjects have been engraved by Brandard, and two by John Pye; the remainder by the best engravers employed on the former numbers.

Next year will commence an entirely new series, connected with the most interesting portion of Indian history.

ENGRAVINGS

FROM

Drawings

BY

WILLIAM DANIELL, ESQ. R.A.

IN THE HARBOUR OF MASCAT (Frontispiece.)
THE ADJUTANT (Vignette Title.)
A RICH MAHOMEDAN . . . . . . Page 16
THE TIGER HUNT 43
THE CHOULTRY OF TREMAL NAIG AT MADURA . . 51
HINDOO TEMPLE AT TRITCHENGUR . . . 59
THE BRAMINEE BULL 71
A HINDOO WOMAN 96
ON THE BALIAPATAM RIVER 105
SCENE NEAR THE COAST OF MALABAR . . . 132
THE SMALL DEER OF CEYLON 141
LION AND BUFFALOE 156
THE MONKEY AND CROWS 173
NEAR MASCAT 182
THE FORTS OF JELLALI AND MERANI MASCAT . . 191
BOMBAY 213
TOMB OF A PATAN CHIEF, OLD DELHI . . . 231
TOMBS OF PATAN CHIEFS, OLD DELHI . . . 243
ON THE ISLAND OF ELEPHANTA 257
ENTRANCE TO THE CAVE OF ELEPHANTA . . . 263
ENTRANCE TO THE LARGE CAVE, SALSETTE. . . 272
THE UPPER CAVES, SALSETTE 284

SCENES IN INDIA.

CHAPTER I.

EMBARK FOR MADRAS.—A HURRICANE.

SHORTLY after the breaking-up of the monsoon, we took our passage to Madras in a country ship: it was a fine vessel, built of teak, and about six hundred tons burthen. Besides our party, there was only one passenger, a lady, on her way to join her husband who had a command somewhere on the Coromandel coast. I occupied a small cabin under the poop, on the right-hand side as you entered the cuddy. The ship was commanded by an old weather-beaten seaman who had lost an eye, over which he wore a black patch, that gave a fierceness to the expression of his countenance, naturally rough and grim, by no means conciliating. He was besides deeply seamed with the small-pox, which imparted to his broad rigid features an asperity that repelled courtesy, and rendered him at first unpopular among his passengers, though he was a prodigious favourite with the crew. The fact was, that although his face presented such an unfavourable index of the inward man, it was really a false interpreter: for, under the most forbidding exterior, this man possessed great kindliness of nature. His coarse boisterous sincerity soon lost its rust, and we saw through the superficial crust that there was the polish of kindly feelings beneath; and he shortly became an object, if not of respect, at least of general well-liking. There were two officers besides the captain, and a crew of forty Lascars. One of the officers was a young man of education and of considerable literary attainments; the other was a much commoner order of person, although esteemed by the men as admirably skilled in the science of seamanship.

On the afternoon of the second day after we had left Calcutta, having cleared the Sunderbunds, we amused ourselves by throwing out a bait for a shark. A large fish soon took the hook, but so desperate were its struggles, that it snapped the rope and escaped. Another tackle, newer and stronger, was immediately prepared, when the same fish almost instantly seized it, and, after a mighty resistance, was drawn up over the ship's side and safely lodged upon the deck. The hook of the first line was stuck fast in its throat, while the last hook was securely fastened in its stomach. Its strength was prodigious, and so furiously did it lash the deck with its tail, as to render it dangerous to approach within its sweep. With a single stroke it overturned one of the guns; the carpenter then severed the dangerous member with the blow of an axe; after which, the savage creature was quickly despatched. It measured nineteen feet. When opened, there was taken from its stomach a piece of solid timber thirteen inches long, and as thick as a man's arm, which it had no doubt swallowed in mistake for something more nutritious; for so ravenous are these creatures, that they have been frequently known to devour greedily not only wood, but even pieces of iron.

Two days after we had fairly got into the bay of Bengal, the weather began to threaten. The previous night had been exceedingly sultry. The air appeared stagnant, as if it had suddenly ceased to circulate, and the heat in consequence became painfully oppressive. In the morning the wind blew fresh, and all the sails were reefed, in consequence of the lowering aspect of the heavens. There was a faint haze over the sun, which gave a brassy tint to its beams, and these were reflected dimly upon the surging waters. The Lascars, who are never fond of preparing against a gale, did their duty sluggishly, and looked grave and uneasy. The captain foretold foul weather, though to an inexperienced eye there was nothing to warrant so unfavourable a foreboding. The wind continued fresh all the morning, but did not materially increase for the first two or three hours. After breakfast the passengers, of whom there were but six, seated themselves in the stern gallery, some watching the progress of the weather, and others making an effort to beguile the dulness of the morning by playing at chess or backgammon. The whole scene was marked by an indefinite dreariness; no one expressed any positive apprehension, yet the captain's unqualified prediction of a stiff gale imposed upon every countenance a gravity not a little ominous of ill. There was something startling in the very unusual appearance of the sky:

a mysterious but omnipotent hand had traced upon its broad expanse mystical characters not to be definitively interpreted, but yet, like the handwriting on the wall in the palace of the Chaldean king, of most portentous aspect. The only lady among us every now and then expressed her fears, when a sudden gust caused the vessel to lurch with an increased momentum, as if the billows were already commencing a fiercer conflict.

By noon the wind had risen to a steady gale, yet there was nothing to excite immediate apprehension. The clouds had by this time obscured the sun, over which they rolled in dark misshapen masses, appearing at intervals as if they had been torn asunder by the wind and scattered in gigantic fragments through the troubled air. The very forms they assumed had that monstrous indistinctness of outline such as the imagination shapes in sleep, bringing before the entranced eye shadowy nothings which impart a vague but actual feeling of terror. Fancy gave them now an indefinite yet palpable existence—I mean a vital existence—and each fantastic volume that passed over the ship changing its form with every fresh burst of the blast, seemed a new harbinger of mischief.

> "The firmament is filled with scatter'd clouds,
> And as they fly before the wind, their forms,
> As in a picture, image various shapes—
> The semblances of storks and soaring swans,
> Of dolphins and huge monsters of the deep,
> Of dragons vast, and pinnacles and towers."*

---

* From the "Mrichchakati," or "Toy-cart," a Hindoo drama.

By four o'clock in the afternoon it blew a perfect hurricane, and the vessel was lying-to under a close-reefed main-topsail. The ports were all fastened down, and the guns drawn in upon the quarter-deck. The hatches were well secured, and every precaution taken which the most vigilant foresight could suggest against the probable devastations of the storm.

While we were seated in the cuddy, not quietly but very uneasily taking our tea, the vessel appeared of a sudden to leap over a gigantic billow, and the moment she had recovered her libration, she rolled so heavily that her bulwarks were nearly under water. The tables were forced from their stays, overturned, and all the tea-things shattered to pieces; we were thrown from our chairs, and for a minute or two the utmost confusion prevailed. Scarcely had we resumed some degree of composure, before one of the guns broke from its lashings, and rolled from side to side of the quarter-deck each time the ship yielded to the fierce impulse of the waters, threatening with every shock, as it dashed against the bulwarks, to force its way through into the deep, to the positive danger of the vessel. In one of its furious migrations, it struck a dripstone, which had been secured in a corner near the cabins, released it from the strong wooden case in which it was confined, and sent it bounding upon the deck, placing in great peril those who were engaged in the necessary duties of the ship. The noise occasioned by these huge masses dashing from side to side, added to the howling of the wind and the fierce lashing of the waters, was painful in the extreme. The Lascars were afraid to oppose themselves to the destructive course of these ponderous bodies, which had so unexpectedly escaped from their assigned stations, and seemed about to add seriously to the mischiefs already fearfully threatened by the storm. At length, the second officer having dexterously cast a noose over the gun, brought the rope suddenly round the capstern, to which the carriage was soon fastened, and here it was suffered to remain for the moment. The stone was now easily secured, and thus our immediate anxiety was quieted.

The wind continued to blow with terrific violence, and the Lascars were evidently becoming indifferent about working the ship. This is one of the characteristics of Indian sailors. In stormy weather, whenever the case appears an extreme one, they abandon themselves to dogged apathy which nothing can rouse: their notions of predestination lead them to imagine that their time is come; and thus, instead of striving to avert the threatened calamity, they sullenly await the apprehended destruction. Ships have been frequently lost by this sluggish and unmanly despair on the part of these blind predestinarians. It has been wisely said by one of their own sages, "danger should be feared when absent, and braved when present;" but they entirely reverse the maxim, and give way to the most superstitious apprehensions. It fortunately happened that we had a few Manilla men on board, who by their active example stirred up the torpid energies of some of the Lascars, which else they might have refused to exercise.

As night drew on, and the hurricane rather increased than abated, every precaution was used to make all secure for the night; but the captain was evidently thoughtful and uneasy, his cheek was flushed and his eye restless. He gave his orders with all the coolness and precision derived from long experience, but it was evident that his mind was labouring under unusual excitement. He turned continually to the weather with an earnest but unquiet gaze; stood frequently by the man at the wheel; watched him as he steered, every now and then seizing one of the spokes with an impulsive eagerness which evinced a highly perturbed state of feeling. I could not help observing this, and it led to conclusions not at all calculated to prepare me for a peaceful night's rest. I began to be extremely disquieted; and though I did not venture to express my apprehension, the saddest ideas were continually crowding upon my thoughts and filling my breast with tumultuous emotions.

The wind was by this time frightfully violent. At intervals the captain vociferated his orders through a trumpet, which sounded amid the howlings of the storm like the hoarse cries of some evil spirit by which its merciless fury was excited and kept in play. The uproar is not to be described! At length all had retired to their cabins save the captain and myself. We were both seated in the cuddy; I upon the carriage of a gun, to which I was obliged to cling to preserve my equilibrium. He was smoking a cigar; and our conversation, now carried on with some difficulty, turned naturally upon the hurricane, against which the ship was at that moment most fearfully labouring. Suddenly, a heavy sea struck her astern, but happily on the quarter, and in an instant carried away the quarter-gallery on that side, swamping the cabin into which the poor lady before spoken of had retired for the night. The force of the water was so great, that it dashed open the door of the cabin, and its fair occupant was borne head foremost into the cuddy, dripping like a mermaid, her hair hanging about her shoulders in long thin strips, when she was rescued by the captain from further mischief. She was drenched to the skin. It was a pitiable sight to see her quick and almost convulsive gaspings—her eye upturned with a deep settled glare of half-consciousness, that seemed as if her mind were in a state between terror and agony, to neither of which she could give expression, as the water had nearly suffocated her. The blood had receded from her cheeks, which were overspread with a dull bluish white. In a few moments she recovered her breath, when she shrieked and fainted. A dry boat-cloak was thrown round her, and the captain gallantly resigned to her his cabin, where she soon recovered, and changed her wet attire. Although the damage done was considerable, yet the breach made by sweeping off the quarter-gallery was immediately stopped by the carpenter, who nailed up a few stout planks, and covered them with a thick tarpaulin.

It was late before I retired to my cot, and some time before I could sleep: weariness, however, at length overcame me, and in spite of the dreadful howling of the hurricane I slept. I remember well my dreams were troubled; I had a confused perception of danger which was more painful than the most vivid sense of peril. The roar of the gale and the heavy booming of the ship as she laboured through the waters broke sensibly upon my ear, in spite of the repelling power of slumber. Every instant I beheld, though indistinctly, objects of horror, which were on a sudden dispersed by the heavy pitching of the vessel, that for a moment restored me to consciousness; but sleep soon again overpowered my senses, and placed her terrifying phantoms before me. I fancied myself upon a rock in the midst of an illimitable ocean, the waters of which were raging around with frightful commotion: a huge raven was perched close at my side, its hideous eyes glaring upon me with an expression that I could not mistake, and which shot through my frame a pang of irrepressible agony. The waters lashed the base of the rock with a fury that made it vibrate to the very foundation, and I felt as if I should be every instant cast among its mountainous billows. The whole surface of the ocean was as red as blood, which disclosed its hideous crimson every time the lightning, that was perpetually breaking from the heavens, illumined the shoreless expanse upon which my eyes were fixed in terror. In the hollows of the waves lay the bodies of the drowned, and of some persons yet alive, struggling in the last agonies of a most appalling death. At this moment the thunder crashed; the lightning glared, struck the rock, and shivered it: the whole mass was riven; it yawned at my feet, and a frightful chasm threatened to engulf me. The raven perched upon my breast, flapped its wings in my face, and I fell backward into the horrible abyss.

I awoke in agony, and to my consternation found

that my cot had struck against the roof of the cabin, where it remained motionless; it no longer swung. For the instant I fancied the vessel was in the act of sinking—I knew not what to think. When my senses had somewhat recovered from the shock and terrible impression of my dream, I sprang from the cot upon the cabin-floor. I heard a dreadful uproar upon deck, and with a half-frantic desperation threw myself into the cuddy. I had no other dress on than that in which I had retired to my cot for the night. The noise upon deck increased, and my anxiety by this time amounted to positive torment. I reached the cuddy door, and opened it with a heart full of wild and tumultuous apprehensions. I had scarcely done this, when a gigantic billow poured over the bow of the ship, hissing and sparkling in the impeded moonlight, and I stood upon the quarter-deck up to my shoulders in water. I clung for an instant to the ladder of the poop, which, as soon as I could recover myself, I ascended. Here I witnessed a scene which I shall never forget to the latest moment of my existence. When memory brings the picture to my mind, with the long shadows of years between it and the reality, it shakes me even now. I never carry my thoughts back to this fearful night that the minutest circumstance of the scene does not recur to my recollection with the most awful distinctness: it is one of those events only to be wiped from the records of memory in that grave "where all things are forgotten."

I looked around me upon a wide world of waters, which were raging with fearful commotion. The lightning streamed over them, pouring like a liquid torrent from the heavens in flashes so quick as to be almost continuous, and illuminating the whole expanse of the ocean. The wind howled so loudly, that I could scarcely hear my own voice, and blew so fiercely, that I was obliged to cling to the rail in front of the poop-deck in order to secure my footing. As I cast my eyes below, the ship appeared absolutely buried in the billows. All the ports were fastened so that no water could escape, and she had shipped no less than five tremendous seas. She was now upon her beam-ends, labouring through the mighty swell with a motion so unnatural, that the captain turned to me, who was alone with him on the poop, and vociferated, with an oath which made me shudder, that we were going down. I quailed under his blasphemy, which the extreme peril rendered the more horrible. He raved and stormed like a madman, and ordered that the lashings of all the ports to leeward should be instantly cut. The vessel now lay like a log upon the sea; the rudder had no power. She was almost under water, while the hurricane was raging at its utmost might, and every billow seemed to rise like a mountain to overwhelm her. She still, however, floated; but the struggle could not last. I had seated myself by the mizen-mast, against which I leaned, expecting every instant to feel the waves dash over and sweep me into the "yeasty deep." To attempt to describe my reflections at this crisis would be a vain effort. I was stunned by the awful scene; my senses were so overwhelmed, that no perceptible image was presented to my mind. I had no positive apprehension of the death which now appeared inevitable; for my imagination was distracted by such a confusion of indistinct and fleeting images, that I could not collect my thoughts into a current of clear and definite ideas. Insensibility was rapidly coming over me; I am satisfied that my senses would have been lapped in complete oblivion before I could have sunk under the surface of the raging sea. While I was in this state of all but complete stupefaction, I heard the welcome sound, though imperfectly through the hoarse brawling of the wind, "Ports all clear!" which had scarcely reached my ear, before the ship righted, and the captain's frightful agitation subsided. The moment the ropes were cut which confined the ports, these latter were forced open by the prodigious pressure of the water, which almost instantly escaped and left the deck comparatively free. The vessel recovered her position, and the immediate peril at once subsided.

She was now put before the wind, and drove under bare poles at the rate of ten knots an hour. I quitted the poop, changed my clothes, and remained for the rest of the night on the deck. At intervals the moon burst from the dark purple masses that hurried rapidly over her fair disk, and poured her clear silvery light upon the turbulent ocean. The lightning diminished shortly after midnight, but the wind continued without the slightest abatement. The Lascars who composed the watch had thrown themselves into the boat, which was fastened between the main and fore masts, and could not be induced to stir until they saw that all immediate danger had subsided. The officer of the watch was obliged to use the most summary methods to induce them to perform their necessary duties: they crawled about with an apathy and indifference which a smart application of the rope's-end, occasionally administered by a very muscular arm, could scarcely dissipate.

Although I had remained so long upon the poop, drenched to the skin, with nothing on but the dress in which I slept, in the very teeth of that terrific hurricane, yet I had not felt in the slightest degree chilled; on the contrary, the excitement from utter hopelessness to the apparent certainty of escape from threatened destruction, produced a glow all over my body, and I continued upon deck, amid the rush of waters and the roar of elements, without the least desire to retire again to my cabin. The officer of the watch, who was a rough sailor, a Newcastle man, about the middle age, and the best portion of whose life had been passed at sea, entertained me with doleful stories of his numerous escapes, and the vessels he had seen go down, describing the cries of the drowning with a melancholy minuteness of detail—all but realizing to my excited mind the horrors by which such dreadful calamities are accompanied. I listened to him with painful interest, which continued until he was relieved, when I quitted the deck and retired to my cot, where I soon fell into a refreshing sleep.

By sunrise the wind had much abated, the foresail was set, and the ship resumed her course. Still there was occasional rain and thunder at intervals:

From the dark womb in rapid fall descend
The silvery drops, and glittering in the gleam
Shot from the lightning, bright and fitful, sparkle
Like a rich fringe rent from the robe of heaven.

Nothing further occurred out of the common course of events until we reached Madras.

The morning was beautiful when we anchored in the Madras roadstead. The Masoolah boats were instantly alongside, and my fellow-passengers and myself gladly proceeded to the shore. There was another boat behind us with several passengers from a ship, which had cast her anchor shortly after we had cast our's. The surf was very high, though the day was fine, and only a slight breeze gently undulated through the air. There was a cross swell, boisterous and difficult, requiring all the skill of the boatmen to get their boat into a favourable position for riding securely over the surf. The catamarans were close beside us, to pick us up in case of accident; for the ground-swell, which is so remarkable all along this coast, was particularly heavy. With some difficulty we were at length safely landed; but the boat behind us was not so fortunate. By some mismanagement, the man at the helm had allowed her to advance too far upon the crest of the breaker, which curled suddenly under her, raised her stern in the air, when another surge instantly succeeding, turned her a complete somerset, stern over head, and sent every person within her sprawling in the surf. They were whirled about in the most violent manner, performing many disagreeable evolutions, their mouths filled with water and sand, until rescued from their jeopardy by the men who followed in the catamarans, and plucked them from the rapacious jaws of the sharks within a very few seconds after the disaster. They presented a sorry picture as they stood upon the beach, dripping, and wiping their faces, when they were beyond the reach of danger. The whole of their baggage was recovered from the impetuous waters. After having liberally rewarded the active fellows who had saved them from a watery death, they proceeded, like ourselves, in palenkeens towards the town.

CHAPTER II.

A RICH MAHOMEDAN.—NAUTCH GIRLS.—A HOG-HUNT.

I REMAINED at Madras for two or three weeks, when, joined by my old travelling companions, we proceeded down the coast, nearly retracing our former route as far as Tanjore. Here we fell in with a wealthy Mahomedan, who showed us particular attention, treating us with great hospitality during our stay, which made our time pass very agreeably. The first visit we paid him was in the afternoon, just after he had taken the siesta, and was enjoying his hookha in the veranda of his dwelling. He was seated on a rich carpet under a magnificent awning, attended by two domestics, one of whom was protecting him from the inconvenience of the sun's rays with a chatta composed of the palmyra-leaf, and the other was waving over him a yak's tail, in order to prevent the impertinent intrusion of flies and mosquitoes. The mussulmaun courteously invited us to his dwelling, which was in the neighbourhood of the city, upon the river Cavery; and we visited him almost every evening during our stay. He had a splendid mansion, with a numerous establishment. One evening, before we quitted Tanjore, he gave a sumptuous en-

A Rich Mahomedan

tertainment, to which we were expressly invited. Our host was about five-and-thirty years of age; he had a tall commanding person, was remarkably courteous in his manners, and of easy, unembarrassed address. Like most persons of his race, he was extremely fond of show, living in a state of almost princely magnificence. In the evening, when we reached his abode, we were ushered into a room almost entirely panelled with English looking-glasses, in gorgeously gilded frames, extending nearly from the top to the bottom of the apartment, and so multiplying its extent, that it appeared all but interminable. The rich Mahomedans frequently live in great splendour, spending large sums of money upon the furniture and decorations of their houses, in which, however, there is much less of comfort than of magnificence. How strikingly do they confirm the wise saying of a Hindoo philosopher!—"Riches amount to just as much as is bestowed in gifts or enjoyed; the rest goes to others."

By the time the room was filled, it seemed to contain a crowd as numerous as Satan's newly raised Pandemonium.

> As bees
> In spring-time, when the sun with Taurus rides,
> Pour forth their populous youth about the hive
> In clusters, they among fresh dews and flowers
> Fly to and fro, or on the smoothed plank,
> The suburb of their straw-built citadel,
> New rubb'd with balm, expatiate and confer
> Their state affairs—so thick the busy crowd
> Swarm'd and were straiten'd.

After a variety of embracings, sprinklings with rose-water, and sippings of an agreeably acidulated drink something like our ordinary lemonade, the party squatted themselves upon small Persian carpets, covered with the most florid devices, spread upon a fine rush mat beautifully white and of the finest texture. When the guests were disposed in proper order, a musician advanced, made his salaam, and gave us an air upon the sarinda;—a rude kind of violin, which he managed with more dexterity than taste. He was shortly joined by several other members of his profession, and for a good half-hour we were doomed to nothing short of a musical purgatory. To my especial relief, this luxury of Oriental melody had its termination, and several nautch girls were introduced. The two principal were extremely pretty, with figures of the most delicate symmetry. They wore silk trousers of a pale scarlet, gathered round the ankles, below which a thin gold bangle embraced the small delicate leg. From these were suspended minute silver bells, that kept a gentle and by no means disagreeable tinkling, as these Oriental figurantes went through the various evolutions of their native dances. Upon the upper part of their persons they wore white jackets closely fitted to the shape, terminating in a short skirt, which descended loosely over the hip, but was left open in front, so as to expose the trousers; under this jacket a transparent petticoat hung as far as the knee. Over the head and shoulders was thrown a veil of beautiful thin gauze, which crossed the bosom, and, when spread open, was made occasionally to hide the entire figure of the dancer; at each corner was a rich tassel of gold or silver bullion. This veil the nautch girls manage with great grace and skill in their dances, one while peeping from beneath it with an arch expression of unequivocal meaning, at another exposing the whole countenance, beaming with a radiance that only makes the beholder regret so much beauty should be allied to so much depravity. The eye is usually lit up with earnest animation, every feature being refulgent with expression, that, but for the revolting leaven of sensuality which appears to give it life, would be entrancing to gaze and to dwell upon.

Nothing can exceed the transcendent beauty, both in form and lineament, of these degraded women, whose lives are as abandoned as their persons are frequently enchanting. Although generally accompanied by the most debauched of their sex, they are nevertheless continually engaged at large entertainments, even by Europeans, for the purpose of amusing their wives and daughters, as well as the wives and daughters of their guests. It must be confessed, however, that when they are admitted into houses to perform before persons of character, they never in the slightest degree offend against propriety; upon these especial occasions, nothing can be more modest than their dress and demeanour, while the gentle grace of their movements and attitudes is often unrivalled. Their dances, generally speaking, are much more decent than those encouraged in the theatres of Europe, which young and innocent girls are permitted to behold and applaud without a blush; and which, I must confess, with some rare exceptions, are to my judgment far more remarkable for their indecency than for their elegance.

The great charm of the Indian dances consists almost wholly in those elegant attitudes which they allow the dancer to display. You see no prodigious springs, no vehement pirouettes, no painful tension of the muscles or extravagant contortions of the limbs; none of that exquisite precision of step and pedal dexterity which constitute the chief charm of European artists. You see no violent sawing of the arms, no unnatural curving of the limbs, no bringing of the legs at right angles with the trunk; no violent hops, and jerks, and dizzy gyrations. The nautch girl advances gracefully before her audience, her arms moving in unison with her tiny naked feet, which, although not like snow in hue, still "fall on earth as mute," gliding through the evolutions of a simple figure without any of that exertion inseparable from European dances as exhibited before public audiences. She occasionally turns quickly round, by which the loose folds of her thin petticoat are expanded, and the heavy silk border with which it is trimmed opens into a circle round her, showing for an instant the beautiful outline of her form, draped with the most becoming and judicious taste. Although in description the perfections of this style of dancing may appear but negative, their effects are nevertheless positive upon the beholder. The ornaments worn by these women are often of considerable value. Their throats are usually encircled with several necklaces, sometimes composed of pearls, sometimes of gold curiously wrought. A large jewel hangs from the right nostril, suspended by a plain gold ring. On the forehead, just between the eyebrows, they always wear an ornament, which has no doubt given rise to the Sevigné now almost universally worn by European ladies. The most unpleasant part of the nautch is the dissonant music with which it is accompanied, and in which the dancers themselves every now and then join with voices as shrill and unmusical as the note of the peacock.

There is little variety in an entertainment of this kind in India. The guests, one and all, squat upon the floor, form themselves into groups, chatter with the most vehement energy of action, or gaze at the dancers, whom they applaud with an animation that frequently drowns the very drums and viols supposed to add such a charm to their favourite amusement. In compliance with the pressing courtesy of our host, we remained until his guests began to separate, accepting an invitation to join him in a hog-hunt on the following day. He had a good stud of horses, from which he promised that we should be well mounted; and we accordingly took our leave, with an assurance that we would meet him the next morning by sunrise.

Shortly after daylight we were mounted and in the field. The sport, for the first two hours, was very tedious and uninteresting, as we saw no game; and I began to think of returning home, when a hog was started from a patch of sugar-cane, and advancing in a diagonal direction across the plain, was pursued by at least a score of horsemen. I was mounted upon a bony country horse, which did not appear to have been much accustomed to the pressure of a European saddle, as it would frequently stop when on the gallop, suddenly turn round, and kick and snort as if it had been stung by a dragon-fly. Happening to be the nearest horseman to the hog when it broke cover, I struck the spur into the flank of my hunter, and thus urged it to full speed, in order to turn the animal's course; but I had no sooner come up with it, than my steed unexpectedly turned short round, threw out its heels with desperate energy, struck the poor hog in the ribs, rolling it upon the plain, and causing me to make a somerset over its own neck; and then, with the most provoking indifference, galloped off, leaving me within two yards of the enraged brute, which I expected every moment would unbutton my waistcoat with its tusks, to the manifest peril of the body underneath. Happily, the kick had so disabled it, that the creature lay for several seconds without attempting to move; of which circumstance I took advantage, and rising with eager celerity, scampered off after my fugitive hunter.

The hog soon recovered, and just as it was prepared to try its speed afresh, our host rode up to it sword in hand, and striking it on the back, completely severed the joint. The vanquished animal fell, and almost instantly died. The body was immediately borne off by some of the attendants. As I could not regain my horse, and being a good deal fatigued with my exertions, I seated myself upon the summit of a small hillock that overlooked a ravine terminating a sheer precipice of at least a hundred feet. From the exalted position I had taken I could command the whole plain, and see the sport though I could not join in it. There was a large tract of thick jungle on my left, upon the borders of which were several patches of sugar-cane, where it was evident some of the swinish multitude had been taking their meals, to the great annoyance of the proprietor of these saccharine plantations. I had not been long seated on this elevated spot, when I saw a boar, pursued by several sportsmen, making its way at full speed towards the precipice. The ground being very uneven, the horses scarcely gained upon the chase, and it appeared to have a fair chance of escape. On it sped, dashing over every inequality of the ground with heedless impetuosity. The shouts of its pursuers seemed to render it desperate; for, nearing the edge of the precipice, it did not attempt to turn, but sprang head foremost over the brink like another Marcus Curtius, if one may venture to compare a hog to a heathen. The spring was so great, that it did not strike the ground until near midway down the precipice, where the face of the escarpment bulged outward. Upon this projection the boar pitched, and, like a newly-inflated football, bounded again into the empty air. After two or three similar bounds, sufficient to have broken the ribs of Phalaris's brazen bull, had it been submitted to a similar process of repercussion, the unhappy brute reached the bottom of the ravine, when, to my astonishment, it rolled over upon its legs, darted into the thicket, as if its precipitous descent had been a mere pastime, and was out of sight in a few moments. I must confess I thought the bold beast deserved to escape, though it was a sad disappointment to its pursuers.

By this time my horse had been caught by one of

the followers, and we repaired to a tent pitched at a convenient spot upon the banks of the river. A chine of the hog which had fallen under the sword of the Mahomedan was soon dressed, and at the top of the table the tusked head appeared with a large orange in the mouth, and garlanded with a wreath—not of laurel, but of some shrub that answered the purpose just as well. Our host, though a votary of the Arabian prophet, had no objection to eating the prohibited food and drinking claret, of which he was excessively fond, in the presence of his domestics; who, he observed, although they might presume to think he did wrong, did not dare to tell him so. Not having a very earnest faith in the religion of his forefathers, he looked upon himself as a free agent: being moreover possessed of the means of exercising his free agency, he took care to employ them to the full extent of his will. He indulged so freely in potations of his favourite beverage, that he was obliged to relinquish his horse for his palenkeen, into which he rolled, and was borne upon the shoulders of four sturdy retainers to his home. The rich Mahomedans in India are fond of European society, and by no means scrupulous in violating the sumptuary laws of the Koran. Those prohibitory canons contained in their scriptures, which restrict them to certain meats and deny them the use of wines, they consider severe restrictions; and though they extol the prophet's wisdom in enacting them, and admit the providential agency that dictated them, they nevertheless sufficiently show how little they deem them worthy of respect, by the open and indifferent manner in which they infringe them. They have various ingenious modes of evading the force of these laws, among which this is one: a single drop of vinegar poured into a cask of wine immediately changes it from a prohibited beverage to one which any pious Islam may drink without scandalizing the prophet. Other religious obligations may be evaded by similar devices.

Before we quitted Tanjore, I witnessed one of those awful acts of superstitious devotion so common in this country. I was riding rather early in the morning upon the banks of the Cavery, when I saw a group of some half-dozen persons descend to the river's brink. The water was here many feet deep. Stopping my horse to see what was going on, I observed one of the group preparing to plunge into the stream. The instant I saw him I suspected he was about to commit an act of self-immolation. My whole frame thrilled with an irrepressible emotion—I was riveted to the spot; and, in spite of the feelings by which I was nearly overpowered, I could not resist the painful temptation of witnessing the whole transaction. The victim was a man somewhat past the meridian of life, but nevertheless apparently in vigorous health. He stood upon the bank of the stream, and on either side of him was a Brahmin, who fastened a large earthenware jar upon his shoulders. After this was done, the man made several prostrations, and entered the river. He slipped off the bank, where the depth was considerable, but the jars prevented him from sinking. The Brahmins folded their arms and looked silently on. They attempted neither to save him from destruction nor to expedite his death. He remained for some time floating, as if in prayer. The surface of the water was unruffled, except where it was disturbed by the motions of his body, and seemed an apt emblem of that apathy with which those ministers of a sanguinary religion looked upon an act of detestable suicide.

The man made several efforts to fill the jars, using the most deliberate exertions to accomplish his abominable sacrifice. Finding that he could not succeed, he at length drew himself to the bank, seized the root of a shrub which was partially bared, and, bending forward, succeeded in turning the mouth of one of the jars towards the stream and filling it. This only served to lengthen the dreadful process of death; for the other jar being empty prevented him from sinking, whilst that which was full drew him sufficiently under water to obstruct his breathing. In his struggles, however, he continually rose and partially recovered, only again to be half-suffocated. Although this continued for several minutes, the wretched man never once attempted to get out of the river; on the contrary, his determination to die was evident to the last moment. Seeing that his struggles were likely to continue, I called out to the Brahmins to break the empty jar; but those haughty functionaries did not condescend to notice my expostulations. At length, one of the bystanders, more merciful than his priests, dashed a stone upon the empty vessel, and the wretched victim sank; a few bubbles rose to the surface, and the water flowed over him, without leaving a visible memorial of that superstitious tragedy. This man was of the weaver caste, and I heard it said that his wife had expressed an anxious desire to die a suttee; but as the husband's body had been probably taken by alligators, and she therefore could not go through the ceremony according to prescribed form, she was spared the necessity of dying a death, distinguished indeed in her eyes, but nevertheless truly horrible.

It is the custom, when a woman of the weaver caste sacrifices herself to the manes of her husband, to descend with his body alive into the grave, which is dug near some sacred river; but if the parties dwell at a distance from any holy stream, then the grave is prepared near the most sacred spot in the vicinity. It is dug very deep and large; and, after a number of initiatory rites, as unintelligible as they are fantastical, the widow takes a formal leave of her friends, who are always present upon these melancholy occasions, and descends into the chamber of death. It frequently happens that she is so stupified with opium as to be scarcely conscious of what she is about, but goes through the necessary forms with mere mechanical insensibility. As soon as she reaches the bottom of the pit, to which she descends by a rude ladder, the latter is withdrawn, and she is left alone with the body of her deceased husband, generally in a revolting state of decay: this she embraces, clasping it to her bosom without the slightest expression of disturbance at the effluvia it emits. Having finished her disgusting caresses, she places it upon her lap, and gives the signal for the last act of this shocking scene to commence, which is even more dreadful than immolation upon the funeral pile. The earth is now deliberately thrown upon her, while two persons descend into the grave to trample it tightly round the self-devoted sacrificant.

During this tardy but terrible process, the doomed woman sits an unconcerned spectator, occasionally caressing the corpse, and looking with an expression of almost sublime triumph, as the earth embraces her body, at the anticipated honours which await her in the paradise of her God. The hands of her own children are perhaps at that very moment heaping around her the cold dust into which she is so soon to be resolved. At length, all but her head is covered, when the pit is hurriedly filled in, and her nearest relatives dance over her inhumed body with those frantic gestures which, whether they betoken ecstasy or madness, it is difficult on witnessing them to decide.

It is remarkable that these immolations are frequently made by women to the manes of husbands who have uniformly treated them with indifference, and often with the most unjustifiable tyranny. Still nothing, in many instances, checks the devoted heroism of the Hindoo widow: no unkind treatment invalidates in her mind the most sacred of all obligations; she forgives every past unkindness, and directs her thoughts to the future; acting upon the beautiful principle of the Persian poet, who has so eloquently inculcated the Christian maxim of rewarding evil with good:—

> "Learn from yon orient shell to love thy foe,
> And store with pearls the hand that brings thee woe;
> Free, like yon rock, from base vindictive pride,
> Emblaze with gems the wrist that rends thy side.
> Mark where yon tree rewards the stony shower
> With fruit nectareous, or the balmy flower.
> All nature calls aloud!—"Shall man do less
> Than heal the smiter and the railer bless?"*

* Hafiz.

CHAPTER III.

MADURA.—CASTE.—HINDOO LITERATURE.

After taking leave of our hospitable friend at Tanjore, we proceeded to Madura, where we arrived upon the evening of the fourth day. This now miserable and dilapidated city is the capital of the ancient kingdom described by Ptolemy as the Regio Pandionis. So early as the third century of the Christian era it was the most celebrated seat of learning in Hindostan. Here was a college which gave birth to some of the greatest lights of Hindoo science. It was visited by learned men from all parts of India; and its professors, up to so late a date as the thirteenth century, were pre-eminent for wisdom among the Hindoos at the most flourishing era of their literature. No persons were admitted as members until they had passed an examination of extraordinary severity; and such was their spirit of emulation, that the wise men of Madura were known and respected throughout all the kingdoms of the East. At that period, knowledge was so universally cultivated among the Hindoos, that it was as rare to find a poor villager who could not read as it is now to find one who can. In fact, their whole social system seems to have undergone a complete revolution. During those ages, when

Europe was enveloped in an intellectual darkness that exposed her to the contempt of the very countries which are now drawing from the stores of her wisdom and science a harvest that bids fair eventually to ripen into universal civilization, Hindostan was distinguished by a race of philosophers who, but for the conquests to which that country has been subjected, and the degrading dominion under which its population has so long groaned, would probably have raised it to an elevation in intellectual and social dignity not inferior to ancient Greece in the brightest period of her glory.

The present odious system of caste is one of those pernicious innovations which have grown out of the barbarous policy that succeeded the decadency of Hindoo literature ; for, until its glories had culminated, those prejudices were few and faint. They have, however, in later times opposed a mighty barrier to the introduction of Christianity among the native population of Hindostan ; and had those bright lights of genius which poured forth the radiance of their luminous minds from the college of Madura not been eclipsed by the bondage of a foreign domination, there is little doubt that the Christian church would have now stood upon the site of many a subverted pagoda, and the worship of a mere rude senseless block have been changed for that of the living God.

It is difficult to ascertain how long the distinctions of caste have prevailed among the Hindoos ; but this is certain, that to however remote a period those political divisions of the popular body may be traced, the narrow prejudices now entertained, and which those divisions tend to encourage and maintain, were kept in abeyance by the wisdom formerly disseminated, and by the national education then extended to all classes of the community. The people were too well informed to succumb to degradation, of which they at once saw the injustice, and which they felt that they possessed mental energies to avert.

Nothing can be a greater delusion than to form an opinion of the intellectual celebrity which the Hindoos once enjoyed by their present ignorant and degraded state. Their social condition is now as deplorable as it was once elevated and enlightened. The acquisition of knowledge was as generally as it was successfully pursued; and the first anxiety of the parent toward his children was to see them furnished with the necessary means of acquiring that knowledge then esteemed the richest earthly treasure. An extract from a letter of Sir Alexander Johnston, a high authority upon all subjects connected with Oriental literature, addressed to Mr. Charles Grant, when President of the Board of Control, will help to justify what I have stated upon the intellectual attainments of the Hindoos, before the Mahomedan conquests.

"Education has always, from the earliest period of their history, been an object of public care and of public interest to the Hindoo governments on the peninsula of India. Every well-regulated village under those governments had a public school and a public schoolmaster. The system of instruction in them was that which, in consequence of its efficiency, simplicity, and cheapness, was a few years ago introduced from

Madras into England, and from England into the rest of Europe. Every Hindoo parent looked upon the education of his child as a solemn duty, which he owed to his God and to his country, and placed him under the schoolmaster of his village as soon as he had attained his fifth year. The ceremony of introducing him for the first time to the schoolmaster and his scholars was publicly recorded, and was attended with all the solemnity of a religious observance; a prayer being publicly offered up on the occasion to the figure of Ganesa, the Hindoo god of Wisdom, which was at the head of every Hindoo school, imploring him to aid the child in his endeavours to learn and become wise."

It is a singular fact that the system of national education, introduced by the late Mr. Bell into this country, and by which his name will be immortalized in its annals, should have emanated from a people whom we have been but too much accustomed, under the erroneous impression excited by the present low ebb of their literature, to look upon as little better than semi-barbarians. The more, however, the treasures of their forefathers' wisdom is brought into view, the more certainly shall we find that in mental resources they were not at all behind the ancient Egyptians.

During the time that the college of Madura flourished, all persons were admitted as members, without any reference to caste, provided they had made the necessary proficiency in those branches of learning required by the canons of the college, which were always most strictly enforced. At that period, as well as now, the Pariahs were a degraded tribe: none of their race had ever become in any degree eminent in the walks of science. Now what remarkably evinces the liberal spirit which prevailed among the literary Hindoos of those days, is the circumstance that a Pariah and his sister not only obtained admission into the famous seat of learning at Madura, but that the former was raised to the presidential chair, and the works of the latter were used as class-books in the college, being to this day esteemed among the gems of Hindoo literature. The name of the former of these distinguished persons was Tiru Valuvir; that of his no less distinguished sister Avyar. When the brother presented himself for admission into that erudite body, being from a stock generally ignorant, and universally despised, he was asked with some bitterness who and what he was. His reply was at once humble and dignified.

"I am a Pariah, but God has endowed me with a power of intellect which elevates me to the first rank among his creatures. I am not to be fettered in those trammels which the foolish prejudices of men cast upon the minds of each other, to debase and enslave them. My mind has a full perception of its own power, and of its own dignity; and I feel that I have a freeborn right to take my station among the wise and good."

He might have answered in the words of an ethical writer* of his own nation—"Greatness is not the fruit of birth: it is not attained but by the greatest exertions; whereas to become insignificant costs no pains. To raise a stone to the top of a mountain requires great labour, but it will descend with the utmost velocity."

* The Pundit Vishnoo-Shurma.

His claim was admitted, and he was shortly afterwards examined with several other candidates. The examiners, anxious to exclude him, for fourteen days subjected him to the most rigid investigation they could devise. He however not only eclipsed all his competitors, but proved that he far surpassed even his examiners in knowledge, which in the issue they ingenuously confessed. The Pariah was admitted, and his sister was considered worthy to be classed with the greatest sages of her time.

Tiru Valuvir became an honour to the college, and was venerated by all its members. Such was his acknowledged superiority, that the year after his inauguration he was raised to the chair, and continued to preside over the college of Madura from that time until his death. He was the author of a work on morals, entitled Koral, which to this day has a high reputation among the Hindoos; and his sister composed several works, written in Tamul verse, and not less esteemed than those of her brother.

Although these persons were Pariahs by birth,—a race now held in such universal detestation among the Hindoos, that whatever their shadow passes over is considered polluted,—they were nevertheless so much respected by all classes of the community for their talents and literary acquirements, that it was esteemed the highest honour to hold communion with them. Their society was everywhere courted: men of the highest caste felt flattered by conversing with the one, and the wives and daughters of princes held it no degradation to be admitted to familiar intercourse with the other. They fully realized the truth of a saying of one of their own people; "Of all precious things knowledge is the most valuable: other riches may be stolen, or diminished by expenditure, but knowledge is immortal; and the greater the expenditure, the greater the increase: it can be shared with none, and it defies the power of the thief." Ever since this period their numerous works have been adopted as class-books for the higher orders of scholars in all the Hindoo seminaries of learning throughout India. This is a sufficient proof that the modern prejudices, which are the bitter fruits of caste, did not exist, or but in a very limited degree, while literature flourished in Hindostan.

The city of Madura, up to the period of the great Mahomedan invasion by Mahmood, was the focal spot at which all the pilgrims met in their journey to the temple of Ramisseram, then the most celebrated in Southern India, and resorted to by pilgrims from all parts of the peninsula. Its importance may be conceived, from the circumstance that the longitude in Hindoo geography was calculated from the meridian of the little island upon which this celebrated sanctuary stood, as the longitude in English geography is determined from that of Greenwich. At Ramisseram the services of the temple were every day performed with Gangetic water, daily supplied at a vast expense for this purpose; and the idol regularly underwent a matutinal ablution with that consecrated element. These pilgrimages were continued, though the concourse was not so great as in earlier times, during that dynasty of which Trimal Naig was so distinguished a member; and it was to the protection offered to the pilgrims, in their periodical visitations to the shrine at Ramisseram, that he is indebted for the reverence with which his name has been handed down to a degenerate but grateful posterity. From the Mahomedan conquest we may date the decay of Hindoo learning, and the destruction of the fairest monuments of ancient Hindoo art. It was not, however, until the worshippers of the Arabian imposter obtained a footing in the southern part of the Indian peninsula, and more especially under the tyranny of Aurungzeb, that Madura became a prey to the ravages of these bigoted and unsparing conquerors.

Aurungzeb, who was an intolerant bigot, and a furious Iconoclast, thought it an act of religious obligation to lay the arm of demolition upon every temple in which a heathen deity was enshrined. Thus some of the finest monuments of Hindoo antiquity were either unsparingly mutilated, or levelled with the dust. Much, however, as the bigotry of these Islam invaders had done to wipe from the fair chronicles of time those noble records of man's ingenuity and enterprise, which were once the pride of the enlightened, and are now the boast of the half-civilized Hindoo, nevertheless the glorious ruins scattered over the face of one of the noblest countries upon earth attest the triumph of human ingenuity, in an age too when the forests with which barbarized Britain was overspread were peopled with a race of savages, and in a country, no less truly than poetically designated "the land of the sun," where now the mental superiority of the descendants of the conquerors of those savages has brought a population of upwards of a hundred million under the control of a wiser and more beneficial legislation.

Madura, at this moment in the proud but dim splendour of her decay, exhibits abundant memorials of her former greatness, though these cannot vie in antiquity with many structures of still grander conception and execution to be seen in other parts of India. Of late years, this ancient city has suffered considerably by the petty chieftains in its vicinity, whose continual struggles for supremacy have perpetually exposed it to the depredations of contending factions. During the Carnatic wars, in the middle of the eighteenth century, it was occupied by a number of turbulent Polygars, who held their dens and fortified castles within the recesses of the thick jungles by which this district was overspread. The city at that time suffered in no small degree from the ravages of these turbulent chieftains; nor was it until the year 1801, when it was transferred to the British government by the Nawaub of Arcot, that it became secure from the depredations of rival princes.

The present aspect of Madura is not attractive to the traveller. The town stands upon an extensive level, though the country around it is much elevated, and about a hundred miles north by east of Cape Comorin. The fort is near four miles in circumference, and environed by a strong wall; this is further protected by a deep ditch, filled from the river Vaylaur; though immediately before the rains, this river becomes exceedingly shallow, consequently the ditch which encompasses the fort, together with the tanks and wells, are nearly all dry. A failure in the fall of rain during the monsoon is attended with serious inconvenience—indeed, a partial famine is the invariable consequence.

The population of Madura has greatly decreased since its cession to the British government in 1801: in 1812 it amounted only to twenty thousand souls. The natives, with very few exceptions, are deplorably poor, living in small filthy huts, exhibiting all the squalid misery of the most destitute condition. The streets are narrow and dirty to the last degree—the drains obstructed; and thus, during the rains, pools of stagnant water everywhere meet the eye, which soon become extremely offensive and unwholesome. Immense quantities of cattle are stalled within the fort; in consequence of which filth of all kinds accumulates to an insufferable extent. It is also crowded with trees, which obstruct the necessary evaporation, at the same time infecting the air with noxious exhalations from their decayed leaves; while the water of the tanks, being seldom renewed, becomes putrid, and emits a most deleterious effluvia. At Madura there is a famous temple, consecrated to the god Vellayadah, to whom his devotees bring offerings of a singular kind: these consist of leather shoes, the shape of those worn by the Hindoos, but much larger and more ornamented. The deity of this place being addicted to hunting, the shoes are intended to preserve his feet when he traverses the jungles.*

Such is the present state of a city once renowned

* See Hamilton's Description of Hindostan, vol. ii. p. 472.

throughout the whole extent of a vast and mighty empire! The only traces which remain of its former greatness are the still noble ruins of those edifices erected by Trimal Naig towards the beginning of the seventeenth century, and the magnificent choultry now standing entire,—a proud evidence at once of his taste and munificence.

While Sir Alexander Johnston's father, who held a high official appointment at Madura, resided in that district, he obtained a grant from the Nawaub of Arcot of a considerable ruin, situated in the jungle about a mile and half from the fort, and originally erected, during the Nayaca dynasty, as a palace from which the court of Madura witnessed the exhibition of gymnastic exercises and wild beast fights at the great Hindoo festivals. This was an extensive edifice, covered by a roof, supported on either side by a double row of massy columns, and overlooking a spacious plain. Mr. Johnston, at great expense, and under the superintendence of his friend, the late Colonel Mackenzie, converted this ruin into a dwelling-house for himself and family, and had it in contemplation eventually to convert the building into a college; and by inducing the most learned Brahmins from Benares, and other places of established repute for literature, to visit it, he was induced to hope that the celebrity of this once famous city as a seat of learning might be revived. He had a zealous and efficient coadjutor in Colonel Mackenzie, whose extensive acquaintance with Hindoo history and science has perhaps never been surpassed. For this the colonel was much indebted to Lutchmin, a learned Brahmin, who has devoted the greater part of his life to the collection of authentic materials for a general history of his country.

Within this ancient edifice Colonel Mackenzie was in the habit of assembling all the most learned Hindoos of the neighbourhood, and of challenging them to discussions in mathematics, as well as in the abstract and physical sciences. He caused large diagrams to be very accurately drawn upon the lofty pillars of the building; those on one side of the area illustrating the science of astronomy according to the Copernican system, and those on the other according to that of Ptolemy; showing, by this simple process, the superiority of the Prussian mathematician over the Egyptian. The system of the latter was that upon which their own appears to have been founded, and the fallacy of it was made manifest by Colonel Mackenzie to many eminently learned Brahmins, who frankly admitted it, and paid a just tribute of their respect to the talents of that most able and highly meritorious officer. Since his death, which was a severe loss to his country and to Oriental literature, the project of converting the building into a college has been abandoned; though there appears some probability of its being revived, as the present proprietor, Sir Alexander Johnston, has offered to cede his right of proprietorship to any body of learned natives who will take up and pursue the original idea of his father.

I cannot better show the cause of Colonel Mackenzie's visit to Madura than by an extract from Sir Alexander Johnston's evidence before the House of Commons, upon the subject of the Mackenzie papers:—"My mother, who was daughter of Mr.

Mackenzie's friend and early patron, the fifth Lord Napier — and who, in consequence of her father's death, had determined to execute the plan which he had formed of writing the life of the inventor of logarithms* — resided at that time with my father at Madura, and employed the more distinguished Brahmins in the neighbourhood in collecting for her, from every part of the peninsula, the information which she required relative to the knowledge which the Hindoos had possessed in ancient times of mathematics and astronomy. Knowing that Mr. Mackenzie had been previously employed by her father in pursuing the literary inquiries in which she herself was then engaged, and wishing to have his assistance in arranging the materials which she had collected, she and my father invited him to come and reside with them at Madura early in 1783, and there introduced him to all the Brahmins and other literary natives who resided at that place."

During our stay at this celebrated city, we joined a party of sportsmen in pursuit of small game in a jungle about six or seven miles' distance. The officers of the garrison made up the party, in order to give us some idea of the sport which the neighbourhood afforded, and we started soon after daylight for the jungle. Several natives of rank, belonging to the Nawaub of Arcot's court, joined us on their elephants; while our's were hired from a sort of jobbing merchant in the town, who was accustomed to lend them by the day for a tolerably extravagant remuneration. The ride before we came to the place where we had agreed

* Lord John Napier, of Merchiston.

to meet the native sportsmen who were to join us was extremely pleasant. The morning was fresh, and the face of the country beautiful, rising gradually as we advanced, and at every turn of the road opening before us into an extensive view of the distant plains which sloped towards the coast, and then swelled into lofty hills towards Cape Comorin. The elephants moved on at a brisk pace, and we were at the ground before the sun was much above the horizon. At first we found the jungles so inconveniently thick, that I began to fear we should lose all chance of obtaining a haunch of venison or the chine of a wild hog, both of which we expected to secure, as there were several of our party who were reputed excellent shots.

We threaded the forest for some time, but neither hog nor deer was roused. As we advanced, and the elephant on which I rode was making its way through a thick tuft of jungle-grass, out started seven or eight little pigs, squeaking and running in all directions between the elephant's legs, preceded by the mother, which escaped into the thicket before any of the party had time to take a deliberate aim at her. Her little family expeditiously followed her, except one, upon which the elephant had trodden in their first unexpected eruption, and crushed every bone in its skin. The underwood was too close and tangled to attempt pursuing the mother of the brood; we therefore took the more practicable part of the jungle, which soon opened into a large space comparatively clear of wood. Upon one side there was an abrupt ascent thinly scattered with trees, and on the top

The Tiger hunt

were a few native huts, composing a small picturesque hamlet in the heart of an extensive forest. While the beaters were in the thicket shouting to scare the game into the open vista, an old elephant upon which one of the officers rode, accompanied by a wealthy native, was seen to fix its eye upon a spot where there was a tolerably thick growth of high grass and underwood. In a short time something was seen to move on this spot, when the elephant, cautiously retreating, forced its body among the bushes of a thorny tree which grew with great luxuriance just on the edge of the vista. A moment after, springing violently forward, its riders were dismounted by the shock, and lodged, together with the Mahoot, among the boughs of the prickly canopy. The sagacious creature having reached the place whence it had previously retreated, with a sudden sharp cry plunged its head into the grass. In a few minutes it raised itself; a tiger crawled from the covert, and lay panting against a bank with two terrific wounds through its body. The elephant, now seeing that no further danger was to be apprehended, went back to the tree, thrust its body among the branches as before, allowed its disconcerted riders to remount, then advanced once more towards its dying enemy, and repeated the infliction; at the same moment a shikarry terminated the tiger's sufferings by shooting it through the head. Having skinned the beautiful beast, we returned with this trophy of our success, and with several fine deer, which we had the good fortune to encounter on our way. Thus, upon the whole, we had reason to be satisfied with our day's sport.

CHAPTER IV.

THE NAYACA DYNASTY.

Although Madura is now so sadly fallen from its ancient splendour, the remains of its public buildings cannot but strike the traveller with a vast idea of the pecuniary and mental resources of their founder. The principal edifices which now claim attention within this once flourishing district, are those raised by the enterprising Trimal Naig, in the early part of the seventeenth century. A brief account of the family of this chieftain will not be out of place here, as it forms the principal subject of the sculptures that adorn a magnificent choultry, built by him to commemorate their power and influence in southern Hindostan.

Madura formerly formed part of a principality subject to a Raya, who presided over fifty-six provinces, from whom their respective princes held them by way of feudal tenure. One of the chiefs of these feudatories was Nagama Nayaca, a man of great influence and extensive resources, but who, in the midst of undisturbed prosperity, was wretched because he had not been blessed with an heir. During a pilgrimage which he made to Casi, the modern Benares, in order to propitiate the deity whom he served, he had a dream, in which the promise of a child was made to him by a venerable man of smiling aspect, which promise was finally accomplished. In due time he had a son, whom he named Viswanat'ha Nayaca. This boy was placed under the ablest masters in every department of education, and grew up to be as much admired as well for his wisdom and skill in arms as for the beauty of his person and the general accomplishments of his mind.

A story is recorded of this youth having severed at a single stroke the head of a buffalo, the horns of which extended backward as far as the tail, cutting sheer through those tough protectors, and thus performing an act of decollation which none of the Raya's officers had the resolution to attempt; it being necessary that this victim of an annual sacrifice to Durga should be immolated by a single blow. This feat of prowess so delighted the Raya, that he loaded the young man with jewels, advanced his rank, and promised him still further honours. Some time after this, several dependant princes revolted, when Viswanat'ha being sent against them, made himself master of their territories, and, having appointed proper persons to govern the conquered provinces in the name of his master, was advanced by him to the highest dignities.

The King of Tanjore having invaded the dominions of the King of Madura and deposed him, the Raya sent Nagama Nayaca against the aggressor, whom he had orders to expel from the conquered province, and to restore the deposed monarch. Nagama immediately marched with a considerable force against the sovereign of Tanjore, and routed him; but, instead of restoring the lawful sovereign, he usurped the government, and, putting the fort of Madura in the best possible state of defence, determined to withstand the siege that was threatened by the Raya, upon his refusing to give up to their lawful prince the territories he had usurped. When this perfidious determination was made known to the Raya, summoning his nobles, he asked which of them was willing to take the command of an army to be employed against his refractory officer. As none of the nobles seemed ambitious of being raised to the dignity of so dangerous a command, Viswanat'ha, who had already rendered his master such signal service by vanquishing the seditious feudatories, offered to head the troops appointed to march against his rebellious parent. The sovereign, though he at first appeared to doubt the sincerity of this proposal, finally gave his consent, and the brave son marched with a powerful force against the usurper. When Viswanat'ha reached the frontiers of Madura, he sent to apprise his father of his presence, and that he was come in his master's name to force him to return to his allegiance. Nagama, surprised and enraged at finding his own son had come to him upon such a hostile errand, bitterly cursed the hour that he had offered up a prayer for a boon, which, as he now averred in his rage, had turned out in the issue to be a bane.

Under the influence of ungovernable exasperation at the foul revolt, as he chose to consider it, of his own flesh and blood, he hastily collected his forces, and, sallying from the fort, attacked the invading army. Several desperate encounters took place, which terminated in the entire defeat of the rebel, who was made prisoner; the Raya, however, pardoned him at the intercession of his son, whom he advanced to still higher dignities. Soon after this, the King of Madura, the successor of that prince who had been restored to his crown by the valour of Viswanat'ha, dying, and his family becoming extinct, the noble son of Nagama Nayaca was advanced to the throne by his sovereign, as a reward for his distinguished services. Immediately upon being invested with the insignia of sovereignty, he departed for his capital, and commenced those improvements at Madura which were so splendidly completed by his successor of the eighth descent, of whom I shall have presently to speak. He enlarged the fort, constructed temples, cut tanks, sank wells, built colleges, raised dams to check the force of the periodical inundations from the river, dug water-courses,—and, in short, did everything which a wise political foresight could suggest to improve his dominions and the general condition of those whom he had been so liberally appointed to govern. He protected travellers and pilgrims proceeding to the sacred shrine at Ramisseram from the rapine of the Polygars, who, under the assumed sanction of their own petty regality, committed the most outrageous violations of the public peace. These were finally reduced to subjection, and the pilgrimages made to the shrine were no longer interrupted.

About this time, Viswanat'ha, having sent a confidential officer with a considerable force to chastise five refractory Rajahs, his troops were defeated, and the Prince was obliged to take the field in person. Uniting his forces with those of his officer, he attacked the rebels; but they fought with such desperate bravery, that he was obliged to retreat with considerable loss. Mortified at this disgraceful issue, and urged by the lamentations of the widows and orphans of those who had fallen in the late conflict, he sent a challenge to the five Rajahs, offering to engage them all in single combat, to prevent the further effusion of blood. The proposal being accepted, the agreement, which was that the territories of the vanquished should devolve upon the vanquisher, was engraved upon a plate of brass, fixed upon a pole, and placed in the centre of the field. The stoutest of the rebels, completely armed and mounted, spurred his horse towards the King, and made a furious stroke at him, which was parried, and the contest continued for some time without a wound having been either given or received. At length, Viswanat'ha, bidding his adversary be upon his guard, raised himself in his stirrups, lifted his ponderous sabre, and, with a force which no armour could repel, struck him on the crest, and completely severed him in two. His companions in arms seeing the fate of their most resolute champion, submitted to the mercy of the conqueror.

The account of this extraordinary contest is related by the Hindoo historian with all the wild exaggerations of fable. The gods are said to have assembled in the air to behold the conflict, and to have showered the most fragrant flowers upon the conqueror. From that period the reign of this excellent Prince was uninterrupted either by domestic or foreign wars. The rest of his life was devoted to the improvement of his kingdom. He died about the middle of the fifteenth century, and was succeeded by his son, Parca Chrisnapa Nayaca, whose life presents nothing memorable, except that he built a village near Palametta, which he called after his own name; dedicated a temple to Siva, dug a large tank, and devoted a number of houses to the accommodation of Brahmins. He died after a tranquil reign of about thirty years, when the crown devolved upon his son, Parcavirapa Nayaca.

During the life of this Prince, part of the royal territory was usurped by a rebel chieftain, who built two strong forts within the district of Madura, in which he alternately held his court. He was finally subdued and reduced to obedience. Parcavirapa died after a tolerably quiet reign of twenty-seven years, and left three sons, who successively sat upon the throne; the last being succeeded by his nephew, who reigned thirty years. He was a munificent prince: following the example of his great progenitor, Viswanat'ha, he built several pagodas, dug tanks, constructed agrars,* and left behind him many noble testimonials of his liberality and public spirit.

It was during this reign that the Ramnad Rajahs established a petty supremacy. The founder of this family, Wodeya Teween, had received authority over a small district covered with jungle and infested by robbers and other tribes of depredators, who not only interrupted the pilgrimages to Ramisseram, the road to which lay through this district, but continually plundered the peaceable inhabitants of the country. It happened that a priest of the King of Madura

* Houses for the accommodation of devotees.

being on a visit to the sacred shrine, then resorted to by every holy man in southern India, was escorted by Wodeya Teween. The priest was so sensible of his good offices, that upon his return he presented him to the King at Madura, and so extolled his loyalty, that the chieftain was appointed to govern that part of the country where he had been of late so actively employed, with an additional grant of territory. Upon this, he built a strong fort at Pogaloor, and in a short time effectually reduced the refractory to obedience, expelling the robbers, and finally making the road to the temple at Ramisseram perfectly free from those incursions which had hitherto rendered it unsafe. He completely subdued the rebellious Polygars, and held so tight a rein over them, that the whole country was soon in a state of profound peace. For these eminent services the King conferred on him the title of Rajah of Ramnad. To him might justly be applied the Hindoo proverb: "A man of excellent qualities is like a flower, which, whether found amongst weeds or worn on the head, still preserves its fragrance."

Wodeya Teween died after a long and prosperous reign, and was succeeded by his son, who trod in the steps of his father, and enlarged his dominion by further conquests. About the same period the King of Madura died, leaving three sons, who successively ascended the throne, the second of whom was the famous Trimal Naig, who built the choultry represented in the accompanying engraving, and recording, in the sculptures by which it is so profusely adorned, the events of his own dynasty. He is said to have laid the foundation, in his kingdom, of ninety-six temples to

Drawn by W. Daniell, R.A. Engraved by J. Lowry.

The Choultry of Trimal Naig at Madura

Siva and Vishnu, and some progress was made during his life towards completing these splendid edifices. Most of them are now expunged altogether from the mighty chronicle of human events, or are only to be faintly traced: of some "the place thereof knoweth them no more;' while of the rest it can only be said, that they remain grand, indeed, but melancholy evidences of the fallacy of human expectations.

Besides these fabrics and the choultry already mentioned, Trimalla Nayaca, commonly called Trimal Naig, erected a splendid palace within the fort of Madura. The choultry, which is always associated with the name of this Prince, is certainly the most remarkable structure of its kind in Hindostan. Intended, as it was, to chronicle, in a material more durable than marble, the deeds of his ancestors and of himself, the founder of this magnificent monument of Hindoo art spared no expense to render it such a structure as should secure the admiration of posterity. Knowing what a powerful agent superstition is to give permanency to, and obtain veneration for, a name, Trimal Naig has so blended the history of his family with the popular mythology, that, until the one shall be exploded, the names of his ancestors and himself will be recorded in the popular annals of his country, and embalmed in the memories of every generation. His munificence is even to this day the theme of many a romance and of many a song; and amid the wrecks of former magnificence at Madura, which seem to point, as with an air of solemn mockery, at the misery of her now poor and scanty population, the proud record of her bygone glory is occasionally heard, like the plaintive song of the nightingale, amid the gloom and loneliness of night.

As Madura was a sort of focal spot, where the pilgrimages met from all parts of India, to the celebrated sanctuary on the island of Ramisseram, Trimal Naig was determined to erect an edifice that should be worthy of such a sacred concourse; and sensible, moreover, of the extreme veneration paid to any sculptured representation of their favourite deities, by placing them in connexion with the effigies of his own ancestors before the eyes of the devotees, whose minds, when about to visit their grand shrine, were always excited to a high degree of devotional enthusiasm, he was fully aware that he should divide their reverence, and attain for his progenitors, and for himself eventually, a sort of popular canonization. Thus, his ambition, though disguised under the plausible mask of public spirit and veneration for the sanctity of religion, was the mainspring of those splendid erections which have immortalized his name in the native chronicles of the southern peninsula of India.

The choultry, of which Mr. Daniell has given so faithful a representation, is in the form of a parallelogram, three hundred and twelve feet in length, by one hundred and twenty-five in width. It consists of one vast hall, the ceiling of which is supported by six rows of columns twenty-five feet high, most of which are formed of single stones, and the whole composed of a hard grey granite. The labour in carving these immense masses must have been prodigious, especially with the rude tools employed by the native workmen, and when the inflexibility of the material upon which they worked is taken into account. Their execution of the figures is extremely clean, and, save where the rude hand of spoliation has defaced them, they are nearly as perfect as at the first moment of their completion. The stubborn nature of the matter from which they were shaped has been their security against the ravages of time.

The view exhibited in the engraving represents half the length of the area between the two central rows of columns. On the second pillar, to the right of the spectator as he faces the door at the bottom, is the figure of Trimal Naig, the founder of this gorgeous structure, in a group with six of his wives, three on one side and three on the other, to whom, on account of their lord's munificence, the Hindoos continue to pay divine honours, as well as to himself. Of the principal wife in the front group a fact is recorded which will convey some idea of the wealth and magnificence of eastern Princes: she was daughter of the Rajah of Tanjore, a Prince who possessed immense treasure and exercised a prodigal liberality.

When the choultry was finished, upon which Trimal Naig had lavished an enormous sum of money, he conducted his wife into it with a certain air of ostentation, as if he expected she would be struck by the extraordinary grandeur of the edifice. Upon his asking her what she thought of it, she coldly cast her eyes around, and told him, with an unmoved countenance, that it was far inferior in splendour to her father's stables. This mortifying declaration so exasperated the royal husband, that he instantly drew a dagger from his girdle and plunged it into her thigh.

Trimal Naig has himself preserved the record of this event, as the figure representing his favourite wife, and standing nearest on the pillar to his own effigy, has a large gash below the hip on the left side. Upon this occasion, when his rage had subsided, he did not suffer the hint given by his royal consort to be lost, but increased the magnificence of the choultry by considerably adding to the richness of its decorations.

Upon the pillars beyond that ornamented with his own image, and on the columns immediately opposite, are other statues, representing his numerous lineage, covered with different groupings, expressive of those events which were considered worthy of commemoration in the respective reigns of his ancestors. Upon the ceiling the zodiacal signs stand out in bold relief; and on the ceiling of the palace it is remarkable that there are several single figures, apparently of angels, from which circumstance it has been surmised that the famous Jesuit, Robertus de Nobilibus, was consulted upon the erection of that celebrated structure. He was a man so eminently skilled in Sanscrit literature, that he translated into this language a work of his own upon the divine unity, in order to confute the doctrines of polytheism, or rather of pantheism, maintained with so much subtlety by the Sanscrit writers.

In different parts of Trimal Naig's choultry there are groups of mythological figures cut in bas-relief, which refer to circumstances by no means obvious to the general observer; but there is one small group of two, separate from all the rest, which tells a lamentable story, recording in imperishable granite the basest act of Trimal Naig's reign. The two architects who designed the choultry appear incarcerated in a cell. This was actually done, in order that they might not erect an edifice elsewhere that should eclipse that raised at such a vast expense by the King of Madura. To prevent the possibility of this, he had them immured in a dungeon, the entrance of which was built up, and they were thus buried alive.

In tracing the histories of tyrants, how generally do we find that death has been the reward where they have been faithfully served! This act of unprovoked and gratuitous cruelty will ever degrade Trimal Naig from ranking with the eminent men of times past, notwithstanding his ambitious prodigality and selfish munificence. He was an ostentatious but not a great Prince; and the more splendid actions of his life descend to posterity sullied by that hue of moral infirmity which was reflected upon them from his personal vices: so true is the beautiful aphorism of a writer* of his own nation—"The lustre of a virtuous character cannot be defaced, nor can the vices of a vicious man ever become lucid. A jewel preserves its lustre though trodden in the dirt; but a brass pot, though placed upon the head, is brass still."

The palace at Madura, which the present ruins show to have been once a noble structure, was one of the numerous edifices with which Trimal Naig adorned his native city, and which suffered considerable injury during the numerous sieges maintained against this capital of a once flourishing empire, between the

* Vishnoo-Shurma.

years 1740 and 1760, when it was frequently in the hands of the refractory Polygars, who desecrated its temples, and destroyed many of its public edifices for the sake of plunder. The lower apartments of the palace, once the abode of the most powerful prince of southern India, are at present used for stalling cattle, and for purposes equally remote from their original destination. Even in its present state of decay there is one chamber especially that cannot be entered without forcing the mind back upon times when kings trod its pavement, surrounded by their retinue of courtiers and nobles. It is conjectured to have been the hall of audience of the Madura sovereigns. The roof is arched and highly ornamented, falling on either side upon richly wrought pillars connected by arches, forming a magnificent gallery, which is supported upon similar arches, terminating in strong massy columns below. The architecture is something of the Saracenic order, blended with the graver severity of the Hindoo. It has all the grandeur of the choultry without its exquisite richness of ornament; the detail, however, is alone wanting to render it a glorious rival. The floor is stuccoed several feet below the present surface, where there is a large reservoir, apparently intended for the admission of water, and supposed by some to have been constructed for the purpose of a bath.

During Trimal Naig's reign, Sadakay Tewen, Rajah of Ramnad, having rebelled, was made prisoner, taken to Madura, and put into irons. This severity having excited the indignation of Sadakay Tewen's subjects, the pillage of pilgrims on their way to Ramisseram was renewed. The King of Madura, in order to put a stop to these outrages, released the Rajah, when they immediately ceased. This Prince dying soon after, was succeeded by his son-in-law, who, to wipe out the stain of his predecessor's rebellion, marched with an army of sixty thousand men against the princes of Mysore, who had invaded Madura, and drove them beyond the ghauts with great slaughter. Trimal Naig was so gratified by this proof of his allegiance, that he released him from his tribute, and made him an independent sovereign, extending the grant to his heirs in perpetuity.* Trimal Naig died in the year 1661, after a reign of forty years. From this period the glory of the family gradually declined. During one reign, and that was when the reins of government were held by a woman, the dignity of the Nayaca dynasty was for a time supported; but the irradiation was transient, and the declension from this time was as rapid as had been its original rise. Madura is now in the possession of the East India Company, who have hitherto shown no disposition to lift it from its present political and social degradation.

Ram Raz, a literary Hindoo of considerable celebrity among his own countrymen, and a correspond-

* The possession of the once powerful kingdom of Ramnad was one of the late cases in dispute before the courts of India. The hearing of the appeal, made by the descendants of her princes, having been put off from time to time, the inconvenience caused to the people of the country by that delay was the ground upon which Sir Alexander Johnston proposed the modification of the Privy Council which now prevails for the hearing of Indian appeals.

ent of the Royal Asiatic Society, has kindly sent to that learned body drawings of all the ornaments in Trimal Naig's choultry, which seem to exhibit every specimen of Hindoo architecture. The Society have had lithographic transcripts made from these curious specimens of native talent, which, though defective as works of art, compared with those of European draughtsmen, are valuable nevertheless as being close copies of the subjects which they represent, and convey a very just idea of the elaborate decoration of that structure which, even at this moment, confers no mean celebrity upon the neighbourhood of Madura.

Drawn by W. Daniell, R.A. — Engraved by J. H. Kernot

Hindoo Temples at Tritchengode

CHAPTER V.

TRITCHENGUR.—HINDOO THEOLOGY.

Having determined to go into the Mysore, to visit the celebrated colossal figure of Buddha, we took leave of our Mahomedan friend, and proceeded much in the same route which we had before taken, as described in the first volume of this work. We again visited the temples of Tritchengur, the most sacred of which is represented in the accompanying engraving. It is one of the most elegant specimens of Hindoo architecture in this part of the peninsula. The ascent to it is by no means tedious, though it stands on the summit of a lofty hill, in which, at intervals, where the slope is very abrupt, there are steps cut in the living rock, in order to facilitate the approach of those numerous devotees who visit this holy shrine. The prospect from the hill at different points is interesting in the extreme; but it is astonishing to see with what besotted apathy the pilgrims, who resort in vast numbers to the temple, look upon the fine features which Nature, in her most bountiful magnificence, offers to their admiration on this elevated spot. But sublimity is beyond the reach of their torpid impulses, and they gaze with sluggish indifference upon a scene that far exceeds the poet's vision, when rapt in that fine frenzy of which one of the greatest sons of genius has spoken in the most beautiful language of poetical inspiration.

Nothing can exceed the glorious splendour of the prospect over which the eye of the traveller ranges from the porch of this celebrated temple. The portico is a fine specimen of early Hindoo architecture. You ascend to it by several flights of wide stone steps. The roof is supported upon eight square massy columns, variously decorated from the pedestal to the capital. The gateway, which is very lofty, and leads into a handsome vestibule, is surmounted by a square pyramidal tower richly embellished with tracery. On the top of the tower is a row of five culices, fixed upon a narrow ornamented ridge, in which the tower terminates. On either side of the gateway is a high and strong wall, built of huge masses of granite, squared and fitted with an accuracy that might bear comparison with a piece of cabinet-work. The most splendid part of the temple is the gateway. The interior of this sanctuary is comparatively plain, and presents nothing particularly to arrest the traveller's eye. The porch was nearly filled with pilgrims when we ascended, and I entered into conversation with an extremely eloquent Brahmin, whose whole soul seemed absorbed in metaphysics; and so deeply did he appear to have dug into the mine of abstract philosophy, that I have no doubt he would have expounded the cabala to his own satisfaction at least, if not to that of more learned Rabbins.

It is quite a mistake to suppose that philosophy is above the study of these heathen priests. Some of the

Hindoo sages have drunk as deeply from the springs of speculative wisdom as the most renowned among the ancient Greeks. This the records which even now exist of their diligence and acquirements will abundantly testify. In confirmation of what I have said, I will present the reader with some recondite reasonings of a Hindoo philosopher, who probably wrote before the earliest of the Grecian sages.

"The Shoonyŭvadees affirm that from nonentity all things arose; for that everything sprung to birth from a state in which it did not previously exist: that entity absolutely implies nonentity, and that there must be some power in nonentity from which entity can spring: the sprout does not arise from a sprout, but in the absence or nonexistence of a sprout. Goutŭmŭ denies that vacuum is the cause of existence, and affirms that the cause is to be sought in concurring circumstances; for seed when sown cannot spring to life without rain; or if a latent principle of life, or an embryo state of existence, be pleaded for, this will subvert the universally acknowledged terms of father, maker, &c. The Shoonyŭvadee admits the necessity of using the terms maker, &c. but maintains that they are mere words of course, and are often used when the things spoken of are in a state of non-existence; as when men say a son will be born, or such a person had a son. Goutŭmŭ now asks, do you mean by this assertion that the living principle in the seed, or that the seed itself, is absent? You cannot mean the former, for that which is destroyed can never become the cause of existence. If, where the principle of life is wanting, existence may be produced, why is not a harvest possible from seed ground into flour? And if you mean by non-existence the absence of the seed, I would answer, that non-existence can produce no variety; but the works of nature are distinguished by an endless variety, and therefore your proposition is confuted. From hence it is plain, seeing existence cannot arise from non-existence as a cause, that the first cause must be sought for elsewhere.

"Goutŭmŭ now engages the Vedantees, some of whom maintain that Brŭmhŭ is the only cause of all things; others that the universe is a form of Brŭmhŭ; and others that the universe is a deception proceeding from Brŭmhŭ; thus excluding every assisting and efficient cause, Brŭmhŭ excepted. Goutŭmŭ, in opposition to these ideas, says, that an assisting cause must be acknowledged; for, unless there were such an assisting cause, we should not see so many changes and fluctuations in the affairs of the universe. The Vedantee says this must be attributed to the will of God. Goutŭmŭ replies, you then admit a something in addition to God, that is his will; and this involves a contradiction of your own opinion, and establishes two causes. If you could admit, for the sake of argument, these two causes, then I would urge that these changes arise only from religion and irreligion; and to affirm that the degrees of religion and irreligion in the world are appointed by the will of God, would be to attach an unchanging destiny to these things, which cannot be admitted. It must therefore be concluded that the fruits of human actions are the causes of the changes and fluctuations that take place in the world."*

So far as appears from the writings of the most eminent among their sages, the religion of the Brahmins has always been decidedly pantheistic. Pantheism, no doubt, prevails in the modern creeds of a large portion of the Hindoo population, of which the immense multitude of their deities, amounting to the prodigious number of three hundred and thirty millions, is of itself a sufficient attestation. In fact, everything in nature is deified. They confound God and the universe, and their notion of the final consummation with respect to man is absorption into the divinity. One would imagine that Spinoza had taken from their abstract theology the pernicious dogmas which he propagated to a generation hungry and ravenous after novelty in religion. The asceticism of many Hindoo visionaries has led them to contemplate God as a mere abstraction, passing their lives in those dreamy contemplations which absorb every perceptive faculty of the mind, and render them the dupes of their own prurient phantasies, placing the ultimate happiness of man in mere uninterrupted quietism. The doctrines of many of their philosophers, who unquestionably had precedence of the Grecian sages in point of time, were in a high degree metaphysical and abstruse. Some of them taught that the deity was identical with what they called nature—the universal plenum, in which everything inert, passive, or ani-

* See Ward on the History, Literature, and Mythology of the Hindoos, vol. ii. pp. 261-2.

mated, formed a positive and integral part of one infinite whole. Even now, many of those modifications of belief which distract the faith of modern Hindoos, may be looked upon as a number of currents, branching in so many meanderings from the one main stream.

The notion that God is a universal principle, permeating all things, both matter and spirit, in whom the latter is finally absorbed at the consummation of man's destiny, seems to have been a doctrine imbibed by Pythagoras from those eastern sages. The esoterick principles propounded by the Samian philosopher to his pupils, after a severe noviciate of years, was evidently adopted, with some modifications, from the Brahminical schools of theology; and these doctrines, by passing through the alembic of his mighty intellect, were purged of much of the dross with which they were originally encumbered, and are no doubt the foundation upon which the fabric of pantheism was erected by the philosophic Jew of Amsterdam.

The belief of many among the modern Brahmins at all learned in theology will be found generally to be a qualified deism, as may be seen from the writings of the late Rammahun Roy, who, though he differed in many respects from the theologians of his own country, did so rather with reference to the forms of their worship, than to the spirit of their doctrine. Although he repudiated the absurdities which form the prominent features of their temple worship, he was nevertheless essentially a Brahmin in faith whatever he might have been in practice. He was rather a rare instance of high moral feeling with a profound reverence for religion in the abstract, apart from all specific creeds. He was tolerant to all believers; and though he expressed the greatest respect for the Christian creed, the deism with which his own national faith had imbued his mind led him to withhold his assent from the fundamental doctrines of Christianity. I do, however, believe, and I owe it to his memory to state it thus publicly, that he had one of the purest minds, and was altogether one of the best of men.

He seems to have felt deeply and to have embodied in his own faith the sentiments so eloquently expressed in Sir William Jones's fine hymn to Narayana.

> Blue crystal vault and elemental fires
> That in the ethereal fluid blaze and breathe;
> Thou, tossing main, whose snaky branches wreathe
> This pensile orb with intertwisting gyres;
> Mountains whose radiant spires,
> Presumptuous rear their summits to the skies,
> And blend their emerald hue with sapphire light;
> Smooth meads and lawns that glow with varying dyes
> Of dew-bespangled leaves and blossoms bright,
> Hence! vanish from my sight!—
> Delusive pictures, unsubstantial shows!
> My soul absorbed, one only being knows,
> Of all perceptions one abundant source,
> Whence every object, every moment flows:
> Suns hence derive their force,
> Hence planets learn their course;
> But suns and fading worlds I view no more:
> God only I perceive;—God only I adore.

After quitting the Temple of Tritchengur our attention was continually attracted by the most affecting scenes of distress. The rains had failed, and a famine had prevailed through the country to an alarming extent. Whole villages were depopulated, and nothing could exceed the misery that prevailed. Mothers frequently came to us and offered to sell their children for a single meal of rice. It was distressing to witness sufferings which we could not alleviate, and to be obliged to turn from supplications to which we could give nothing but our sympathies; for our united means would, as an aggregate, have been but as a drop in the ocean towards ameliorating the general distress. The calamity was dreadful beyond description. I have seen groups of miserable Pariahs, almost maddened by hunger, scrape up the ordure of our baggage bullocks, and absolutely fight for it with desperate ferocity. This, when obtained, they washed for the occasional seeds of gram* which were to be found in it. During this melancholy season I witnessed scenes of the most appalling misery.

I remember walking out one morning just about sunrise. Within a few yards of a village I saw a poor woman seated upon the ground in a state of complete exhaustion. Her back was supported by a large stone; and her hands hung, as it appeared, insensibly by her side. From the waist upward she was entirely naked, and the squalid misery of her appearance defies description. Her eyes were closed, her chin had fallen, her lips moved so gently as scarcely to indicate the presence of life. Her long hair hung over her shoulders, and partly hid her countenance, which had the ghastly expression of death when the spirit quits its prison with a fierce conflict. Her frame presented the appearance of a skeleton covered with a

* Gram is a sort of vetch upon which cattle are fed in India.

loose skin, through which every bone was hideously prominent. It hung in folds upon her almost fleshless body. At her breast an infant clung trying to draw the nutriment which nature no longer provided. The poor babe was likewise macerated nearly to a shadow; still it cried with anguish when her bosom refused the maternal supply. I took in mine the hand of the dying mother. I put my finger to her wrist: the pulse was like the agitation of a thread just stirred to the gentlest vibration. She could not speak. In a moment the lips slightly quivered, the mouth became fixed, and the soul was no longer associated with the form on which I gazed. I took the child in my arms and carried it to my tent. The poor infant had evidently partaken of the severe sufferings of the parent. Whether the person to whose charge I confided it treated it properly, I know not,—but it died in the course of the day. I would have given anything I possessed to save that child. I saw it die without a groan. The mother became a prey to the jackals and vultures. In that village near which she died many perished on the same day. The vulture, the adjutant, the kite, and the Pariah dog here held a horrid carnival. A miserable half-starved Hindoo attempted to scare them from their banquet.

> And he saw the lean dogs beneath the wall,
> Hold o'er the dead their carnival,
> Gorging and growling o'er carcass and limb,
> They were too busy to bark at him.

I cannot forbear recording another circumstance, of which I was a melancholy witness, as it will show how stubborn the prejudices of caste are, and that they operate with indomitable pertinacity even in the agonies of death. On the day after the event just recorded, I entered the dwelling-house of a poor Hindoo, detached from the village a few hundred yards. A lean Pariah dog, foul with mange, and attenuated to a mere outline, raised its head as I stepped over the threshold, turning its dull eye upon me with a still sickly glare, as if the lustre of life had departed, and it had been moved in the socket by some mechanical impulse independent of that animal volition which gives to motion at once such an expression and charm. Leaving the starved brute "to die unhonoured and unmourned," I entered the chamber where the emissaries of death had been executing his awful purpose, under circumstances peculiarly harrowing. In one corner of the hovel appeared the corpse of an aged woman, in which the dreadful process of corruption was so actively going on that it was frightful to behold, whilst the atmosphere was charged with those horrible fumes of decaying mortality, at once disgusting and sickening to inhale. In the centre of the floor was a man of middle age, stretched upon a ragged palampore, apparently in the last extremity. His wife lay on the bare earth, scarcely a yard from his feet, much in the same state: beside her a dead child, about two years old. A little girl was kneeling on the other side, and kept continually striking the mother's face, and asking in a tone of bitter petulance, to which extreme hunger had excited it, for rice. The wretched parent only answered by turning her eyes upward with so slow and evidently painful a motion, that

I thought it was the last effort of departing life. I called to a servant, who had accompanied me, to bring a basket of provisions, which I opened before the child. The unhappy father turned his eye upon me with a look of horror, threw out his arms like a maniac, seized the infant, dragged it from the polluted food, and fell back dead. The mother was too far gone to notice the action. I desired the servant to lift her up. She breathed, though her respirations were scarcely audible; but she was insensible to everything around her. She died in my servant's arms. It was altogether the saddest scene I ever witnessed. The child survived its parents, and was claimed by some of its relatives, who were fortunate enough to escape the destruction to which so many fell victims during this season of scarcity.

Nothing can exceed the sufferings endured by large masses of the population in Hindostan when the periodical rains fail to scatter over the land that fertility of which they are the fruitful and annual source. It sometimes happens that those accustomed supplies are withheld, or only partially distributed; and then famine, either partial or general, according to the circumstances, invariably ensues among the poorer natives, who are too indolent and withal too improvident to lay up a store against such a melancholy but by no means unusual contingency. When the visitation does come upon them, it is but too frequently accompanied with horrors to which the greatest privations of the poor in more civilized countries would be comparative though negative blessings. And yet these horrors are witnessed by the wealthy among their countrymen with an apathy that deplorably shows the unbenign influence of a religion which neither encourages nor admits the operation of human sympathies. What a different lesson does Christianity teach, and what a different practice does it enforce!

Drawn by W. Daniell, R.A. — Engraved by [illegible]

The Braminee Bull.

CHAPTER VI.

BRAHMINEE BULLS.—SERINGAPATAM.

Upon quitting Salem, we crossed the Cavery and proceeded towards Seringapatam. On the banks of the river, in the neighbourhood of a small pagoda, we saw a couple of Brahminee bulls, so sleek and fat as to form a perfect contrast with the population around them, everywhere suffering from the sad scarcity of grain, while the bones of these sacred animals were loaded with an encumbrance of consecrated flesh. It was melancholy to see, that while thousands of human beings were starving, the bulls dedicated to the stern divinity, Siva, were so pampered that they would eat nothing but the most delicate food, and this was generally taken with a fastidious and palled appetite. These bulls were very small, but very beautiful; the dewlap of one of them, hanging from his throat and between his fore-legs, almost touched the ground. I could not help feeling deeply the sad fact that the miseries of their fellow-creatures were looked upon with cruel indifference by the wealthy members of the Hindoo community; while before the dumb creatures devoted to their gods, and those senseless blocks which formed the disgusting effigies of their divinities, that food was scattered which would have saved whole families from perishing with hunger.

The Brahminee bulls are generally about the size of calves of two years old, except in some districts, as in Guzerat, where they are sometimes found as large as the Durham ox. Upon their haunches there is an emblem of the god Siva, to whom they are devoted, and held in such high reverence, that no one is permitted to strike them, or to prevent them from feeding precisely where and upon what they please. They are almost always to be seen in the bazaars, where they unceremoniously enter the shops, begin to munch the grain exposed for sale, and frequently turn over everything in their way, to the great annoyance of the sedate Hindoo, who nevertheless bears it all with a religious patience, allowing the sacred intruder to continue its freaks so long as it may fancy agreeable.

One of the bulls represented in the engraving chose to take a dislike to a small, rough-haired, terrier dog, of the Scotch breed, which I had with me, and, unexpectedly raising him on its horns, nearly flung him into the river. Snap, not at all pleased at such uncourteous treatment, no sooner recovered his legs, than he rushed upon the bull, seized it by the lip, to which he clung with such persevering obstinacy, that though the animal, with a stifled roar, galloped off at its utmost speed, the terrier still maintained his hold for at least five minutes; and when at length he did relinquish the bull's lip, the enemy did not show the least disposition to renew the encounter, but sought the shelter of a pagoda, whither its companion actively followed.

We did not stay long in the Mysore, which is generally unhealthy; but while we remained there, we took the opportunity of visiting the celebrated Jain statue near the village of Sravana Belgula, thirty-three miles north of Seringapatam. There is a small choultry close by the spot on which the figure stands, where our bearers rested with the palankeens while we proceeded to view this gigantic idol. It is an image of Gomuta Raya, the divinity of the Jains; a sect differing in several particulars both from the Brahminical and Buddhist forms of worship. This part of the Mysore was formerly the principal seat of the Jain sect, once so prevalent in the south of India; and the statue, which is still to be seen, is a remarkable memorial of the power possessed by them in this neighbourhood at that period. It stands seventy feet three inches from the summit of a huge pedestal, consisting of a hill of granite upwards of two hundred feet high.

This stone divinity is composed of the same material as the pedestal, and is supposed to have originally formed the cone of the mountain, which the ingenious sculptor converted into an image, hewing away the lateral substance of the rocky hill, until the figure stood revealed to sight in all the majesty of size, though certainly not of symmetry. The statue, though formed, upon the whole, with tolerable exactness, is deficient in harmony of proportion. It is manifest to a very cursory glance, that the artist had by no means a profound knowledge of anatomy. The figure, nevertheless, is minutely defined in all its parts; but, although elaborately wrought, there is an evident rudeness in the execution, from absence, not of labour, but of skill. The effect, however, is extremely grand when this colossal image bursts upon the sight on emerging from the jungle by which it had been previously hidden. It appears to start up into the sky like the Demiurge of eastern superstition, as if it could hold communion at once with heaven and earth, upon the latter of which it seems to look down from its sublime elevation with the immobility of stern and inflexible power.

The associations on first beholding this gigantic sculpture are of the most exalted description. You forget for the moment that you are looking upon a mere inert mass of granite; but the ideas of power, vastness, and other attributes of divinity, are irresistibly associated in the mind, while a feeling almost amounting to awe is kindled; until the eye is turned from the mighty mockery by the natural impulse of mental reaction, and you are suddenly brought to the humiliating consciousness that it is nothing more than a huge lump of senseless rock.

In the neighbourhood of Cabul there are statues of similar colossal proportions with this at Sravana Belgula, which have been well described by Lieutenant Alexander Burnes, in his travels into Bokhara. "There are no relics of Asiatic antiquity," says this intelligent writer, "which have roused the curiosity of the learned more than the gigantic idols of Bameean. They consist of two figures, a male and a female; the one named Silsal, the other Shahmama. The figures are cut in alto-relievo on the face of the hill, and represent two colossal images. The male is the larger of the two, and about a hundred and twenty feet high:

it occupies a front of seventy feet, and the niche in which it is excavated extends about that depth into the hill. This idol is mutilated, both legs having been fractured by cannon, and the countenance above the mouth is destroyed. The lips are very large, the ears long and pendent, and there appears to have been a tiara upon the head. The figure is covered by a mantle, which hangs over it in all parts, and has been formed of a kind of plaster, the image having been studded with wooden pins in various places to assist in fixing it. The figure itself is without symmetry, nor is there much elegance in the drapery. The hands, which held out the mantle, have been both broken. The female figure is more perfect than the male, and has been dressed in the same manner. It is cut in the same hill, at a distance of two hundred yards, and is about half the size. It was not to be discovered whether the smaller idol was a brother or son of the colossus, but from the information of the natives.

"I have now to note the most remarkable curiosity in the idols of Bameean. The niches of both have been at one time plastered and ornamented with paintings of human figures, which have now disappeared from all parts but that immediately over the heads of the idols; here the colours are as vivid and the paintings as distinct as in the Egyptian tombs. There is little variety in the design of these figures, which represent the bust of a woman, with a knob of hair on the head, and a plaid thrown half over the chest; the whole surrounded by a halo, and the head again by another halo. In one part I could trace a group of three female figures following each other: the execution of the work was indifferent, and not superior to the pictures which the Chinese make in imitation of an European artist.

"The traditions of the people regarding the idols of Bameean are vague and unsatisfactory. It is stated that they were excavated about the Christian era by a tribe of Kaffirs, infidels, to represent a king named Silsal and his wife, who ruled in a distant country, and was worshipped for his greatness. The Hindoos assert that they were excavated by the Pandoos, and that they are mentioned in the great epic poem of the Mahaburat. Certain it is that the Hindoos on passing these idols, at this day, hold up their hands in adoration: they do not make offerings, and the custom may have fallen into disuse since the rise of Islam. I am aware that a conjecture attributes these images to the Buddhists, and the long ears of the great figure render the surmise probable. I did not trace any resemblance to the colossal figures in the caves of Salsette, near Bombay; but the shape of the head is not unlike that of the great tri-faced idol of Elephanta. At Manikyala, in the Punjab, near the celebrated 'tope,' I found a glass or cornelian antique which exactly resembles this head. In the paintings over the idols I observed a close resemblance to the images of the Jain temples in Western India, on Mount Aboo, Girnar, and Politana, in Kattywar. I judge the figures to be female; but they are very rude, though the colours in which they are sketched are bright and beautiful. There is nothing in the images of Bameean to evince any great advancement in the arts, or what the most common people might not have easily executed. They cannot certainly be referred to the Greek invasion, nor are they mentioned by any of the historians of Alexander's expedition. I find in the history of Timourlane that both the idols and excavations of Bameean are described by Sherif-o-deen, his historian. The idols are there stated to be so high, that none of the archers could strike the head. They are called Lat and Munat, two celebrated idols which are mentioned in the Koran. The writer also alludes to the road which led up to their summit from the interior of the hill. There are no inscriptions at Bameean to guide us in their history; and the whole of the later traditions are so mixed up with Ali, the son-in-law of Mahommed, who we well know never came into this part of Asia, that they are most unsatisfactory."

Not far from Sravana Belgula is a neighbourhood remarkable for a tribe among whom there exists a custom as singular as it is absurd. When a mother betroths her eldest daughter, she pierces her ears as an initiatory ceremony, by which the girl becomes plighted to her future husband. Before, however, the parent can accomplish this mystical perforation of the daughter's ears, she is herself obliged to undergo the amputation of the first joints of the third and fourth fingers of her right hand, and with the mangled limb performs upon her child this singular ceremony of matrimonial inauguration.

The amputation of the mother's finger-joints is accomplished by a very summary process. The operator is generally the blacksmith of the village, who simply lays her finger upon his anvil, places the edge of a blunt chisel upon the joint, and with one stroke of a heavy hammer off flies the divided member, whilst the sufferer seems to think no more of the matter than she would of a corn being cut. In spite of this clumsy method of operating, it is surprising how soon the wound heals; a poultice of turmeric is applied, and in a few days the hand appears relieved from all pain or inconvenience. So pure is the state of blood in these people, that the severest wounds heal in an incredibly short space of time. Such a thing as mortification is seldom or never heard of. They are, however, very subject to tetanus, from slight punctures in the feet, which invariably proves fatal.

The tribe to which I have just referred is, I imagine, confined to two or three districts of the Mysore, and perhaps do not altogether embrace a population of twenty thousand souls. I believe they are a low caste, and associate with no one out of their own community. When a girl is betrothed, should she happen to be an orphan, the mother of the affianced husband is obliged to submit to the loss of her finger-tops, provided she has not already undergone the necessary mutilation. When that is the case, any further membral disfigurement is dispensed with, though, such is the excess of joy evinced by parents at the marriage of their children, that had the mother fifty fingers, and the law of superstitious custom prescribed that she should leave the tips of every one of them in the shop of the village blacksmith, she would cheerfully undergo the mutilation, to see her daughter provided with a husband—the greatest earthly blessing in the estimation of a Hindoo woman. It frequently happens that parents will expend everything they possess in the world upon an entertainment given on the marriage of a child, and readily encounter the severest privations during the rest of their lives, in order thus to gratify a momentary vanity.

I was much amused by an occurrence at a small village through which we passed on our way toward the Courg district, whither we directed our course after we quitted Sravana Belgula. In a narrow enclosure, behind a small hovel, we saw a woman tied to a stake, and a man standing over her administering severe chastisement with a thick bamboo, which he occasionally applied to her naked shoulders so earnestly, that she screamed with a piercing but dissonant expression of suffering. She bore the infliction for some time without manifesting the slightest disposition to retaliate; but at length, goaded by the unbending severity of her tyrant, she made a sudden spring at his leg as he advanced to repeat the castigation, and, seizing him by the calf with her teeth, bit it so energetically, that he howled like a scourged whelp. Springing aside, however, he got beyond her reach, and then administered the discipline of the bamboo at so furious a rate, that I thought the woman's bones in jeopardy. She now bore the blows without wincing, fixing her full dark eyes upon him with an expression of calm triumph which seemed to say, "You may kill me, now I have had my revenge!" The rattling of the hollow bamboo against her ribs might have been heard, I am sure, at the distance of a hundred yards: still she did not move a muscle, but sat sullen and enduring, while the man's rage appeared to kindle in proportion to her non-resistance.

There were several persons looking on with perfect unconcern, from whom I learned that it was a domestic despot beating his wife for some act of social dereliction. Becoming uneasy at seeing the merciless mode of chastisement pursued by the enraged Hindoo, I sent one of my native attendants to expostulate with the man upon his undue severity. The moment he attempted to interpose in this family disagreement, the woman released herself from the cords by which she was bound, rushed upon my unhappy messenger, threw her head into his stomach with the fury of an excited tigress, and poured upon him a volley of such eloquent abuse for interfering between a husband and wife as perfectly astounded me, though it only excited a smile on the countenances of the generality of the bystanders. She had no sooner put to flight the man whom I had sent as a pacificator, for he scampered away from the scene of combat as if he had been stung by a scorpion, than she took her station at the stake, to which her better half again bound her, and proceeded to thump her to her heart's content and his own.

It is a strange anomaly in human nature, but with the Hindoo wife passive endurance is at once a virtue and a social obligation. She esteems her husband in proportion as he maintains what she conceives to be the dignity of his character; and this, in her mind, is most properly maintained when he makes the wife feel his power and her own impotence,—when he obliges her to treat him with the deference due to a master, and forces from her the subserviency of a slave. Nothing would so soon cause a Hindoo woman to rebel against the authority of her husband as the circumstance of his using that authority mildly. So strong an impression has she of her own inferiority in every respect as a rational and social animal, that her most active contempt would be excited were she to be treated by the lord of her heart with that equality which can alone render the married state one of mutual confidence and happiness. If her husband were to allow her to eat in his presence, she would despise him; if he were to permit her to approach when he is taking his refreshment, she would no longer respect him: in short, if he did not use her as the mere instrument of his pleasure and of his comfort, she would consider him a degraded member of that community to which it is his and her pride to belong.

The state of utter ignorance in which women are kept in India may in some measure account for the perversity with which they adhere to and even venerate customs that operate so oppressively upon themselves. They never receive the slightest education, and defer to their male relatives in every instance where the passions do not interfere with reason and assume the ascendancy; which, indeed, now and then may be observed among some of the lower and more profligate classes. A Hindoo writer has said, "A woman can never be independent; in childhood she must be subject to her father, in youth to her husband, and in old age to her sons." This is literally true.

It is indeed pitiful to see women, often lovely beyond what conception can shadow forth in the mere external graces, or what may be called the accidents of form and feature, yet lapped in an ignorance so profound as to stifle the sweetest associations to which the sight of beauty, under whatever aspect, must give rise, and realize the humiliating reality of the mere animal, in which the mind is utterly merged and almost brutalized. I should impute the social degradation of the modern Hindoos much to the ignorance in which their women are suffered to live, and the domestic tyranny to which they are subjected; for it has ever been found that man becomes refined in proportion as woman is intelligent, and that where there is not a high and delicate respect for the gentler sex, there never can be a perfect civilization;—of which the moral disorder, now so distorted a feature in the character of Hindoo society, appears to me a sad but irrefragable evidence.

However the native of Hindostan may look upon woman, a proof of the beauty of her mind and the noble powers of her intellect is exhibited in every community where those powers are permitted to expand by a suitable culture. Mind, in the abstract; has no distinction of sex; and what is there to prevent the mental faculties of woman from reaching to the highest intellectual elevation, if they are directed with the same fervency of purpose and ardour of pursuit as have exalted the brightest names in our literature to those dignities which posterity has gratefully assigned to them? In our own country, Mrs. Somerville may stand forth an illustrious example of the supremacy of mind under the control and direction of a woman, and how high a woman may rise in the scale of intellectual attainment merely by her own inherent principle, which is the secondary source of knowledge, and therefore, in accordance with Lord Bacon's well known axiom, the germ of power.

> "The mind alike,
> Vigorous or weak, is capable of culture,
> But still bears fruit according to its nature:
> 'Tis not the teacher's skill that rears the scholar.
> The sparkling gem gives back the glorious radiance
> It drinks from other light; but the dull earth
> Absorbs the blaze, and yields no gleam again."*

With all their failings, nothing can exceed the intensity of affection which Hindoo mothers feel towards their offspring, of which I once happened to witness a remarkable instance.

I was one morning riding upon the banks of the river that flows almost immediately under the walls of Poonah, in the Deccan, when I saw a very interesting Hindoo woman, with an infant in her arms about two years old, descend to the edge of the river to bathe. She laid her child upon the bank, which was here about three feet above the water, while she walked into the stream. The rains had not long ceased, and therefore the course of the river was at this time more than usually rapid, especially near the bank, where the water was deep. Here the channel curved; and as the water was turned off from its direct course, the resistance of the bank increased its

* Uttara Rama Cherita.

impetus. The mother was busily employed in washing her long black hair, when a sharp quick shriek from one of the bathers called her attention to the spot on which she had laid her infant. She only saw the ripple on the surface of the stream, but this was enough to satisfy her that the object of her maternal yearning was in jeopardy. She instantly threw her dripping hair back upon her shoulders, her dark eye dilating with the intense expression of her resolved and holy purpose, and dashed fearlessly into the deep turbid waters. She rose buoyantly upon their surface, and, having reached the spot where her child had sunk, disappeared beneath them. She rose again at a considerable distance, made for the shore, and cast herself upon the ground in despair. Her agony was intense; and as every expression of consolation from her companions seemed only to aggravate it, she was soon left by the other bathers upon the ground bewailing her bereavement. I could not venture to intrude upon the sacred privacy of her grief, as I knew it would only be adding the pain of imagined pollution, which my immediate presence would have inflicted, to that of her present desolation.

The issue of this melancholy event was still more sad. The body of the child was recovered some hours after it had fallen into the river, and the wretched mother mourned over it day after day, until it was in such a state of dreadful decomposition, that no one could approach it without disgust. The poor woman was a few days after attacked with fever, and died. She was the wife of a Sepoy. I had the curiosity to go and see her the day after the accident. She was bewailing the death of her babe in the most pathetic strains: I did not venture to interrupt her grief, but looked on in painful silence. She was evidently unconscious of my presence, her whole mind being absorbed by her sorrows. There were two or three women near her, who looked on with heartless indifference, chattering to each other, and occasionally addressing to the mourner a few words of callous and repulsive consolation. Among the Hindoos in general, and especially among the women, it is surprising how little the sympathies are excited. Their affections are strong towards their own offspring, but seldom radiate beyond the domestic circle; and thus we find this strange moral anomaly among them, that although they feel a domestic loss of the kind just related with extreme intensity, they never appear to sympathise with those whom they may happen to see suffering under a similar bereavement. One of the women, on the present occasion, said to the miserable parent in a sharp tone of rebuke, "Why do you weep? Have you nobody else to care for but the child who is gone away from you? Is he worth lamenting when he has caused you so much sorrow? Why did he go away, if he cared anything for his mother? Either he was not fit to be with you, or you were not fit to be with him, and therefore it was proper that he should go. This is your punishment, and you ought to bear it with patience. You must have done something very wicked in a former birth, and this is the bitter fruit of your crime. Come, come, dry your tears, and be happy."

These words of coarse reproof fell upon the mourner's ear like snow upon water—they were absorbed without leaving an impression. I quitted the scene, giving the husband a few rupees to meet the expenses of the poor babe's obsequies, little thinking then that he would so soon have a second blank left upon his domestic hearth. The man was considerably affected, but the loss of his child smote him much more severely than the death of his wife, towards whom, however, I found he had the character of having proved at least a forbearing if not a tender husband; which is much to say, since among the Hindoos tenderness does not commonly class with the conjugal virtues.

It is really melancholy to witness the social misery common to the domestic state in India. From the ill-judged indulgence of parents, their children usually grow up to be intractable and rebellious. If the least check is opposed to their forwardness, they resist with the vehemence of maniacs, and in defiance of all parental authority act according to the impulses of their unruly wills. We cannot be surprised, under such circumstances, at the filial atrocities so frequently witnessed on the banks of the Ganges, where almost daily parents are suffocated by their offspring with the mud of the sacred river.

CHAPTER VII.

SERINGAPATAM.—HYDER ALI.—TIPPOO.

Before we proceed, it will not be out of place to give a short account of the capital of Mysore. At the spot near which this city stands the river Cavery branches off into two streams: these, after diverging obliquely to the right and left, again move towards each other; then, after a course of about four miles and half, unite, enclosing the city of Seringapatam which stands upon a conical island, about half a league wide at the upper end, and a league and half in length. The Cavery is here of considerable width, and pours a large body of water rapidly through a deep channel, interrupted by huge fragments of rock, over and between which, during the periodical rains, the river struggles and foams with great turbulence. The island of Seringapatam is low, and extremely unhealthy. The jungle fever, induced by the malaria so constantly rising from this flat unwholesome spot, is very prevalent; and those whom it has once attacked seldom entirely recover from its pernicious effects. The country in the immediate neighbourhood of this city is watered by canals, which are supplied by the river. Dams are thrown across the stream, and the water thus forced into the canals irrigates the country to some extent.

The fort stands at the west end of the island, and is a large building, designed by one evidently less skilful as an architect than as an engineer, though built with great strength. During the memorable siege of Seringapatam, the glacis was found to be in many places so high and steep as perfectly to shelter the assaulting party from the fire of the besieged. All the public buildings in the city are clumsily constructed, bearing little appearance of architectural symmetry; on the contrary, looking mean and even rude. They are chiefly surrounded by a lofty wall composed of mud and stone. Hyder Ali's palace, which he called the Laul Baugh, situated at the eastern extremity of the island, is an exception to this rule. Although entirely constructed of mud, it has all the light, airy elegance of the better Mahomedan structures, and the convenience as well as beauty of a modern palace. Near it is the tomb of the renowned Hyder, enclosing likewise the bodies of his wife and of his son, Tippoo Sultan; they are deposited under slabs of black marble raised a few inches from the ground. There is still kept up at the expense of the British Government an establishment of priests, who daily perform the customary services for the welfare of departed souls over the graves of those distinguished persons.

The suburbs of this capital are built on the highest part of the island,—about the middle of it; they are composed for the most part of small mean tenements, the whole occupying the space of five furlongs square. There is a palace called Dowlut Bang, or the garden of riches, and which was, I believe, built by Hyder Ali, but improved by Tippoo. It is rather an ordinary building, and is now in a state of dilapidation. When Captain Basil Hall visited Seringapatam he slept in this palace, "but," says he, "I paid dearly for my temerity: indeed, I believe this island is nearly the most unhealthy spot in the East Indies. What is curious, however, I felt none of the effects of the malaria poison as long as I remained on the high level of the Mysore country; but within a few days after reaching the sea-coast of Malabar, was seized with what is called the jungle fever, of which I feel the consequences to this hour. The Duke of Wellington, then Colonel Wellesley, when Governor of Seringapatam, lived in the same palace, which he rendered more commodious than it had ever been in the days of Tippoo Sultan, or even of his father Hyder Ali. He filled it with European furniture, and made it less unhealthy by placing glass sashes in all the windows, by which some portion of the noxious air of the night could be kept out."*

The public buildings in this once powerful capital of one of the greatest princes whose actions modern history records, are now turned into military offices, and residences for different functionaries of the East India Company's government. Hyder's palace is converted into the dwelling-house of the resident surgeon; his harem into an hospital for European troops. The private apartments of Tippoo's harem are now the abode of a British Resident, and the rest of the build-

* See Basil Hall's Fragments of Voyages and Travels, third series, vol. ii. p. 238.

ing has become an artillery barrack. Although some of these edifices in the palmy days of the Mahomedan glory, under Hyder Ali in the Mysore, were occupied by persons of the first distinction in the state, they afford but indifferent accommodation to our countrymen, who are especially partial to air and light, neither of which are very liberally admitted into these structures, they being for the most part heavy without, as well as close and inconvenient within.

In Tippoo's time the population of Seringapatam was estimated at upwards of a hundred and forty thousand souls, a considerable population for so confined a spot. The Sultan had a numerous and well-appointed army, and such was his hostility to the English that nothing less than their utter extirpation would have satisfied his sanguinary antipathy. Like the father of the great Carthaginian general, Hyder Ali transmitted to his son his own detestation of those national foes who had obtained a footing in India, which seems likely only to be extinguished with their existence as a nation.

It was this very hostility that proved in the issue the cause of his family's downfal, and the extinction of a dynasty which he had established at so much cost of labour and of blood. The energies of that mind which established and bequeathed to Tippoo Sultan such a powerful principality in southern India, bore in their own fierce strength the elements of ruin which finally overwhelmed it under the weaker domination of his son. Although Hyder Ali was a sagacious man, he was neither honest nor truly wise, for he made everything subserve his ambition, and the ferocity of his passions was like an incubus upon the loftier aspirations of his intellect. No man ever more completely realized the Hindoo proverb, "a wicked person, though possessed of wisdom, is no more to be trusted than a serpent with a jewel in its head." The fierceness of hostility bequeathed by him to his successor, coloured the whole of that Prince's political life, and drove him perpetually to attempt the infliction of retribution upon those who were the objects of his bitter hatred, his rash perseverance in which precipitated his fall, and in that fall the utter ruin of his family was involved. Had Tippoo courted an alliance with, instead of provoking the enmity of, the British government in India, his banners might be now floating over the battlements of Seringapatam.

The fall of this city is one of the most memorable events in the annals of British India. It was stormed on the 4th of May 1799, by the army under General Harris, the garrison amounting to eight thousand men. "In less than seven minutes from the period of issuing from the trenches the British colours were planted on the summit of the breaches. It was regulated, that as soon as the assailants surmounted the rampart, one half of them should wheel to the right, the other to the left, and that they should meet over the eastern gateway. The right, which was led by Colonel Baird, met with little resistance, both as the enemy, lest retreat should be cut off, abandoned the cavaliers, and as the inner rampart of the south-western face was exposed to a perfect enfilade. The assailants on the left were opposed in a different manner.

Lieutenant Dunlop, by whom it was commanded, received a wound in the ascent, and the Sultan passed the nearest traverse as the column quitted the breach. A succession of well-constructed traverses were most vigorously defended; and a flanking fire of musketry from the inner rampart did great execution upon the assailants. All the commissioned officers attached to the leading companies were soon either killed or disabled, and the loss would at any rate have been great, had not a very critical assistance been received. When the assailants first surmounted the breach they were not a little surprised by the sight of a deep, and, to appearance, impassable, ditch, between the exterior and interior lines of defence. A detachment of the Twelfth regiment having discovered a narrow strip of the terreplein, left for the passage of the workmen, got up the inner rampart of the enfiladed face without much opposition, and wheeling to the left, drove before them the musketeers, who were galling the assailants of the left attack, and they at last reached the flank of the traverse which was defended by the Sultan. The two columns of the English on the outer and inner rampart then moved in a position to expose the successive traverses to a front and flank fire at the same time, and forced the enemy from one to another, till they perceived the British of the right attack over the eastern gate, and ready to fall upon them in the rear; when they broke and hastened to escape. The Sultan continued on foot during the greater part of this time, performing the part rather of a common soldier than of a general, firing several times upon the assailants with his own hands. But a little before the time at which his troops resigned the contest, he complained of pain and weakness in one of his legs, in which he had received a severe wound when young, and ordered a horse. When abandoned by his men, instead of seeking to make his escape, which the proximity of the water-gate would have rendered easy, he made way for the gate into the interior fort. As he was crossing to the gate by the communication from the outer rampart, he received a musket-ball in the right side, nearly as high as the breast, but still pressed on till he arrived at the gate. Fugitives from within as well as from without were crowding in opposite directions to this gate, and the detachment of the Twelfth had descended into the body of the place, for the purpose of arresting the influx of the fugitives from the outer works. The two columns of assailants, one without the gate and one within, were now pouring into it a destructive fire from both sides when the Sultan arrived. Endeavouring to pass, he received another wound from the fire of the inner detachment; his horse also being wounded, sank under him, and his turban fell to the ground, while his friends dropped rapidly around him. His attendants placed him in his palenkeen, but the place was already so crowded and choked up with the dead and the dying, that he could not be removed. According to the statement of a servant who survived, some English soldiers, a few minutes afterwards, entered the gateway; and one of them offering to pull off the sword-belt of the Sultan, which was very rich, Tippoo, who still held his sabre in his hand, made a cut at him with all his remaining strength. The man, wounded in the knee, put his firelock to his shoulder, and the Sultan, receiving the ball in his temple, expired."*

When the city was taken, and the sons of Tippoo secured, " the Sultan was to be searched for in every corner of the palace. A party of English troops were admitted, and those of Tippoo disarmed. After proceeding through several of the apartments, the Kelledar was entreated, if he valued his own life or that of his master, to discover where he was concealed. That officer protested, in the most solemn manner, that the Sultan was not in the palace; that he had been wounded during the storm, and was lying in a gateway on the northern side of the fort. He offered to conduct the inquirers, and submit to any punishment if he was found to have deceived. General Baird and the officers who accompanied him proceeded to the spot, covered with a promiscuous and shocking heap of bodies wounded and dead. At first the bodies were dragged out of the gateway to be examined, it being already too dark to distinguish them where they lay. As this mode of examination, however, threatened to be very tedious, a light was procured, and Major Allen and the Kelledar went forward to the place. After some search, the Sultan's palenkeen was discovered, and under it a person wounded, but not dead. He was afterwards ascertained to be the Rajah Khan, one of Tippoo's most confidential servants, who had attended his master during the whole of the fatal day. This person being made acquainted with the object of the search, pointed out the spot where the Sultan had fallen. The body being brought out and sufficiently

* Mills's British India, vol. vi. page 115.

recognized, was conveyed in a palenkeen to the palace. It was warm when first discovered; the eyes were open, the features not distorted, and Major Allen and Colonel Wellesley were for a few moments doubtful whether it was not alive. It had four wounds, three in the trunk and one in the temple, the ball of which, having entered a little above the right ear, had lodged in the cheek. His dress consisted of a jacket of fine white linen, loose drawers of flowered chintz, the usual girdle of the east, crimson-coloured, tied round his waist, and a handsome pouch, with a belt of silk, red and green, hung across his shoulder. He had an amulet on his arm; but his ornaments, if he wore any, were gone."*

Upon quitting the neighbourhood of the once flourishing capital of Mysore, we bent our course towards the coast of Malabar, where we concluded we should find some vessel about to sail up the Persian Gulf, in which we might procure a passage to Mascat, whither we were very anxious to proceed. On our way towards the Ghauts that separate Malabar from the upland country, we were delighted with the abrupt massy grandeur and extreme diversity of the scenery. A new prospect was presented at every point, or rather the aspect of the country seemed so altered by change of position within the intervals of a few hundred yards, that it had all the appearance of exhibiting a different view, unless where some remarkable object existed to show its identity. Upon our approach to a small town, my attention was arrested by the beauty of a large tank, surrounded with

* Vide Mills ad loc.

fine masonry, and having a capacious and highly-decorated choultry at one end. In the distance was the pyramidal tower of a pagoda. Near it, leaning with her back against a wall, upon which was the statue of a sacred bull, formed of brick and covered with chunam, stood a young Hindoo woman, of high caste, dressed with a more than usual degree of splendour. She had several rich necklaces round her throat, a costly sevigné, or an ornament precisely similar to it, upon her forehead, and long pendulous earrings, composed of gems apparently of value. Her wrists were encircled with broad gold bangles, and over her left shoulder, crossing the body and falling over the right hip, hung a muslin scarf of the finest texture and richly embroidered. The tali, or marriage-knot, as Southey has called it in his masterly poem, The Curse of Kehama, was round her neck, which showed that she was a married woman.

> Her limbs with fragrant oils were dyed,
> Her hair with pearly fillets tied;
> Her neck fresh wreaths of chumpa* prest.

I was much struck with the easy and natural grace of her form and attitude as she reclined carelessly against the wall where first she had arrested my attention. Upon passing her, under the shadow of the wall, on her right hand, a few yards beyond, lay two of the most beautiful children I had ever beheld. They appeared about five or six years old, were as near as possible the same size, and so much alike that it

* The chumpa is a tree venerated by the Hindoos; it bears a very fragrant flower of a saffron colour.

A Hindu Woman

would have been very difficult to distinguish them apart. They were evidently twins, and the children of the beautiful Hindoo whom we had just passed. Being roused by the noise of our approach, they ran to their mother, as if for protection. They were both straight, and admirably formed; their little limbs exhibiting a gracefulness and precision of outline, which showed that they had not been cramped into obliquity according to those refinements exclusively practised by the great in more civilized Europe.

I was arrested by the premature sagacity developed in the countenances of these children. They were shy but not timid, and shrank from my approach rather with the seeming of considering it an unauthorised intrusion, than from any apprehension of harm. I expressed my admiration of them to the mother, who said nothing, but received my laudations with a slight graceful inclination of body; yet the relaxed expression of her eye satisfied me my praises were not unwelcome: and as if to show that she appreciated my commendation, she turned the boys round, when to my astonishment I perceived that from the nape of the neck to their heels the whole body behind was covered with a short thick hair, as black and glossy as the feathers on a raven's throat. In front their skins were as smooth as the cheek of a beautiful woman, and without the least speck of deformity. Their legs were feathered behind like those of a high-bred spaniel, and nothing could exceed the strange contrast presented by the front and back of their little bodies. They had come into the world, as I at length ascertained from the parent, with the same hirsute mantle in which they then stood before me. Strange as the thing appeared, there was nothing disagreeable in the back aspect of these children, for the hair was so short that it did not in the slightest degree conceal the figure, and of so soft a texture as to excite an impression rather of delicacy than of coarseness in these beautiful brothers.

On the day that followed our meeting with those children and their lovely mother, a serious event occurred which interrupted our progress for some time. One of the coolies engaged in transporting our baggage having thrown himself down under the shade of some aloes to take his usual rest at our first halting-place, was bitten in the side by a venomous snake. In a short time he became violently sick, foamed at the mouth, and exhibited symptoms of extreme agony. It unfortunately happened that no one present had the means of administering to his positive relief; he therefore lay in a deplorable state, being in strong convulsions, and the effects of the poison becoming every minute more and more powerful, he was evidently in a state of great suffering, and writhed fearfully. At a venture, I poured a small quantity of brandy down his throat, which for the moment seemed to arrest the strong muscular action, and give a little comparative ease; but the spasms soon returned with aggravated violence, and all hope of saving him vanished. He continued the whole day in a dreadful state; during the night delirium came on, which subsided after some hours, leaving him lethargic and speechless.

Finding his case hopeless, some of his companions

sent for a sort of seer in the village near which we had halted, who professed the power of curing diseases by a spell, and pretended that the poison of the most venomous reptile could not resist the potency of his mystical but curative charm. The poor cooly at the time of this man's arrival was lying upon his back, still breathing indeed, but in a state of perfect unconsciousness as to what was passing around him, and obviously at the last extremity. The professor, nothing abashed by the apparent impossibility of resuscitating a dead man, or a man all but dead, audaciously declared that the bystanders should see the sufferer rise in his strength in a few minutes,—such was the form of his declaration. He began accordingly to gesticulate, to mutter, to hum, to look wild and mysterious; but in the midst of his afflatus, the bitten cooly gave a quick gasp and died. As soon as it became apparent to the empirical Hindoo that his patient was actually dead, he expressed neither surprise nor emotion, but gravely averred that the man had been guilty of some unpardonable crime, and that as his soul was to go into the body of a snake in the next birth for his sins in this, the great Siva's minister was prevented by the sinner's destiny from exercising the efficacy of his spell; "but," he continued, pointing to the body, "had that been a good man, I could have rendered the poison of the reptile as harmless as milk."

It may excite surprise that these imposters are never suspected. Their failures expose them to no discredit. They have a ready excuse which is always received, and their infallibility becomes so settled an opinion among their superstitious dupes, that they always continue to retain an influence as morally pernicious as it is socially degrading.

Mr. Forbes, in his Oriental Memoirs, relates a circumstance which completely eclipses the magnetising of Mesmer, and leaves the question still one to be answered, whether other mortals besides Faust have not their Mephistophiles. "At Baroche," says he, "I was intimate with a Banian, named Lullabhy, the richest man in the city, and of great influence in the Purgunna. He was universally believed to possess the power of curing the bite of venomous serpents by a knowledge peculiar to himself, which he never imparted to another. By this art he certainly recovered many natives from a desperate state, after being wounded by the Cobra de Capello and the scarlet snake of Cubbeer-Bur, without touching the patient, or prescribing anything inwardly. The talent of Lullabhy seemed to have no affinity with that of the ancient Psylli, or the modern snake-charmers, but probably was not unlike the science professed by Mesmer and Doctor de Mainoduc. Be that as it may, his fame for effecting these cures was everywhere established. Mr. Perrott, then second in council, and some other of the civil servants at Baroche, were satisfied with a cure of which they had been frequent witnesses."

"Of all the Europeans I am acquainted with in India, Mr. Robert Gambier, at that time chief of Baroche, was, perhaps, the most incredulous respecting talismans, charms, divinations, and preternatural pretensions of the Brahmins. His opinion of Lullabhy's talent was publicly known. A circumstance in his own garden now afforded a fair opportunity of detecting its fallacy. One of the under-gardeners, working between the pavilions, was bit by a Cobra de Capello, and pronounced to be in danger. Mr. Gambier was then holding a council in an upper pavilion, and, at the desire of Mr. Perrott, immediately sent for Lullabhy, without informing him of the accident, of which he remained ignorant until ushered into the chief's presence. The gardener was lying on a slight bed of coir rope,* in a veranda adjoining the council-room. Being asked if he could effect a cure, Lullabhy modestly replied, that by God's blessing he trusted he should succeed. The poor wretch was at this time in great agony and delirious; he afterwards became speechless; still Lullabhy was not permitted to commence his operation. The members of council anxiously waited the chief's permission, especially when Lullabhy asserted that any farther loss of time would render it too late. Mr. Gambier examined the man's pulse by a stop-watch, and when convinced his dissolution was inevitably approaching, he allowed Lullabhy to exert his influence. After a short silent prayer, in presence of all the company, Lullabhy waved his catarra, or short dagger, over the bed of the expiring man, without touching him. The patient continued for some time motionless; in half an hour his heart appeared to beat, circulation quickened; within the hour he moved his limbs, and recovered his senses. At the expiration of the third hour Lullabhy had effected his cure. The man was sent home to his family, and in a few days recovered from the

* Rope made from the exterior coat of the cocao-nut.

weakness occasioned by convulsive paroxysms, which probably would never have been so severe, or of such long continuance, had the counteracting power been sooner applied."*—Those Indians are in truth strange deluders!

* Forbes's Oriental Memoirs, vol. iii. pp. 249-50, quarto edition.

CHAPTER VIII.

COORG.—ROBBERS HANGED.—PHANSIGARS.

We now descended the ghauts through a very picturesque country, and pitched our tents in the territories of the Coorg Rajah. As he was an ally of the British government, to which he was much attached, we expected to be well received by him; nor were we disappointed. The morning after we had made the descent of the ghauts, I was on horseback a little after daylight, when, suddenly turning an angle of the road, my horse started at something which appeared to obstruct its further progress. As the light was not yet very perfect, from the unexpected wheeling of the animal, I could not for the moment discover what had alarmed it, but, upon a nearer inspection, I found it to be the body of a man suspended from the arm of a tree that nearly extended across the road. It was in a dreadful state of decay; but so common are offensive odours of all kinds in India, that the traveller is never surprised at being half suffocated without seeing anything to account for his annoyance. Thus, though I had for some time breathed an atmosphere neither wholesome nor agreeable, I had nevertheless not the slightest suspicion of my proximity to such a loathsome object. I turned away from the sickening sight with shuddering disgust. I had not advanced very far, before a similar object appeared, in all the revolting deformity of decay and mutilation. It hung so low, that the jackals had been enabled to gnaw the flesh from the legs so far as the knees; and the frightful distortion of feature, from the summary and clumsy mode of strangulation adopted by the native executioner, altogether exhibited a picture which I can never easily forget. I passed hastily on; but my annoyances in this way were not yet at an end.

I had not proceeded above a few hundred yards before a third spectacle, still more revolting than the two former, met my view: this was the body of a woman hanging by the legs from a rude gibbet set up by the roadside. This person had been hanged in the usual manner, but the cord having snapped, some passengers had probably reversed her position, by way of expressing their indignation at her crime, of which I shall have presently to speak. The face was horribly disfigured by jackals, all the flesh having been eaten away, and presenting the mask of a grim and hideous skeleton. The vultures were kept off by the continual passing of travellers; else these bodies would not have remained twelve hours unconsumed: when I saw them they had been hanging since the previous morning. I counted no less than eight of those objects in the course of my ride.

Upon inquiry, I ascertained that they were the bodies of a dacoit-gang, called Phansigars, who had been detected in attempting to murder a subject of

Drawn by W. Daniell, R.A. Engraved by J. C. Armytage

On the Palinkatam River

the Coorg Rajah some distance down the coast. Sixteen of the gang were taken and executed, eight at one extremity of the Rajah's territory, and eight at the other: among them was one woman. I had an account of the whole affair from an intelligent native, who was present at the executions of the eight whose bodies I saw, which may not be uninteresting to the reader, as characteristic of national habits, and as showing the summary mode in which the laws deal with criminals not within the British jurisdiction.

Upon the banks of the Balliapatam river, on a very elevated spot, was situated the palace of a native independent chieftain, who was said to protect different tribes of robbers, from whom he received a considerable tribute. This is not an uncommon practice among the petty chieftains in different parts of India, by which they obtain no trifling addition to their revenue; for the robber-tribes to whom they extend their protection always make them a liberal return in plunder for the benefit thus enjoyed. In the district of Madura this base system of political delinquency was adopted to a most disgraceful extent in the middle of the last century by the Polygars in that province and in those districts immediately bordering upon it.

The building of which I have spoken stood upon a remote but romantic hill, almost inaccessible, except by a strongly fortified path, the river flowing beneath with a deep placid current. The seclusion of the neighbourhood rendered it the frequent scene of robberies, and even of murders.

It happened that a Coorg horseman was passing near the spot, when he was accosted by an interesting-looking girl, who told him a piteous story of having been robbed and maltreated, and besought his assistance in her difficulties. Excited by the appeal of a handsome woman in distress, he offered to take her behind him on his horse, and thus assist her a few miles on her journey. She readily assented to his proposal, with many protestations of gratitude, and immediately mounted. Having engaged the unsuspecting traveller in conversation, she suddenly passed a noose over his head, and drawing it with all her strength, endeavoured to pull him from his saddle. At this moment a number of persons started from the neighbouring thicket and surrounded him. Being a man of great strength and resolution, he contrived to foil the diabolical designs of the robbers. Luckily, at the moment the noose was applied he was in the act of stooping his head, so that when the woman tightened the instrument of death it passed over his mouth instead of round his neck, and he seized it firmly between his teeth. The murderess, fancying she had sufficiently secured her victim, slipped from the horse; but the Coorg, striking his heels into the animal's flanks, it flung out its hind-legs with great violence, struck to the ground the girl, who immediately relinquished the cord. The man, finding himself free, released his head from the noose, drew his sword, and cutting his way through the robbers, effected his escape. He wounded two of them severely. These men were shortly after taken, and through their means twelve others fell into the hands of the Coorg

Rajah's judicial functionaries, including the girl by whom his subject had been betrayed into so dangerous a snare. They were all executed as I have described.

We cannot be surprised at the numerous classes of robbers with which every part of India abounds, when we consider the civil degradations to which such a vast proportion of her population is subjected. The prejudices of caste are so inflexible and exclusive as to produce moral mischiefs which never can be got rid of until those prejudices shall be repudiated. When men are degraded below the dignity of their species, they will naturally make reprisals upon their oppressors, and cause them to reap the fruits of that harvest of tyranny which the latter are perpetually sowing. The oppressed looks upon his oppressor as his natural foe; and when those links that bind him to the conditions by which all civilized societies are governed are once snapped by the violence of arbitrary customs, and he has the means of revenge within his grasp, he seldom fails to exercise them with a reckless and malignant spirit. In India thousands are forced from that pale of kindred communion consecrated by the imposition of certain civil and social laws, which it is held a disgrace to infringe. They are cast from the bosom of society, and, while encircled in the vast coil of pollution, are flung into the arena of guilt and crime. Can we then wonder that, thus forced from the contact of virtue into an atmosphere of moral contagion, they should be imbued with the pestilence, and that the infection should extend instead of yielding to the mild process of moral influence. Gang-robbery in India, which is carried on to a most dreadful extent, is one of the bitter fruits of that exclusion peculiar to the laws of caste, which are the most pernicious ever introduced among human communities.

Some time after the capture of these Phansigars, I passed the place where they had attempted to murder the Coorg. It was a retired spot upon the bank of the river, but at the same time so exceedingly picturesque, that I almost wondered how such a scene could be selected for the perpetration of such a crime. Here was everything to withdraw the mind from all vulgar associations and to lift it from nature up to nature's God. A mangrove-tree raised its roots from the water, exhibiting one of those apparent anomalies in nature which unites wonder with admiration. This singular tree is certainly one of the most extraordinary productions of the vegetable kingdom: it grows to the height of from twenty to thirty feet; and is found chiefly on the margin of rivers not far from the sea, where its roots are nourished by the salt-water. It is likewise found in low grounds overflowed by the sea. A great number of long lateral branches project on all sides from the trunk to a great length; these are covered with clear glossy leaves of an elliptical form, and nearly half a foot long.

Nothing can well exceed the strange appearance which this tree presents on first beholding it. The roots seem like a coarse network upon the surface of the water, above which the trunk is elevated several feet. From this there branch out a number of flexible shoots, that take a circular direction downward, and, continually intersecting each other, resemble a reticulated bower, which a prurient fancy might take to be the abode of dryads, hamadryads, and water-fairies. The interlacings of these shoots are sometimes so thick, that nothing larger than a small reptile could pass between them. They are frequently covered with oysters, and it is no uncommon thing for the crews of boats to gather from these strange beds a generous meal of those crustaceous luxuries.

The seed of the mangrove-tree begins to germinate while the fruit in which it is enclosed is yet hanging from the branch. At the top of the cell that confines the seed a minute fibre gradually protrudes to the length of ten or twelve inches. This process continues, in fact, until the weight of the mass separates it from the parent branch, and it falls vertically into the mud, the seed being disengaged from the cell in which it was enclosed, when the soft loam that covers it quickly excites the germinating principle.

These trees frequently grow in such thick clusters as to form an impenetrable grove. Upon one of the branches of that represented in the vignette, when I saw it, there was a large Adjutant, a bird of the crane kind very common in India, but of which some account to the mere English reader may not be unwelcome.

This bird is full five feet high, and when the wings are extended, measures nearly fifteen feet from one extremity to the other. The bill, which opens far back into the head, is of so vast a size, that it will readily enclose a full-grown goose: it is near three feet long. The head and neck of this bird are bare, but deformed by small spongy excrescences like warts, and thin patches of strong curly hair. A long pouch hangs from the bottom of the neck over the breast, thinly covered with a short feathery growth, and terminated by a tuft of long hair resembling a stunted tail. The shoulders, when the wings are closed, appear to project considerably from the inosculation of the neck with the trunk, and are edged with soft white feathers; the wings and back are blue.

At a distance, these birds look like human beings pacing to and fro on the margin of the sea, where they are continually seen looking for whatever the tide may cast upon the beach, calculated to appease the voracity of their appetite. So ravenous are they, that they will swallow large bones, and even tortoises have been found entire in their stomachs. They will devour hares, rats, some of which are as large as a small cat, snakes, lizards, frogs, and all kinds of vermin, which pass into their stomach so readily, that, when shot, snakes have been taken alive from them several hours after they had been swallowed. I once knew an instance of a tame bird of this species having devoured a hind quarter of kid which the cook of the party, to whom it belonged, had inadvertently placed within its reach. The adjutant is naturally timid, but when excited will open its huge bill with an aspect of formidable menace, and emit a hoarse dissonant roar as loud as that of a bear or buffalo. It would seem to have derived the name of adjutant from the singular circumstance of its appearing at a distance like a person in military undress, which in India consists of a white jacket and trousers. Its stately march and erect figure gives it an official air, until a nearer proximity dispels the delusion, and one of the most unsightly birds in nature is presented to the view.

These creatures may be truly called the scavengers of India, as, especially near the sea-coast, they remove immense quantities of filth, which, if left to corrupt upon the earth, would be a perpetual cause of pestilence.

An idea prevails among the Hindoos, that the bodies of adjutants are possessed by the souls of Brahmins; shooting them, therefore, they consider an act of unpardonable wickedness: indeed, many persons profess to believe that they bear a charmed life, and are utterly proof against the murderous influence of powder and shot. In deference to these prejudices, they are seldom molested by Europeans.

CHAPTER IX.

PHANSIGARS.

WHILE Europeans have generally travelled through India in comparative security, arising from the dread inspired by the power and dominance of the British government, the path of the native has been beset with perils by the hordes of ferocious robbers which everywhere abound, from the highest regions of the Himalaya mountains to the southern extremity of Hindostan.

This is one of the sad fruits of imperfect legislation, that, by an unpardonable tolerance of delinquency by the petty governments into which this vast country is divided, leaves the public peace exposed to outrageous violations. Impunity is an encouragement to crime, and until the laws which emanate from the native tribunals of India are enforced with strict and impartial severity, man will prey upon his fellow with that sanguinary ferocity which nature dictates to the wild beasts of the forest only.

Encouraged by the general apathy of the native princes, tolerated desperadoes commit their depredations with comparative impunity; and in many instances their extraordinary dexterity is equalled only by the savage brutality with which they perpetrate their deeds of blood. Despised but dreaded by every class of the community, save only those outcast tribes with whom alone they maintain any intercourse, they look upon themselves to be the common enemies of mankind, and act generally therefore upon a principle of fierce retaliation wherever they make their base reprisals for the general odium in which they are held.

Among the most detestable of the dacoit tribes in India, are the Phansigars, a race of robbers probably unequalled in any part of the world for cold-blooded and heartless depravity. Their system of plundering is as peculiar as it is horrible: when they rob they invariably murder, except where the victim happens to escape, which is a circumstance of rare occurrence.

These robbers derive their name of Phansigars from the instrument with which they accomplish their atrocious murders. Phansigar signifies a strangler, and they employ a phansi, or noose, which they suddenly cast over the heads of those whom they intend to plunder, and strangle them. By this method of murderous precaution, their victims are unable to raise any outcry; for the compression of the noose upon the throat effectually prevents the voice from rising to the lips. They thus secure their booty without resistance, and with little chance of detection, acting invariably upon the maxim that dead men tell no tales.

It is strange that these tribes belong to no particular caste, but are made up of all, being composed of Hindoos and Mahomedans, Pariahs and Chandellahs:—even Brahmins are frequently found among them. This arises from the circumstance of their never destroying the children of those persons whom they rob and murder. The children they take care of and bring up to their own horrible mode of life, which at once accounts for the strange mixture of castes composing their community. Brahmins, however, degraded by their own class, have been occasionally known to join them, though this is not often the case.

A gang of these robbers varies from a dozen to sixty or seventy persons. They always commit their depredations at a distance from their place of common resort, being frequently absent for several months; and they return to their homes to spend the proceeds of their ill-gotten booty in the most revolting debauchery. Their victims are travellers whom they happen to fall in with on the road. Assuming the garb of pilgrims, or appearing as families removing to a distant part of the country, by their peaceable and homely guise, they beguile the unwary, who, when thus lulled into security, become easy victims. Each company of these murderers has a chief, to whom they scrupulously defer. He directs all their operations, but in general is not actively employed, except in gaining intelligence, and in those less hazardous offices which require more astuteness than courage or manual promptitude.

When upon active service, they usually separate into parties of from eight to twelve, who again subdivide into twos and threes, following each other within sight, in order to take immediate advantage of any casualty that may occur favourable to their sanguinary purposes. They then instantly unite, and from their numbers easily hush their victim or victims in everlasting silence. None of the parties into which the main body divides on these occasions ever keep far asunder: thus, if one division requires a reinforcement, it is soon obtained, and they have a sort of telegraphic mode of communication, known only to themselves, by which their chief is soon apprized how they are going on.

These parties frequently meet at small towns and villages as if by accident, where they unite as occasion may require; but their murders are usually committed in places distant from public resort, as they are little likely to be interrupted. Having with them a number of children of different ages, they escape suspicion. The children who accompany them being always ignorant of their practices, can never betray them by any unguarded prattle, and their artlessness is generally a presumptive guarantee to the traveller of his own safety. Before a party of Phansigars commit a murder they remove their youthful companions from the scene.

Two or three of them will sometimes take up their station in a choultry, and when a victim appears their companions are instantly apprized; these latter then drop in under the guise of travellers, engage in casual conversation as if strangers to their own party, and having lulled the unsuspecting traveller into perfect security, accomplish their purpose while he sleeps; or rather, they violently rouse him, and when he starts from his recumbent position in sudden surprise, they cast the noose over his head and strangle him.

A single traveller is never attacked by less than two Phansigars, and if there is the least chance of resistance, the two are always joined by a third; but such is the skill which they employ in their deadly trade, that they are scarcely ever frustrated in the accomplishment of their purpose.

The usual mode of perpetrating their murders is as follows: when their victim is lulled into perfect security, one of the party suddenly passes a noose formed of a twisted handkerchief, or a strip of thin muslin, over his head, and drawing it dexterously round the neck, instantly tightens it with all his strength. The moment this is accomplished, a companion strikes the struggling man on the joint of his knees behind, which causes him to fall forward, and thus to accelerate this summary process of strangulation. When he is prostrate, they kick him violently in the temples until his sufferings terminate, which is generally within the space of a minute. The whole thing is so rapidly and adroitly performed, that the sufferer has no power to make resistance; and whatever his strength may be, it is seldom or never of any avail against these practised adepts in murder.

Such is the plan commonly pursued; and although there may be an occasional deviation in the details of the process, yet the method of strangulation is never departed from. So cautious are these monsters, that they do not attempt a robbery, which, as I have said, is invariably accompanied with murder, until they have taken every practicable precaution against surprise, and secured themselves, so far as human foresight can extend, against the possibility of failure. They have been known to follow their victim for weeks before the desired opportunity has occurred, and their patience in waiting for this is only equalled by the heartless ferocity with which they finally accomplish their purpose. They are deterred by no consideration, either human or divine, from the atrocities of their profession; and so lightly do they value the life of a fellow-creature, that they will often take it for the few rags which cover the body of the poorest traveller. Should any person unexpectedly pass upon the road before the body of their victim is removed, they throw a cloth over it, making doleful lamentations, as if for a departed relative; or one of them will fall down, and writhe in apparent agony, in order to divert the attention of the unwelcome passengers from the object of their pretended sorrow. If the opportunity presents itself, they usually perpetrate their deed of blood near some jungle, and, as I have already stated, at a distance from the frequented track of travellers. They prefer the proximity of a nullah, as the body is more easily disposed of; but they always bury it, if possible, in some remote spot, where the soil is light or sandy, as this favours the necessary expedition of all their proceedings. Here a grave is quickly prepared, into which, after having barbarously mutilated the corpse, they cast it with its head downward. It is gashed all over to prevent its swelling, and thus raising a tumulus, or causing cracks, which might attract jackals and other beasts of prey, and lay open their guilt to the casual passenger. Sometimes the legs are disjointed at the knees and hips, and turned back upon the body, when haste obliges them to dig too small or too shallow a hole, which is then hastily filled. But if there should appear no chance of interruption, the murderers sometimes pitch a tent upon the spot, and regale themselves over the dead body which they have just consigned to so melancholy and succinct a burial.

The calculating caution of these people, under circumstances so revolting to our common nature, is a distinguishing feature of their system of plunder. They seem to leave unconsidered no circumstance that can in the slightest degree tend to wrap their crimes in concealment: everything appears to be prepared with almost philosophical foresight; and the provision made against the chance of detection is so perfect, that it is all but impossible to trace them in their career of blood.

When they have committed a murder in a place unfavourable for the burial of their victim, they enclose the body in a sack and cast it into a well, or hide it in some secluded part of a neighbouring jungle, secure from the ravages of vultures, jackals, and other beasts of prey, until a favourable place is discovered, whither it is removed, and disposed of as already described. Should a dog happen to accompany the person whose life they take, it is always killed, lest the faithful creature should lead to the discovery of its master. So systematic are they in their detestable vocation, that if they fail in the performance of a single particular in the regulations established among them for putting to death the object of their plunder, the Hindoo Phansigars consider they have committed an offence against the sanguinary deity to whom they tender their daily homage, and make an oblation as an offering of expiation. They esteem it a meritorious act to present to their dumb divinity a portion of the gains obtained by the death of a fellow-creature; and, in truth, it is not surprising that they should be so perfectly reconciled to the shedding of human blood, if they can persuade themselves that the deity whom they are taught to worship as the one great source of all things, can accept, as an act of grateful adoration, such abominable offerings.

Thus we see that religion is made a sanction for the blackest crimes. With such perversion of mind, we can scarcely wonder at the extent of human depravity.

The Phansigars, though they most commonly attack single travellers, have been known to destroy a whole party of eight or ten persons. Sometimes the booty they obtain during their excursions is very large, though at others it is so trifling as scarcely to supply them during these predatory journeys with the common necessaries of life. When they have collected their plunder, a division is regularly made, the most valuable portion of it being set apart for the Polygars, or petty chiefs who connive at their depredations, and are thus liberally remunerated for their protection. Another portion is appropriated to the expenses of religious offerings, which they never fail to make after a successful expedition; and the priests, with a heartlessness of purpose only second to that of their tributaries, make large demands upon them for the benefit of their spiritually kind offices with the deities whom the plunderers are desirous to propitiate.

Inured as these people are to the most appalling crimes, they are rigidly scrupulous in performing the rites of their abominable worship, and willingly devote a great portion of their gains to the shrines of their idol divinities. After these two important portions are taken from their booty, the remainder is divided among them in certain proportions, according to their admitted claims. To their chief is appropriated a double share, he being considered the animating spirit of the society. The person who casts the noose and actually strangles the victim receives a share and half; so does he who mangles the body. All who were present, but not actually engaged, have each one share; and they who were not present half a share. These divisions are made with such regularity, that there is neither bickering nor dissatisfaction. Each person disposes of his portion as he pleases, and it is generally sold to the readiest purchasers for at least a twentieth part of its value. To obviate suspicion, it is always got rid of at a distance from the scene.

The reason these people give for mutilating and burying the bodies of those whom they despatch is as follows:—They relate that a certain goddess, to whom they pay especial adoration, used to relieve them from the trouble of interring the corpses of their victims by devouring them—thus securing the murderers from all chance of detection. Upon one occasion, after having despatched a traveller, the body was, as usual, left unburied. One of the Phansigars employed, unguardedly looking behind him, saw the epicurean divinity in the act of feasting upon it. Irritated at this prying upon her carnivorous indulgence, she vowed — and the vows of heathen divinities are irrevocable — that she would never again devour a body slaughtered by Phansigars, they having by that one act of audacious curiosity forfeited all title to her future protection. As something like an equivalent, however, for thus withdrawing her divine patronage, she condescended to pluck one of the fangs from her celestial jaw and presented it to them, stating that they might use it as a pickaxe, which would never wear out. She then opened her ethereal side, pulled out one of her ribs, which she gave them for a knife, annealed to such a temper that no contact with any earthly material could ever blunt its edge. Having done this, she stooped down, tore off the hem of her garment, spun in the bowers of Paradise from the looms of industrious Suras,* and presented it to them for a noose which would never fail to strangle every person about whose throat it should be cast. She moreover commanded them for the future to mutilate and bury the bodies of those whom they destroyed. Thus they pretend to a divine sanction, while they are committing the most frightful outrages against the common peace of society. Acting as they do under such a persuasion, we can scarcely be surprised at the crimes of men

* Good spirits.

who can implicitly resign their reason to a thraldom so odious and besotted.

Such is the utter moral aberration of these wretched beings, that they do not appear conscious of any real degradation being attached to their savage profession. Their usual reply to those who ask them how they can be guilty of so outrageous a crime as that of shedding human blood, is,—" My father and mother were Phansigars, and I must pursue that to which they brought me up. How should I live, if I did not follow the business with which I am best acquainted?" They do not for a moment admit that it is a greater sin to put to death a human being than a dumb animal; and being generally predestinarians, if they happen to be taken, they express not the slightest dread of execution, conceiving their time is come, and therefore the best thing they can do is to make up their minds to meet death with fortitude, especially since they cannot obviate the fixed course of destiny by shrinking from a doom which, in some form or other, is the common lot of man.

If you ask a Phansigar, when apprehended, how he has obtained his livelihood, he will not hesitate to tell you, nor blush to confess the number of murders he has committed; he will also recount, with savage delight, his celebrity among the tribe of which he was a member for his dexterous application of the fatal noose.

CHAPTER X.

PHANSIGARS CONTINUED.

WHEN we look at the depravity of the various dacoit gangs so common in India, we are to consider this, as I have already said, one of the evils of that defective legislation which prevails through all the native governments. The whole social system is radically defective; and where a large mass of men is cast from the bosom of the community into degradation and contempt, the spirit of retaliation for wrong will prevail among them, and the desperate reaction of crime must be the natural consequence. Where man forces his fellow-man to become his enemy, by casting upon him a moral taint and shunning him as a moral pestilence, it is natural to expect that the fiercest passions of his nature, then loosed from the restraint of all civil ties, will rebel against the tyranny, and that he will put them in array against his oppressors. The justice of this inference is practically proved in India every day and every hour. Where there are many outcasts from society, there must be as many enemies; and to those rigid and exclusive laws which separate men from each other by an impassable wall of partition, elevating one class at the expense and to the positive degradation of the other, are we to attribute the rise and progress of those desperate bands of plunderers which swarm over the fertile plains of one of the finest countries under heaven. Nor let us imagine that the most ferocious even among the Phansigars are not rather fair claimants for our pity than for our detestation; since, ferocious though they be, they are, perhaps, rather the victims of depraved education than by nature the fell ministers of crime. From infancy they are taught to look upon murder and upon plunder as their just and lawful occupation. They are gradually inured to scenes of bloodshed, and taught to believe that their destiny has forced upon them the avocation which they are destined to follow. Monsters as they may appear in the eyes of the pious Christian, whose religion has kept him from falling into a moral desuetude so shocking to the feelings of our better nature, yet, if we look upon them as the wretched dupes of a horrible delusion, we shall perhaps abate something of the fierce indignation with which we are naturally apt to regard such delinquents, and rather feel our regret awakened at the existence of those restrictions which have raised a race of desperadoes, driven to embrace the desperate alternative of vice because they are denied all encouragements to virtue. Their ferocity and hardness of heart is the natural consequence of their education; for how can we expect that the blander sympathies of humanity should be reflected from bosoms upon which no gentle emotion has ever been impressed, but which have been hardened from the earliest period of life by a progressive initiation in practices the most sanguinary and revolting.

All Phansigars bring up their children to their own profession, unless prevented from pursuing it on account of constitutional weakness, or from some bodily defect. In that case they are left to follow the bent of their propensities, which generally inclines them to pass their lives in sluggish inaction.

The process of initiation is progressive: a boy at the age of ten years is first permitted to accompany a party of Phansigars upon an expedition of plunder, having been gradually prepared for this by being inured to sights of cruelty apart from their profession almost since the period that perception first dawned upon his mind. Upon those occasions, when the boy is to be initiated, he is placed under the guidance of an ustade, or tutor, who is usually one of his near relations, and whom he is taught to treat with extreme deference and respect, submitting with perfect acquiescence to everything his preceptor requires of him. He first serves him in a menial capacity, carrying his clothes, taking messages, dressing his food, washing his linen, and performing various other acts of servile employment. Upon many occasions the father becomes his son's instructor, but the boy is no more obedient to him than to a tutor not related to him: in both cases the authority is absolute and the obedience implicit.

Should the child happen to be questioned by any travellers in the road, so well is he prepared against betraying the slightest hint of his companions' occupation, that he always renders a plausible account of their object and destination, and this being given with the apparent artlessness of childhood, he passes almost invariably unsuspected. Even should suspicions arise, the traveller has no means of realizing them; and whenever the Phansigars are conscious of being suspected, they always change their route, and soon put themselves beyond the reach of a too vigilant scrutiny. It is one fundamental law of their community never to expose themselves to any risk of detection where this can be safely avoided; and so inviolably do they adhere to this cautious regulation, that no prospect of gain, however great, can tempt them to violate it, where the violation would expose them to obvious hazard.

The protection which they receive from the Polygars secures them in most cases from molestation. The child under initiation is instructed to consider his interest as opposed to that of society in general, by whom he is detested, and against whom, therefore, he is to look upon himself as in a state of perpetual hostility. This is one of the natural consequences of exclusion. To deprive a fellow-creature of life is represented to him as an act of no more enormity than the common and often necessary act of killing a reptile which insidiously lies in his path, and would bite or sting him as he passes. The boy is not at first allowed to witness the murders; while these are taking place he is sent with one of the watchers to a distance from the scene, lest the reaction of terror at beholding a deed so revolting to humanity should create a shock that would withhold him from embracing the inhuman profession of phansigary. He is merely permitted at first to view a dead body, his mind being gradually prepared for the sight; after which the dreadful secret of his trade is communicated to him by degrees. So soon as he expresses a wish to be engaged in this horrid service, the whole process is at once disclosed. Meanwhile he is allowed a small share of the booty in order to whet his appetite for murder, since it is only by murder that this booty is obtained. He is from this time permitted to assist in matters of minor importance, while the crime is perpetrating; or if there is nothing for him to do, he is allowed to be present, in order that he may observe how this essential part of the Phansigar's business is managed. It is not, however, until he has attained the years of manhood, and evinced both prudence and resolution, combined with bodily strength and activity, that he is allowed to apply the noose—an advancement in dignity to obtain which he usually devotes at least eight or ten years of his life.

Before he can claim the full privilege of committing murder, he must have been formally presented by his ustade with a dhoute—the ordinary name of the instrument of death employed by these systematic murderers. This ends his noviciate, and sets him loose upon the world a licensed man-slayer. When the ceremony of presenting the dhoute is to take place, a fortunate day is fixed upon, and the grand festival of the Dusserah is considered the auspicious period. All being duly prepared, the tutor takes his pupil apart, and presents him with a new noose, which he solemnly enjoins him to use with skill and discretion, as it is to be the means of his future subsistence, and as his safety will depend upon the dexterity and judgment with which it is employed. The moment he receives the dhoute he is released from all restriction, and tries his skill at strangulation the next opportunity that offers.

The veneration which the Phansigar entertains for the person by whom he has been initiated into the abominable mysteries of their vocation, continues through life. Whenever he meets him, after a long absence, he touches his feet, as a mark of profound respect; frequently divides with him the plunder which he has obtained in many successful excursions; and when his tutor becomes old and helpless, he provides for him with an anxiety worthy of a better state, until death removes him beyond the influence of his anxiety or the need of his care.

The course of education which the Phansigar undergoes is so progressive and so exciting; such expectations are held out, and such advantages anticipated; the spirit of emulation is so successfully roused, and the field of adventure so attractively portrayed, gradually winning the heart to a love of that by which our common nature is shocked and repelled, and warping it by gentle degrees to the most revolting prepossessions, as to cause in the members of this singular community such an intense attachment to their detestable occupation—that nothing can induce them to relinquish it. Although some of them have been employed in the Company's armies, they have never entirely abandoned their original mode of life, but have always returned to it when opportunity offered of a successful enterprise.

Even when so bowed by the weight of years as to be unable to take an active part with the younger members of their tribe, they do not quit the service, but act as watchers, procure intelligence, and decoy the unwary traveller by a well-feigned tale of distress, into some remote spot, where he is silenced for ever, and sleeps his last sleep in the solitude where no human eye ever beholds his grave. The old or disabled wait upon the younger, prepare their food, and perform all the various servile offices to which the more efficient members of their community have neither time nor disposition to attend. The social elements which unite together this strange race, abhorrent as they are from every tie of humanity, are of so binding a nature, that few of its members ever secede to take a higher stand among their less degraded fellow-creatures. They unite more nearly, by intermarriages, those bonds of conjunction in which they are so closely held together. Thus the tie of relationship is so extended, that their union becomes the more fixed, from the mysterious influence of that indissoluble link attached by the wisdom of the Creator to our finest sympathies, to keep alive the desire of mutual communion for which man was especially constituted, and without which he could have no real happiness.

Desperate and degrading as their employments are known to be, the Phansigars frequently marry into families that have the name of being respectable; it not being much the custom in India for women who are about to enter into connubial engagements to inquire very scrupulously into the characters of those whom they intend to espouse. Among these robbers, the wives are seldom ignorant of their husbands' proceedings. Though they do not assist them in their atrocities, they not only feel no repugnance at them, but enjoy the fruits of those atrocities with as keen a relish as if they had been the gains of an honest industry. These murderers rarely admit into their community persons of mature age; and even when they do, it is after a long and severe trial of their fidelity.

The most odious circumstance in the character of Phansigars is, that they often strangle their victims from the mere love of inhumanity, and for the sake of exercising dexterity in their horrible calling; in too many instances they cannot shield their crimes under the palliative, weak as it may be, of pecuniary temptation. One remarkable feature in these people is, the utter indifference they feel at being looked upon as human monsters. They do not hesitate to acknowledge that they are mere brutes endued with reason, which renders them the more formidable to society, against whom they wage a savage and perpetual war. They unblushingly compare themselves to tigers, maintaining, with a plausible logic every way worthy of their occupation, that as those ferocious beasts are impelled by irresistible necessity, and but fulfil the design of their creation in preying upon other animals, so the proper victims of Phansigars are men, whom alone it is profitable to them to destroy, and who therefore are their natural and lawful prey. They further maintain that those persons whom they strangle were predestined to be murdered, and that therefore they only fulfil the irrevocable decree of destiny in putting them to death. It is their professed belief that they are as surely destined to become Phansigars as their victims were to be killed, and consequently express surprise when they hear themselves traduced as murderers. They are all fatalists, and imagine themselves to be actuated in whatever they do by an invincible necessity; we shall therefore be the less surprised that compunction is a stranger to their bosoms.

However great the sufferings of those unfortunate beings who happen to fall into their hands, they behold them with indomitable indifference, and frequently make their writhings the subject of their coarse and brutal jests. Although such a state of hardened insensibility may appear, upon a superficial view, justly to challenge our detestation, nevertheless, in spite of the horror with which a contemplation of their enormities must naturally fill our bosoms, the calm and philosophic Christian will readily perceive that in their condition there is in truth far more cause for the exercise of pity than for that of any severer feeling. They are the wretched creatures of stern and debasing circumstance; they are the moral victims of a system of social legislation subversive of all civil union, except among parts and parcels of the community.

It is to be remembered that they have never tasted the fruits of virtue. They have been reared in an atmosphere of vice, where nothing but pollution could thrive. They have imbibed with their maternal aliment the frightful principles which direct their lives. Religious fanaticism and the dark policy of a barbarous superstition have cast around them the fetters of a spiritual slavery, from which they are not likely to emancipate themselves until those causes are greatly abated or entirely removed. It has been said by a wise man of their own country, that "religion is the ladder by which men ascend into heaven;" but their religion is a ladder by which they descend into the lowest depths of guilt and infamy.

Like all classes of persons addicted to habits which the laws do not recognise, the Phansigars are licentious in an extreme degree. The booty they acquire during their marauding excursions they spend in the vilest debauchery, and when it is all got rid of they go in pursuit of more. They are generally in a state of intoxication, except while in quest of plunder, when, with their usual habits of caution, they rigidly refrain from any indulgence likely to lead them into danger. They commonly inhabit places on the border of some jungle, near a river or a tank, where they can perform their ablutions, and on the banks of which there is usually a small temple devoted to the worship of their favourite deity. Here their wives and daughters, who seldom take part in their robberies and murders, may be seen enjoying the luxury of the morning bath, or performing the abstersions exacted by their creed. In these romantic seclusions they live apart from, and despised by, the more respectable classes; but as they scrupulously forbear exercising their horrid avo-

Drawn by W. Daniell, R.A. Engraved by W. J. Cooke

Scene near the Coast of Malabar.

London, Published Sept. 1, 1835, for the Proprietor, by Edward Churton, 26 Holles Street, Cavendish Square.

cations near their own abodes, they excite no terror among those who happen to reside within their vicinity. Their deeds of robbery and of death are committed at a distance from their homes, in order that those domestic sanctuaries may not be disturbed by the officers of justice; and should detection follow a murder, they are always apprehended in the neighbourhood of the spot where the murder is perpetrated.

Although the society of these plunderers is composed almost entirely of men, yet women are occasionally admitted, and upon some occasions allowed to apply the dhoute; as was the case in the attempt upon the Coorg already mentioned. They sometimes select a handsome girl, and place her in a convenient spot, where, by her beauty or a well-feigned story of distress, she may interest some unsuspecting passenger, whom she betrays to almost certain destruction. Should he be on horseback, she will induce him to take her up behind him; after which, when an opportunity offers, she throws the noose over his head, leaps from the horse, drags him to the ground, and strangles him.

Besides the Phansigars, there are in India other tribes of robbers far more numerous, indeed, but none so sanguinary. The Pindarees, who of late years have been so formidable as to require an army to crush them, are now nearly if not quite exterminated; but the Bhills, a race of mountaineers inhabiting the hilly tracts of Candeish, Malwa, and Rajputana, are still a daring race of marauders. "Existing," says Sir John Malcolm, "as they have hitherto done,* under despotic governments, which placed them beyond the pale of civil society, and which not only gave them neither encouragement nor protection, but authorised the lowest of the fiscal officers to take their lives without trial; considering themselves a proscribed and contemned race; ignorant to a deplorable degree; believing in witchcraft, blindly obedient to the orders of their chiefs, subject to extraordinary privations, and constantly exposed to danger from their fellow-creatures, and from the ferocity of the wild beasts with whom they shared the forests, the Bhills have in consequence become the enemies of order and peace. They have cherished predatory habits as the means of subsistence; and receiving no mercy or consideration, they have sought, from natural impulse, to revenge the wrongs they have sustained. Time has interwoven their habits of life and feelings with their superstitions, until they actually believe that they were created to prey upon their neighbours. 'I am Mahadevas thief,' is the common answer of a Bhill detected in a crime; and his promise of amendment is usually so qualified as to period, that it seems more like a truce than a pact of permanent good conduct. Nevertheless, from what has occurred since this tribe became subject to the British government, we may anticipate a gradual, and ultimately a complete, change in their character and condition. The men, though habituated to a life of rapine, are not sanguinary; and the females of the tribe, who possess great influence over them, are of kind

* See a paper in vol. i. of the Transactions of the Asiatic Society.

dispositions, and many of them are intelligent and industrious."

With all their rapacity, the Bhills have certain notions of honour, to which they are known so scrupulously to adhere, that no traveller ever doubts their pledge of protection. With a Bhill guide, a person may travel through the districts most infested by them without the slightest molestation. They would put any one of their tribe to death who should rob a person so protected. Their skill in robbery is extraordinary. They have been known to make a hole through the wall of a bungalo, and carry on their depredations so stealthily as to clear the room, and even take the bed-clothes from a person asleep without waking him. When they enter a house or a tent, they are always naked, and so covered with oil that it is almost impossible to seize them. Upon each arm is usually fastened a sharp knife, with the blade projecting upwards; thus, if they are laid hold off in the dark, the person seizing immediately releases them:—indeed, they are very rarely taken.

An officer, with whom I was acquainted, had a narrow escape from death by attempting to seize a Bhill who was in the act of robbing him. It happened in the neighbourhood of Guzerat. This person was asleep in his tent, when, suddenly waking, he felt the quilt slightly twitched: suspecting that some one was not far from his bedside, he soon began to breathe hard, as if he were in a sound sleep. In a short time the twitch was repeated with some additional force. Satisfied that there was a robber near him, he suddenly sprang from his bed: a Bhill as suddenly rose, and attempted to escape through an opening which he had previously made in the canvas. The officer, being a strong and active man, dexterously tripped up the heels of the robber, who instantly fell, and the other, laying hold of his arm, received a severe wound, which made him immediately relinquish it. In a moment the Bhill was on his feet, and rushed towards the opening. My friend, regardless of the gash already inflicted upon him, made a second attempt to seize the intruder; but the latter having disengaged one of the knives from his arm, struck him with it in the face, laid his cheek completely open, and effected his escape. The wound was so desperate, that for several days the officer's life was despaired of.

CHAPTER XI.

A WILD DOG. THE COORG RAJAH.

While we halted at a village in our progress towards the Coorg capital, a native offered me for sale one of the wild dogs of the ghauts, which I was anxious to see. Having been recently taken, and confined in a cage, it looked sulky and fierce. It was about the size of a small hound, strongly limbed, with a large head and a long bushy tail. The head was of extraordinary length in proportion to the body, but very narrow; the jaws opening much higher into the skull than in any other species of dog with which I am acquainted. From the great elongation of the forehead, the eyes appeared seated so near the nose as to impart a particularly repelling expression to the face. When any one approached the cage, the animal growled fiercely, at the same time manifesting symptoms of fear; but the moment a piece of meat was thrown in, it devoured it with ravenous eagerness.

I declined the purchase, knowing the difficulty of taming those creatures, especially if caught after they are full grown. Even if taken quite young, their natural ferocity is never effectually overcome.

These dogs hunt in packs, destroying deer, hogs,

N 3

and buffaloes. They are even said to hunt the tiger, which they surround, and having wetted their thick bushy tails with their own secretions, whisk them in the tiger's eyes, and while the enraged animal is suffering from this unexpected infliction, they fall upon it in a body, and it thus becomes a comparatively easy prey. I state this upon the testimony of the natives, who relate it as a generally known and admitted fact.

The claws of these dogs are exceedingly strong and sharp, approaching nearer to those of the feline than the canine races. Thus armed, their great strength and ferocity render them formidable even to the most savage beasts of the forests. They always tear out the eyes of their prey; their attack is therefore invariably at the head. Though not extremely swift of foot, yet such is their patience and capability of endurance, that they proceed regularly through the jungle in the track of their victims, until the latter are exhausted; they then commit frightful havoc among the herds of harmless animals. When urged by extreme hunger, they have been known to attack and destroy travellers, though they are so alarmed at the discharge of fire-arms, that a pistol loaded with powder is a sufficient security against any invasion from those ferocious creatures.

These dogs are found in most of the hilly districts, but are said to abound chiefly in the western ghauts. Very little seems to be known of their peculiar habits, and I believe the species has not hitherto been noticed by European naturalists. They are not frequently seen, and from their natural ferocity it appears impossible to domesticate them. The natives are much afraid of them, and relate a great number of fabulous stories respecting them, always expressing satisfaction whenever they capture or destroy any of them.

The dog offered for sale upon the occasion just referred to had been taken in a trap, and was no doubt eventually destroyed, if the person to whom it belonged had not the good fortune to find a purchaser within a short period of the capture, as the voraciousness of the animal would have rendered it an intolerable burden on the finances of a poor Hindoo.

Nothing particular occurred during our further progress to the capital of the Rajah, by whom we were received and welcomed with a munificence and hospitality worthy of a liberal and enlightened prince.

When we reached the Coorg capital, we selected a convenient place about a mile and half from the town, where we pitched our tents. Next morning we were waited upon by a functionary of the Rajah, bearing us a civil message from his master, desiring that we would visit his palace on the following day. We accordingly repaired to the palace at the time appointed, and were received by the Prince in a large hall of audience, where his levees were always held, and where, in fact, the public business of his government was usually transacted. Round the room were hung several pictures of Englishmen who had distinguished themselves in India, among which were portraits of Lord Clive, and Colonel Wellesley, now Duke of Wellington. The room was extravagantly fitted up with a profusion of European furniture and ornaments. Several guns and pistols in cases, all of British manufacture, were placed in different parts of the room, the lids of the cases being open in order that visiters might be able to inspect the genuineness of the instrument.

The Rajah was a handsome man about the middle age; he had quick penetrating eyes, which occasionally fixed upon you with such ardency of expression that it was painful to encounter their gaze. He had the character of a worthy prince, and seemed to me fully to ratify in his own person an apt saying of one of his own countrymen, "The heart of an excellent man resembles the cocoa-nut, which, though hard without, contains refreshing water and delicious food within."

He was exceedingly attentive, and anxious to show us his partiality for cabinet-work made by British artisans, receiving our approbation with evident satisfaction, but was much more familiar than I with the names of celebrated makers in this country of the different European articles which his taste directed him to procure. He had several splendid looking-glasses, and four or five pianofortes made by Clementi, of whom he spoke as if that great composer had been a visiter at his court, and his Highness had received instructions from him in the science of musical sounds. He was very proud of his guns, near which there were two or three highly ornamented matchlocks, as if to show that the native gunsmiths were not without taste and ingenuity in embellishing their arms, though they were far behind those of Europe in skill of construction.

Drawn by W. Daniell R.A.

The small Deer of Ceylon

The Rajah continued in conversation with us for some time, and when he dismissed us, invited us to repeat our visit whenever it might be agreeable. On the following morning we strolled into a sort of park, in which he had a great number of curious animals, and among these were two small deer from Ceylòn, the most beautiful little creatures I had ever seen. They were about the size of a fox, of a deep reddish brown, the body covered with bright spots, which gave them quite a refined beauty, as if they were creatures fit only to be the pets of royalty. This species of deer is the smallest of the cervine tribe, and has no horns, in some respects corresponding with the Cervus Guineensis of Linnæus. They abound in Ceylon, where they are taken in traps, and disposed of on the coast for a mere trifle. It is the most exquisitely formed creature that can be imagined, its small taper legs being scarcely larger than a lady's finger. Its flesh is esteemed a particular delicacy, and remarkably wholesome. These tiny animals are caught in great numbers in the interior of Ceylon, and almost daily taken to Columbo and other towns, where they are sold for about two shillings. On the peninsula they are esteemed a rarity, and are frequently purchased rather for the exquisite symmetry of their forms than for the delicacy of their flesh, which, however, is far superior to that of any other deer. The Rajah had several, and highly valued them, having a great fancy for animals of all kinds. Those we saw were quite tame, allowing us to approach within a few yards of them without appearing in the slightest degree disturbed by our proximity. They are called the moose-deer by the Cingalese, though, further than is usual with creatures of the same race, they bear no resemblance to that animal, of which they may be mutually said to constitute the antipodes, the one being the largest and the other the smallest of the deer tribe.

Besides these creatures, the Rajah prided himself upon his collection of more savage animals, having sundry lions and tigers in cages, some of which were under such control, that I have heard he was in the habit of introducing them into his palace before his guests, without even submitting them to the restraint of a keeper. He had a great passion for animal-fights, which he often indulged; and we were told that in a few days he intended to entertain us with a sight of what some of his subjects could do against those ferocious animals. This was confirmed on the following morning by the arrival of a messenger from his Highness, who informed us that his master purposed having an exhibition of animal-fights and native gymnastics on a specified day, to which he hoped we would favour him with our company. These fights are common in the Mysore during the Dusserah feast, and are celebrated throughout this part of India. The Oriental athletæ, who use the cestus, are, I imagine, peculiar to that district, and Hindoos of low caste, yet as perfectly distinct and unmixed in their generation as the highest among the social divisions of the people. They are a strong and hardy race of men, and their whole lives are devoted to the acquisition of dexterity in their favourite pursuit. They are called Jetties, and perform feats of strength as remarkable for their variety as for exhibiting the muscular capabilities of the human form. Nothing can exceed the fine manly symmetry of proportion which these men display, nor is their activity inferior to their strength.

On the day appointed we repaired to the palace. After a liberal entertainment, in which several dishes were served up in the European fashion, with a plentiful supply of Port wine, Claret, and Madeira, we retired to a gallery that overlooked a large area full a hundred yards square. The sports commenced as soon as the Rajah arrived. A small but sturdy goat was introduced into the enclosed space. Upon its forehead was fixed a steel spur, like that placed upon the leg of a game-cock when armed for battle. This instrument was four inches long, about as thick at the base as a man's middle finger, and exceedingly sharp. It was strapped across the forehead at equal distances between the eyes and the sockets of the horns; for of these the animal had been deprived, in order to give it more freedom in the encounters to which it was trained. It paced the area with a firm proud step, as if aware that it was about to have an opportunity of exhibiting its prowess to the Prince of the country.

When all was ready, the door of a large cage was slid aside, and a boar started out with a grunt that betokened a desire of freedom, but no relish at having to show its valour before company. It was immediately urged towards the goat, which erected its stiff wiry mane, reared upon its hind legs, and retreated; but whether this was an impulse of fear, or a feint to draw its adversary into a more favourable position for attack, was not so evident. The boar stood perfectly still, striking its jaws together with a sharp, quick champ, and covering its tusks with a creamy foam that flowed copiously from the mouth, and occasionally fell in flakes upon the ground. As the goat retired, it was brought forward by one of the attendants on the sports, and placed near its foe, which turned upon the armed adversary its small glittering eyes, champing as before, but continuing perfectly still. The goat, at length, emboldened by the apparent immobility of its antagonist, made a butt with its forehead; the boar, suddenly turning, received the spear in its shoulder, but striking its enemy in the flank at the same moment, inflicted a long ghastly wound, which disabled it from continuing the conflict.

A second goat was introduced, which the boar, in spite of its wound, soon disabled. It was now attacked by a third. This was a much larger animal than either of the former; and the boar's energies being reduced by its exertions and the wound already received in its shoulder, the match did not appear very equal, though, from the quickness of its motions in its two former conflicts, I confess, I apprehended that it would come off victorious in this third encounter. The moment the large goat was brought forward, it advanced fiercely to the attack, receiving and avoiding its adversary's charge without sustaining any injury beyond a slight opening of the skin on its left haunch. As if exasperated by the wound, it turned furiously upon its foe, and buried the spear with which it was armed in its body, just below the ribs. The boar rolled upon its side, when the infliction was again repeated, and the goat borne off in triumph, crowned with a garland, by its keeper.

The next scene was of a far more awful character. A man entered the arena, armed only with a Coorg knife, and clothed in short trousers, which barely covered his hips, and extended halfway down the thighs. The instrument, which he wielded in his right hand, was a heavy blade, something like the coulter of a plough, about two feet long, and full three inches wide, gradually diminishing towards the handle, with which it formed a right angle. This knife is used with great dexterity by the Coorgs, being swung round in the hand before the blow is inflicted, and then brought into contact with the object intended to be struck, with a force and effect truly astounding.

The champion who now presented himself before the Rajah was about to be opposed to a tiger, which he volunteered to encounter almost naked, and armed only with the weapon I have just described. He was rather tall, with a slight figure; but his chest was deep, his arms long and muscular. His legs were thin; yet the action of the muscles was perceptible with every movement, whilst the freedom of his gait, and the few contortions he performed preparatory to the hazardous enterprise in which he was about to engage, showed that he possessed uncommon activity, combined with no ordinary degree of strength. The expression of his countenance was absolutely sublime when he gave the signal for the tiger to be let loose: it was the very concentration of moral energy—the index of a high and settled resolution His body glistened with the oil which had been rubbed over it in order to promote the elasticity of his limbs. He raised his arm for several moments above his head when he made the motion to admit his enemy into the area. The bars of a large cage were instantly lifted from above; a huge royal tiger sprang forward and stood before the Coorg, waving its tail slowly backward and forward, erecting the hair upon it, and uttering a suppressed howl. The animal first looked at the man, then at the gallery where the Rajah and his court were seated to see the sports, but did not appear at all easy in its present state of freedom:—it was evidently confounded at the novelty of its position. After a short survey, it turned suddenly round, and bounded into its cage, from which the keepers, who stood above, beyond the reach of mischief, tried to force it, but in vain. The bars were then dropped, and several crackers fastened to its tail, which projected through one of the intervals.

A lighted match was put into the hand of the Coorg; the bars were again raised, and the crackers ignited. The tiger now darted into the arena with a terrific yell; and while the crackers were exploding, it leaped, turned, and writhed as if in a state of frantic excitement. It at length crouched in a corner, gnarling as a cat does when alarmed. Meanwhile its retreat had been cut off by securing the cage. During the explosion of the crackers, the Coorg stood watching his enemy, and at length advanced towards it with a slow but firm step. The tiger roused itself and retreated, the fur on its back being erect, and its tail apparently dilated to twice the usual size. It was not at all disposed to commence hostilities;

but its resolute foe was not to be evaded. Fixing his eyes intently upon the deadly creature, he advanced with the same measured step, the tiger retreating as before, but still presenting its front to its enemy. The Coorg now stopped suddenly; then moving slowly backward, the tiger raised itself to its full height, curved its back to the necessary segment for a spring, and lashed its tail, evidently meditating mischief. The man continued to retire; and as soon as he was at so great a distance that the fixed expression of his eye was no longer distinguishable, the ferocious brute made a sudden bound forward, crouched, and sprang with a short, sharp growl. Its adversary, fully prepared for this, leaped actively on one side, and as the tiger reached the ground, swung round his heavy knife, and brought it with irresistible force upon the animal's hind-leg just above the joint. The bone was instantly severed, and the tiger effectually prevented from making a second spring. The wounded beast roared; but turning suddenly on the Coorg, who had by this time retired several yards, advanced fiercely upon him, its wounded leg hanging loose in the skin, showing that it was broken. The tiger, now excited to a pitch of reckless rage, rushed forward upon its three legs towards its adversary, who stood with his heavy knife upraised, calmly awaiting the encounter. As soon as the savage creature was within his reach, he brought down the ponderous weapon upon its head with a force which nothing could resist, laid open the skull from ear to ear, and the vanquished foe fell dead at his feet. He then coolly wiped the knife on the animal's hide, made a dignified salaam to the Rajah, and retired amid the loud acclamations of the spectators.

His Highness informed us that this man had killed several tigers in a similar manner; and that, although upon one or two occasions he had been severely scratched, he had never been seriously wounded. The Coorgs, moreover, are known often to attack this terrible animal in the jungles with their heavy, sharp knives, and with almost unfailing success. Upon the present occasion, nothing could exceed the cool, cautious, and calculating precision with which the resolute Hindoo went through his dangerous performance.

In order to vary the sports, several men were introduced into the arena, armed with sticks in the form of a crescent, tapering towards one end like a Scotch mull, and loaded at the other with iron. They are from twenty-six to thirty inches long at the largest extremity, and about as thick as a child's wrist. By persons accustomed to the use of this instrument it is thrown with astonishing dexterity, as was proved upon the present occasion. A frame, nearly two feet square, containing a flat surface of clay, four inches thick, was placed at a distance of forty-five yards from the spot where the man stood who was to throw. In the centre of this frame was stuck a circular piece of iron, about the size of a cheese-plate. The first who threw the stick was a short Hindoo, with a robust, muscular frame, of more strength than symmetry. Fixing his eye intently upon the object which it was his aim to strike, his left foot being forward and his body slightly curved, with a rapid evolution of the arm he discharged the loaded wood. It whizzed through the air, and hitting the iron, forced it through the clay to the distance of several yards. The man now made his salaam with an expression of conscious triumph, and gave place to one of his competitors, who advanced, and with equal skill sent his instrument through the aperture made in the clay, striking the wall beyond, with a force that showed such a weapon in battle to be scarcely less formidable than the matchlock or musket. Four others tried their skill, but not with equal success. Each struck the frame and forced his instrument through; but not one hit the centre, though the man who made the fifth throw was very near it. They all, nevertheless, seemed to think themselves entitled to the applause of the company; and he who had been least successful appeared much disappointed that the plaudits which followed his performance were so faint and few.

After these men had retired, a person entered with a sort of quarter-staff, full six feet long, and as thick as a man's thumb, with a wooden ball at either end, enclosed in a quilted cotton bag. He was followed by three slender Hindoos, with sticks nearly a yard in length, and of much the same thickness as the single-stick used bythe players at that rustic game in England. When all was ready, this party commenced their play; he who had the long staff defending himself against the attacks of the three with extraordinary agility and adroitness. His evolutions were so rapid, that he appeared every instant to present his front to each of his antagonists; and the instrument, which he held at the centre of the shaft, he turned with such amazing rapidity, protecting his back and front at the same instant, that every attempt to hit him was completely foiled. His body, all but naked, was covered with foam with the violence of his exertions. At first he acted solely on the defensive, when seeing his assailants somewhat off their guard, with the rapidity of lightning he struck one of them upon the head with a forward stroke from the padded end of the staff, and as rapidly darting it backward, met another directly upon the temple with such force that both instantly fell. The third man immediately leaped within his guard, and gave him a blow upon the ribs that rang through the arena. Starting aside, he swung round his weapon with tremendous velocity; but his antagonist, by actively stooping, escaped for a moment the intended visitation. No sooner, however, had he raised himself, than he received the ball plump upon his forehead, which sent him upon his back as if he had been shot. The little Hindoo, who had so skilfully foiled three adversaries, was now proclaimed victor, received a nod of approbation, and retired with the fallen champions, who did not seem at all satisfied with the issue. This was, altogether, the most interesting exhibition of skill I had ever beheld. The amazing activity of the man who played with the quarter-staff,—so to speak, for it was very similar,—altogether defies description. It was, moreover, a bloodless conflict, which rendered it by no means painful to see, though it must be confessed that the blows inflicted were sufficiently severe.

A pair of wrestlers now appeared before us to contend for the honour of the Rajah's smile,—a reward as highly prized by them as a mural crown by the ancient Romans. One was tall and thin, the perfect model of an Indian Apollo. His chest was broad; his waist remarkably taper; his gait erect, and every motion full of decision and grace. His arms were long; his hands small as a woman's. His adversary was at least three inches shorter, with a very robust body, but ill-formed legs; these being rather bowed, stumpy, and destitute of muscle. His arms, however, exhibited a legible index of muscular energy that could not be mistaken. They were long and covered with hair, like those of a huge bear; whilst his broad, expansive chest, no less sinewy and hirsute, showed evidently that he would prove a formidable opponent. The expression of his countenance was mild, but determined; and he eyed his more graceful adversary with a smile that seemed to acknowledge his personal advantages, but at the same time indicated that they were not likely to win for him the palm of superiority in the coming encounter.

The handsomer wrestler had a restless and ardent motion of the eye, that gave the spectator an impression either of want of confidence in his own powers or an apprehension of his adversary's physical superiority; nevertheless he did not quail, but advanced to the struggle with a calm yet fearless determination. The head of both champions was perfectly bare, with the exception of a single lock of hair about three inches long. which grew from the crown and hung rather quaintly over the left ear; the bald cranium imparting a look of keenness and delicacy to the countenance of the handsomer competitor, though it detracted somewhat from the general dignity of his form and lineaments.

The men wore no clothing, except a narrow strip of cloth round the waist; and thus they advanced to the encounter. For some time they did not close, but remained at a certain distance from each other, making a variety of sudden springs, and throwing their bodies into strange contortions, as if to show their amazing suppleness, and the extraordinary power they possessed of putting them into positions out of the ordinary course of nature. It was obvious that these preliminary movements were adopted merely to distract the attention, in order that any advantage might be taken of a momentary lapse of caution on either side. This skirmishing continued so long that it began to be fatiguing, when the Rajah showing much impatience, it was communicated to the wrestlers, who, by mutual consent, immediately came to close quarters, and prepared in good earnest to strive for the mastery. Each grasped the other firmly by the wrist, and placing their heads together they began to push, as if to try each other's strength. The taller man appeared to have the advantage when they first joined hands, as he stood over his antagonist, and from the superior length of his limbs kept him for some time at arm's length, thus preventing the prompt exercise both of his strength and of his skill. At last the shorter wrestler, having succeeded in closing, placed his arm round the neck of his opponent, which he appeared to grasp with the clutch of a Hercules. The struggle now became excessively animated; the combatants writhed and twisted round each other without much apparent superiority, though it was manifest that the shorter was the stronger of the two. At length, the latter suddenly striking his heel in the joint of his adversary's knee, and seizing him firmly by the hip at the same moment, gave him a violent fall. The taller wrestler, by an active turn of the body, succeeded in preventing what in India as well as in England constitutes the triumph of wrestling, a fair back fall, and pitched with his shoulder upon the ground. Notwithstanding the force of the shock, he was on his legs in an instant, and approaching his antagonist, whom the late advantage appeared to have put somewhat off his guard, seized him with a vigorous grasp, and quick as lightning flung him completely over his head, but the man pitched upon his legs like a cat.

The struggle was now renewed with increased energy, yet the superior strength of the shorter wrestler was becoming more apparent;—the other had evidently less stamina. He appeared distressed, and in proportion as he felt his energies decreasing, the more desperate became his struggles. Having, as it seemed, collected all his powers for one final effort, he lost his balance; the lesser champion, seeing his opportunity, grasped him by the thigh behind with his left hand, and placing the right upon his chest, threw him upon his back with a force that seemed to shake every fibre of his frame. The man, however, rose in a moment, and with a disconcerted look made his salaam to the Rajah, then bounded from the arena with the activity and fleetness of an antelope, as if to show that he was nothing the worse for his exertions, however mortified he might feel at his defeat.

The victor awaited another competitor: in a few moments a gigantic fellow advanced, at least six feet high, with a broad iron frame, but the muscles, though prominent, seemed to want that firmness of texture and closeness of tension which are the great indications of elastic vigour. This man was past the middle age, and had gone beyond the prime of his strength. His ponderous body seemed, notwithstanding, to make fearful odds against the lighter candidate, already weakened by a long and arduous struggle. The big Hindoo advanced with a surly aspect, which completely turned the balance of sympathy against him, and the bout commenced with many clumsy evolutions upon his part, and as many active ones on that of his opponent. At length they closed, but the smaller wrestler clung so close to his Herculean antagonist, that the latter could not throw him. He exerted his great strength to no purpose, the quickness and elasticity of his rival foiled all his attempts. He snorted with his exertions, and at length became visibly excited. He had been a successful champion in his better days, and was loth to yield to younger men the reputation he had once enjoyed. His limbs no longer retained their wonted pliancy; and though from his large muscular frame and superior weight he was still a formidable opponent, these, nevertheless, could not countervail the superior advantages of youth and greater flexibility of limb. He moreover showed so much less skill than the man to whom he was opposed, that it was evident he owed his former reputation chiefly to his immense strength, of which sufficient remained to show that in the prime of his days he must have been a person of uncommon physical capabilities. His excitement was manifestly increasing every moment, and by a fortunate turn of his leg he succeeded in throwing his man upon the face. The prostrate wrestler immediately extended his legs and arms like the spokes of a wheel, and stiffening the muscles, defied all the efforts of his huge antagonist to turn him upon his back. In this position he lay for several minutes, and when he found that the large Hindoo relaxed his efforts, he suddenly sprang upon his feet, and closing with him, renewed the contest with undiminished vigour. He had recovered his breath during the time he lay on the ground, whilst his adversary had exhausted his in the fruitless exertions he made to throw him. The little man now clearly felt his advantage, for he caused his huge opponent to reel and stagger in a way that made it clear to all how the contest must terminate.

Upon a sudden, to our astonishment, we saw the big wrestler lifted from his legs and thrown completely over the head of the smaller with a force quite astounding. The poor fellow pitched upon his crown, falling upon his back senseless. The blood gushed from his ears and nose, and I certainly thought he was dead; but within a minute he rose, made a sullen obeisance to the gallery, and waddled from the arena, evidently much mortified at the issue of his exertions. The victor received the smile of his Highness with an inelegant salaam; for he happened to be an exception to the general rule, the Hindoos being almost universally elegant in all conventional acts of external courtesy. He then retired, and the sports closed for the day.

CHAPTER XII.

WILD BEAST FIGHTS.—JETTIES.—JUGGLERS.

NEXT morning, we again repaired to the palace at an early hour; the Rajah was ready to receive us, and after a slight refreshment we took our station in the gallery to witness the second day's sports. We were prepared for an unusual sight. A lion was to be turned into the arena with an African buffalo, purchased by his Highness some months before, and which still remained uncommonly wild and fierce. The buffalo of Africa is larger, and consequently more powerful, than the buffalo of India, and it is said frequently to kill the lion when it encounters the latter in their native jungles, though the lion generally obtains the mastery. A conflict between them sometimes terminates in the death of both. Even in India the buffalo is a formidable creature, and when one is ejected from the herd, it runs at everything that comes in its way, until destroyed either by its own violence, or by the superior strength of some wild animal.

I once knew an instance of a buffalo, maddened by being expelled from the community of its fellows—which is often the case, though from what circumstance is not, so far as I know, ascertained—and, fearless of the odds, which were evident in such

Drawn by W. Daniell, R. A. — Engraved by R. Brandard

Lion and Buffaloes

an unequal contest, rush, with its nose between its fore legs, its tail in the air, and exhibiting every symptom of frantic hostility, towards an elephant, upon which a friend of mine was mounted. The wary animal calmly waited its approach, with head declined and its tusks projected;—the maddened buffalo plunged forward and was completely impaled. After a moment, the elephant shook the quivering carcass from its tusks, pushed its huge foot upon the still panting body, and passed quietly on its way.

We had not long taken our station in the gallery, before the buffalo was driven from its stall. The moment it entered the enclosure it began to bellow and plunge violently, throwing the dirt from its heels into the air at least a dozen feet high. It was a bony animal, as large as a Durham ox, though not, perhaps, quite so tall, its legs being short in proportion to its size. It had an immense head, with long horns, that curled like those of a ram, whilst its large projecting eye and dilated nostril gave it an expression of extreme fierceness. There was scarcely any hair upon its body, except on the neck and tail: at the extremity of the latter appeared a large tuft, very thick and coarse. It was altogether a noble creature, full of strength and fury,

> "Crook-knee'd and dew-lapp'd, like Thessalian bulls."

After a few moments the bars of the lion's cage were raised, and the kingly animal bounded forward. It was one of the finest I had ever seen. A Hindoo sage has said that "the elephant, the lion, and the wise man seek their safety in flight; but the crow, the deer, and the coward, die in their nest." In the present instance, however, the lion was fully vindicated from the obloquy of such vulgar wisdom, as will be presently seen.

It stalked majestically forward, but, seeing the buffalo, dropped upon its belly, swept the ground with its tail, and then uttering a short growl, made two or three leaps, and sprang upon its adversary's neck without further preliminaries. The sudden shock brought the buffalo upon its knees; but immediately recovering, the latter threw back its head with a violence that dislodged the lion, casting it with prodigious force against the strong wooden palings of the enclosure, at the same time striking one of its horns into the flank of its assailant and opening a hideous gash. The lion was for a moment stunned; nevertheless, before its enemy had time to take advantage of its condition, it was on its legs, and had again sprung upon the buffalo's neck, which it lacerated dreadfully. There was now a deadly struggle; but the latter, repeating the same action which had before disengaged it from the gripe of its tawny foe, threw the lion again against the palings with still greater violence than before, and there gored it with an animation and goodwill that soon entirely disabled the noble beast from renewing the contest.

The buffalo was by this time so exhausted that it fell by the side of its prostrate enemy. After some exertion the keepers got it upon its legs and led it from the scene of combat. The lion was with difficulty dragged into its cage, but in a few days appeared little the worse for the punishment it had received from the horns of its formidable antagonist, which died the day after the combat. The lacerations in the neck were so extensive, and it became so furious under the pain of its wounds, that no one could venture to apply any thing to repair the mischief.

This was altogether a painful sight; I almost sickened at witnessing the fierce and deadly ferocity with which those two powerful animals strove to destroy each other. Though the strength of the buffalo evidently exceeded that of the lion, this was more than counterbalanced by the activity of the latter, and the deadly weapons with which it was armed; although, moreover, it appeared to have had the worst in the encounter, yet the result proved the reverse to be the case.

After this a few other animal fights of minor importance and little interest took place. A pair of native Mysore boxers then appeared before the Rajah to exhibit their skill in an art practised upwards of two thousand years ago in Europe, and perhaps even before that period in Asia. These boxers are called Jetties, from the instrument, a sort of cæstus, with which the right hand is armed. It is made of buffalo horn, with four sharp projections like knuckles. There is a fifth near the little finger of greater prominence than the rest. These horny knobs are very sharp, and a blow inflicted with this instrument, if delivered with the full force of a muscular man, would cleave open a man's skull; but as it is placed upon the fingers between the lower joints and the main knuckles of the hand, the fingers passing through a narrow opening below the knobs, just large enough to receive them when the fist is doubled and the instrument thus secured, the power of hitting is considerably lessened. A heavy blow would probably dislocate the fingers of the striker, from the awkward position of the weapon, which does not cover the knuckles, but, as I have said, is fixed immediately between them and the finger-joints. The mode of hitting is by a sharp perpendicular cut, which instantly makes an incision and lays the flesh open to the bone. The Jetties are never allowed to strike below the head; but wrestling forms the principal feature of their contests, which are decided more by their skill in this art than by the use of the cæstus; that being a mere accessory, though in truth a most formidable one, as the parties are frequently so disfigured in these encounters that, when they are over, scarcely a feature remains perfect.

A good deal of skill is displayed in these combats, and sometimes a considerable period elapses before a successful blow is struck, the combatants being very dexterous in defending their heads from the stroke of that formidable weapon with which their right hands are armed. They are generally fine men, perfect models in shape, and larger than the generality of Hindoos. They are a distinct caste, and their profession is traced as far back as the remotest historical records of Mysore. Their choicest champions exhibit yearly at the great festival of the Dusserah, when many couples of them contend at the same time before their prince. They are much feared by the peaceable inhabitants of the neighbourhood in which they dwell, though a race, I believe, in general of sober habits; but the circumstance of their possessing the means of inflicting summary chastisement upon aggressors, forces a kind of constrained outward respect from those around them, who inwardly despise both their caste and their occupation, which in every country is a degraded one. The native princes have at all times given great encouragement to these and similar stern trials of skill, and though the reward obtained by the vanquisher falls far short of the punishment received, still such is the stimulus imparted by the mere ambition of obtaining the approbation of their prince, that these men will occasionally undergo an almost incredible degree of infliction merely to gain his smile, accompanied with the trifling, though more substantial, reward of a few rupees.

The two Jetties who now entered the arena were young men of fine forms, about the middle height, neither very robust nor very muscular, but with frames remarkable for compactness and admirable proportion. Their attitudes were imposing, and they exhibited a natural grace and apparent refinement altogether different from those persons who pursue occupations of a similar character in Europe. They approached each other, holding up and crossing their left arms, and putting themselves into position for the strife. They shortly separated, making various motions with the left hand, and frequently shifting their position with great activity, in order to withdraw attention from the meditated point of attack,—but their eyes were mutually fixed upon each other with a keen and intense expression which nothing could divert. Several blows, struck with the rapidity of lightning, were as successfully parried,

P 3

and it was difficult to guess upon which side the advantage was likely to turn, so equally did they appear to be matched. Every now and then they mutually produced a short clapping noise by striking the palm of the left hand upon the muscles of the right arm. This was frequently repeated; and although several minutes elapsed before any decisive blow was struck, yet it was by no means uninteresting to see the activity which they displayed, and the fine muscular development of their well-proportioned limbs as they moved before each other with the intense earnestness of men seeking to obtain superiority in manual skill.

An opportunity was at length afforded to one of the combatants, who, rushing upon his adversary, hit him a smart blow upon the cheek, laying it open to the bone. The wounded man suddenly stooped and lifted his adversary in the air, when he received another blow upon the crown from the cæstus, which in a moment covered his neck and shoulders with blood. He, however, succeeded in throwing his man, who in rising received in his turn a gash on the temple, that again sent him backward. The rapidity with which he sprang upon his legs was surprising. Both the men now closed and planted several successful blows, by which they were shortly so disfigured that it made me quite sick to behold them; when the Rajah, at the anxious solicitation of one of the company, in which we all eagerly united, gave the signal for them to desist. They were both liberally rewarded for the skill and courage they had shown, with which they were so well satisfied, that one of them said he should be very happy to receive a similar punishment every day, if it were to be followed by a similar recompence.

After the struggle was over, it was pleasing to witness the good humour that seemed to exist between these two combatants. They remained within the arena looking on at the sports, squatted upon the ground, and chatting with perfect good fellowship, notwithstanding the severity with which they had so lately punished each other. I am told that these encounters do not in the slightest degree interrupt the personal friendship often existing between these men; neither does their friendship prevent them from inflicting the severest punishment during those encounters, in which their proudest ambition is to obtain manual superiority.

To me the most interesting part of the sports was the performance of the jugglers, a party of them being now introduced. The usual preliminaries took place, such as swallowing the sword, eating fire, and a few other tricks, common to every exhibitor at the provincial fairs in our own country. After which, one of the men taking a large earthen vessel, with a capacious mouth, filled it with water and turned it upside down, when all the water flowed out; but the moment it was placed with the mouth upwards, it always became full. He then emptied it, allowing any one to inspect it who chose. This being done, he desired that one of the party would fill it: his request was obeyed; still, when he reversed the jar, not a drop of water flowed, and upon turning it, to our astonishment, it was empty. These and similar deceptions were several times repeated; and so skilfully were they managed, that, although any of us who chose were allowed to upset the vessel when full, which I did many times, upon reversing it there was no water to be seen, and yet no appearance of any having escaped. I examined the jar carefully when empty, but detected nothing which could lead to a discovery of the mystery. I was allowed to retain and fill it myself, still, upon taking it up, all was void within; yet the ground around it was perfectly dry, so that how the water had disappeared, and where it had been conveyed, were problems which none of us were able to expound. The vessel employed by the juggler upon this occasion was the common earthenware of the country, very roughly made; and in order to convince us that it had not been especially constructed for the purpose of aiding his clever deceptions, he permitted it to be broken in our presence: the fragments were then handed round for the inspection of his Highness and the party present with him.

The next thing done was still more extraordinary. A large basket was produced, under which was put a lean, hungry Pariah bitch; after the lapse of about a minute, the basket was removed, and she appeared with a litter of seven puppies. These were again covered, and upon raising the magic basket a goat was presented to our view; this was succeeded by a pig in the full vigour of existence, but which, after being covered for the usual time, appeared with its throat cut; it was, however, shortly restored to life under the mystical shade of the wicker covering. What rendered these sudden changes so extraordinary was, that no one stood near the basket but the juggler, who raised and covered the animals with it. When he concluded, there was nothing to be seen under it; and what became of the different animals which had figured in this singular deception, was a question that puzzled us all.

A man now took a small bag full of brass balls, which he threw one by one into the air, to the number of thirty-five. None of them appeared to return. When he had discharged the last there was a pause of full a minute; he then made a variety of motions with his hands, at the same time grunting forth a kind of barbarous chant; in a few seconds, the balls were seen to fall, one by one, until the whole of them were replaced in the bag: this was repeated at least half a dozen times. No one was allowed to come near him while this interesting juggle was performed.

A gaunt-looking Hindoo next stepped forward, and declared he would swallow a snake. Opening a box, he produced a Cobra de Capello not less than five feet long, and as big as an infant's wrist. He stood, however, apart, at some distance from us, and, like his predecessor, would not allow any person to approach him, so that the deception became no longer equivocal. He then, as it appeared to us, took the snake, and putting its tail into his mouth gradually lowered it into his stomach, until nothing but the head appeared to project from between his lips, when, with a sudden gulp, he seemed to complete the disgusting process of deglutition, and to secure the odious reptile within his body. After the expiration of a few seconds, he opened his mouth and gradually drew forth the snake, which he replaced in the box, making a salaam to the Rajah. This was by no means a pleasing sight, but his Highness laughed heartily, and threw the performer a handful of rupees; thus clearly showing that his pleasure was no counterfeit, like the juggler's trick.

The next thing that engaged our attention was a feat of dexterity altogether astonishing. A woman, the upper part of whose body was entirely uncovered, presented herself to our notice, and taking a bamboo, twenty feet high, placed it upright upon a flat stone, and then, without any support, climbed to the top of it with surprising activity. Having done this, she stood upon one leg on the point of the bamboo, balancing it all the while. Round her waist she had a girdle, to which was fastened an iron socket; springing from her upright position on the bamboo, she threw herself horizontally forward with such exact precision that the top of the pole entered the socket of her iron zone, and in this position she spun herself round with a velocity that made me giddy to look at, the bamboo appearing all the while as if it were supported by some supernatural agency. She turned her legs backward until the heels touched her shoulders, and grasping the ankles in her hands, continued her rotation so rapidly that the outline of her body was entirely lost to the eye, and she looked like a revolving ball. Having performed several other feats equally extraordinary, she slid down the elastic shaft, and raising it in the air, balancěd it upon her chin, then upon her nose, and finally projected it to a distance from her, without the application of her hands. She was an elderly woman, and by no means prepossessing in her person, which I conclude was the reason that the Rajah, though he applauded her dexterity, did not give her a proof of his liberality. We, however, threw her a few rupees, with which she appeared perfectly satisfied.

The next performer spread upon the ground a cloth, about the size of a sheet: after a while, it seemed to be gradually raised; upon taking it up, there appeared three pineapples growing under it, which were cut and presented to the spectators. This is considered a common juggle, and yet it is perfectly inexplicable. Many other extraordinary things were done which have entirely escaped my memory; but the concluding feat was too remarkable to be easily forgotten.

A tall, athletic fellow advanced, and making his salaam to the gallery, threw himself upon the ground. After performing several strange antics, he placed his head downwards with his heels in the air, raised his arms, and crossed the mover upon his breast, balancing himself all the while upon his head. A cup, containing sixteen brass balls, was now put into his hands; these he took and severally threw them into the air, keeping the whole sixteen in constant motion, crossing them, and causing them to describe all kinds of figures, and not allowing one of them to reach the ground. When he had thus shown his dexterity for a few minutes, a slight man approached, climbed up his body with singular agility, and stood upright upon the inverted feet of the performer, who was still upon his head. A second cup, containing sixteen balls, was handed to the smaller man, who commenced throwing them until the whole were in the air. Thirty-two balls were now in motion, and the rays of the sun falling upon their polished surfaces, the jugglers appeared in the midst of a shower of gold. The effect was singular, and the dexterity displayed by these men quite amazing. They were as steady as if they had been fixed into stone, and no motion, save that of their arms and heads, was visible. At length, the upper man, having caught all his balls and replaced them in the cup, sprang upon the ground, and his companion was almost as quickly upon his legs.

After a short pause, the man, who had before exhibited himself with his body reversed, planted his feet close together, and standing upright like a column, the smaller juggler climbed his body as before, and placing the crown of his own head upon that of his companion, raised his legs into the air, thus exactly reversing the late position of the two performers. At first they held each other's hands until the libration was complete, when they let go, the upper man waving his arms in all directions to show the steadiness of his equilibrium. The legs were kept apart sometimes, one being bent, while the other remained erect; but the body did not seem to waver for a single instant. After they had been in this position for about a minute, the balls were again put into their hands, and the whole thirty-two kept in motion in the air as before. It was remarkable that, during the entire time they were thrown, neither of them once came in contact,—a proof of the marvellous skill displayed. It is certain that the manual dexterity of these men is not exceeded, if approached, by the jugglers of any other country in the world.

When they had done with the balls, the upper man took a number of small cylindrical pieces of steel, two inches long; several of these he placed upon hi nose, producing a slender rod full a foot in length, which, in spite of his difficult position, he balanced so steadily that not one of the pieces fell. He then crossed the taper column with a flat bar of copper, half an inch wide and four inches long; upon this he fixed one of his little cylinders, and on the top of that a slight spear; the whole of which he balanced with perfect steadiness, finally taking off every separate piece and throwing it upon the ground: thus concluded this extraordinary performance. Grasping hands as before, the little man sprang upon his feet, and made his obeisance to the gallery.

This feat appears to have been something similar, though much less extraordinary, to one mentioned in the autobiography of the Mogul Emperor Jehanguire; the truth, however, of which I am much disposed to question, as it appears to me to involve physical impossibilities.

"One of seven men," says the imperial author, "stood upright before us, a second passed upwards along his body, and, head to head, placed his feet upwards in the air. A third managed to climb up in the same manner, and planting his feet to those of the second, stood with his head upwards; and so alternately to the seventh, who crowned this marvellous human pillar with his head uppermost. And what excited an extraordinary clamour of surprise, was to observe the first man, who thus supported upon the crown of his head the whole of the other six, lift one foot as high as his shoulder; standing thus upon one leg, and exhibiting a degree of strength and steadiness not exactly within the scope of my comprehension."* I confess I should be disposed to doubt the authenticity of the manuscript from which this record is taken, as it relates a number of circumstances manifestly impossible, and, to my mind, completely contradicts the historical character of Jehanguire.

The sports having terminated, we made our bows to the Rajah and retired.

* See Memoirs of the Emperor Jehanguire, written by himself, and translated from a Persian manuscript by Major David Price.

CHAPTER XIII.

THE COORG RAJAH AND HIS SUCCESSOR.

We were altogether much gratified with the kindness of the Coorg Rajah during the short stay that we made at his capital. When we took our leave, he made us presents of shawls; and we quitted him with a favourable idea of his generosity and hospitality. This prince always entertained a high respect for our countrymen, showing those who visited his territories the greatest attention. To the last moment of his life this feeling never subsided. Though his passions were violent, and his anger was soon roused, yet he was readily appeased, and then his enmity instantly vanished. His alliance with the British government was singularly cordial and sincere; and I have heard it said of him that, with reference to his good faith towards that government, he was fond of quoting the words of a philosopher of his own nation, no less beautiful than true:—"The friendship of a good man is not easily interrupted, and if lost, is soon regained: a golden bowl is not readily broken, but if broken, is soon repaired. The friendship of the vicious is soon lost, and never regained but with great exertion: an earthen bowl is quickly broken, and cannot be repaired, even with the greatest labour."

The successor of this prince has by no means followed in his father's steps. Having ventured to put himself in hostile array against a power which no native force has yet been able successfully to oppose, he has lost his principality, and is now a state-prisoner, his possessions having fallen into the hands of the East India Company. The present Rajah and the interesting boy mentioned by Captain Basil Hall in his visit to the Coorg district, are identical. That boy, in his manhood, has shown himself to be a cruel tyrant, and in his reverse of fortune we can follow him neither with our respect nor with our sympathies. I cannot forbear mentioning here a circumstance which took place when he quitted his capital a prisoner: it was related to me by an eyewitness, as a marvellous proof of animal sagacity. The Rajah had an extensive stud of fine elephants, among which was one that had been in the habit of carrying a taper before the prince when he retired to rest, and of performing various domestic offices. When the royal Coorg quitted the town, this elephant approached the palenkeen in which its master was reclining, fell upon its knees, made several salaams, exhibiting every token of the profoundest respect, and appearing to feel acutely its sovereign's disgrace. This is not all:—the poor beast, after the Rajah's departure, began to pine, and when my informant quitted the country was reduced to a state of deplorable infirmity; by this time it has more than probably ceased to exist. The attachment of these creatures, where they are kindly treated, frequently puts human friendships and human attachments to shame.

Drawn by Wm. Daniell R.A.

Engraved by R. Brandard

The Monkey and Crows

I do not stay to describe our journey to the coast, which had nothing particular to render it interesting. We determined to proceed forthwith to Cochin, expecting there to be able to procure a passage in some vessel that would take us up the Red Sea. We stopped a few days at Tillicherry, where a curious incident occurred, which, as Mr. Daniell has thought it worth making the subject of a picture, I cannot but think it worth recording.

In the jungles about this neighbourhood there is a large species of monkey, frequently tamed by the natives, and at a village a short distance from this celebrated seaport we had an evidence of the remarkable sagacity of this animal. A few yards from the house of the person to whom it belonged, a thick pole, at least thirty feet high, had been fixed into the earth, round which was an iron ring, and to this was attached a strong chain of considerable length, fastened to a collar round the monkey's neck. The ring being loose, it easily slid up the pole when he ascended or descended. He was in the habit of taking his station upon the top of the bamboo, where he seemed perched as if to enjoy the beauties of the prospect around him;—this was really striking. The crows, which in India are very abundant and singularly audacious, taking advantage of his elevated position, had been in the daily habit of robbing him of his food, which was placed every morning and evening at the foot of the pole. To this he had vainly expressed his dislike by chattering, and other indications of his displeasure equally ineffectual; nothing that he could do was of any avail to scare away these unwelcome intruders upon his repasts. He tried various modes to banish them, but they continued their periodical depredations. Finding that he was perfectly unheeded, he adopted a plan of retribution as effectual as it was ingenious.

One morning, when his tormentors had been particularly troublesome, he appeared as if seriously indisposed: he closed his eyes, drooped his head, and exhibited various other symptoms of severe suffering. No sooner were his ordinary rations placed at the foot of the bamboo, than the crows, watching their opportunity, descended in great numbers, and, according to their usual practice, began to demolish his provisions. The monkey now began to slide down the pole by slow degrees, as if the effort were painful to him, and as if so overcome by indisposition that his remaining strength was scarcely equal to such exertion. When he reached the ground, he rolled about for some time, seeming in great agony, until he found himself close by the vessel employed to contain his food, which the crows had by this time wellnigh devoured. There was still, however, some remaining, which a solitary bird, emboldened by the apparent indisposition of the monkey, advanced to seize. The wily creature was at this time lying in a state of apparent insensibility at the foot of the pole, and close by the pan. The moment the crow stretched out its head, and ere it could secure a mouthful of the interdicted food, the watchful avenger seized the depredator by the neck with the rapidity of thought, and secured it from doing further mischief. He now began to chatter and grin with every expression of gratified triumph, while the crows flew around, cawing in boisterous chime, as if deprecating the chastisement about to be inflicted upon their captive companion. The monkey continued for a while to chatter and grin in triumphant mockery of their distress; he then deliberately placed the captive crow between his knees, and began to pluck it with the most humorous gravity. When he had completely stripped it, except the large feathers in the pinions and tail, he flung it into the air as high as his strength would permit, and, after flapping its wings for a few seconds, it fell on the ground with a stunning shock. The other crows, which had been fortunate enough to escape a similar castigation, now surrounded it, and immediately pecked it to death.

The expression of joy on the animal's countenance was altogether indescribable; and he had no sooner seen this ample retribution dealt to the purloiner of his repast, than he ascended the bamboo to enjoy a quiet repose. The next time his food was brought not a single crow approached it, and I dare say that, thenceforward, he was never again molested by those voracious intruders. The scene was, in truth, well worth witnessing.

On our way down the coast to Cochin we found the country extremely picturesque. The houses of the natives were frequently buried amid thick groves of palms, mangoes, jacks, and plantains, skirting the bottoms of the small hills which here and there dot the surface of the landscape. Above them are magnificent woods of forest-trees perfectly free from rattans and other climbers, which mar their growth and greatly injure the timber. The teak and black-wood abound in these jungles, the former frequently attaining to the majestic height of one hundred and fifty feet. Scarcely any part of the hills in this province is cultivated; the lower elevations are covered with rank wiry grass, and other useless growths of a superabundant vegetation.

The Tiers of this district, and indeed throughout the whole province of Malabar, are a fine race. They are the cultivators of the soil. Nothing can exceed the beauty of their women, who are models of the human form, possessing countenances of great symmetry. Their complexions are a clear light brown, much like those of the women of Italy, only far more uniform and brilliant. The more respectable classes among them wear no covering on the upper part of their bodies, and yet there is not the slightest indication of immodesty in their actions or address. They consider this exposure of themselves a mark of delicacy; for women of bad character among them invariably cover the neck and shoulders, which they affect as the distinction of their avocation.

The better classes wear a hat made of chip matting, the top of which is encircled by a wide brim; this they put on with a good deal of taste, allowing it to droop over the right shoulder, thus showing to advantage their small handsome features. There is nothing remarkable in the appearance of the men except the air of cleanliness which universally distinguishes them, forming a strong contrast with many of the tribes by whom they are surrounded. Among these are the Niadis, an outcast tribe not numerous, but of very filthy habits. They are reckoned so impure that not even a slave of caste will touch them. They occupy wretched hovels built under the shade of trees, and generally wander about in small companies, keeping at a distance from the public roads. When they see a passenger approaching they howl like a pack of hungry jackals. They eat carrion and offal of every description, and are altogether in a destitute condition.

The Tiers, though seldom wealthy, are generally in good circumstances, living upon the produce of their land, which they cultivate with sufficient industry, but with no great skill. The Nairs are a superior caste to the Tiers. They are the pure Sudras of Malabar, and all pretend to be born soldiers, though they embrace various professions. Those of the highest rank among them perform the distinguished office of cook; for, as every Hindoo desires that his food should be dressed by persons of higher rank than himself, the office of cook is one of distinction. There are eleven classes of Nairs, and from this caste the militia of Malabar is formed. They are governed by Rajahs, to whom they pay the most abject homage. These princes hold a despotic tyranny over them. A Nair would not hesitate a moment to cut down a Pariah who happened to pass within the length of his arm.

The Nairs marry in infancy, but the wife always remains with the parents, and cohabits with any person she chooses of equal rank with her own. This practice is not considered in the slightest degree disgraceful, nor does the husband reject the offspring of his wife, even though none of her children should be his. Such a system of social degradation, as may be supposed, does not tend to elevate the characters of this caste, and they have generally all the vices which a course of systematic immorality must inevitably engender. They are a debased tribe, though they rank higher than the Tiers, who are far their superiors in moral dignity and social respectability.

I may mention here a singular circumstance which occurred among some Nair children while a military friend of mine was stationed at Cannanore, a town upon the sea-coast of this province. A number of boys, none of whom exceeded the age of twelve years, and some of them were considerably younger, whilst in the charge of their flocks—for they were goat-herds—which grazed near the parade-ground of the British regiment stationed at Cannanore, had there an opportunity of witnessing the mode of punishment adopted in the British cantonment. Struck, as it appears, with its justice, they established among themselves a punitive discipline precisely similar. It was determined that any instance of theft detected among them should be punished with death. Having witnessed the military execution of a soldier and flogging, they came to the resolution that graver and minor offences among them should be visited with chastisements of equal severity. A short time after they had established their system of legislation, a boy was detected in having appropriated to his own use—a direct violation of their laws—some seeds of the jack fruit with which he had been intrusted. He was immediately subjected to a kind of court-martial, found guilty, and sentenced to be hanged upon a tree. The sentence was accordingly carried into execution, and the boy was actually found dead within a few hours after. This circumstance caused a great sensation at the time; but, from the youth and number of the offenders, it was considered inexpedient to proceed against them with rigour. Their confederacy, however, was broken, their laws were abrogated, and the fear of punishment prevented the recurrence of any similar extra-judicial acts among these juvenile legislators.

"The villages of Malabar," says Hamilton,* "are the neatest in India, and much embellished by the beauty and elegant dress of the Brahmin girls. The houses are placed contiguous in a straight line, and built of mud, so as generally to occupy two sides of a square area, a little raised, and kept clean and free from grass. The mud is of excellent quality, and in general neatly smoothed, and either white-washed or painted; but the houses being thatched with palm-leaves, are extremely combustible. Both bazaars and cottages have been introduced by foreigners; the Nambouries, Nairs, and all the aboriginal natives of Malabar, living in detached houses surrounded by gardens, and collectively named Desas. The higher ranks use very little clothing, but are remarkably clean in their persons, cutaneous distempers being never observed, except among the slaves and the very lowest castes."

In the neighbourhood of Cochin we found a large number of persons afflicted with elephantiasis, which is scarcely seen in any other part of this coast. Here

* See "Description of Hindostan," &c.

we purchased a vessel for eight thousand rupees, about eight hundred pounds, and changed her Dutch name of Yong Vrouw Jacomina to that of the Cornwallis. She was a sloop of eighty tons burthen.

We now changed our minds of going up the Red Sea, on account of rumours that the plague was raging, and shaped our course towards the Persian Gulf. The morning was beautiful, and as we passed gently up the coast with a light breeze, the distant mountains of Travancore rose majestically above the level country with a grand and imposing magnificence. For miles we found the water covered with a thick, tawny scum, which, upon examination, appeared to be composed of very minute leaves, of oblong shape and yellowish hue. We coasted for thirty days, but without making much progress, and our daily amusement was catching dolphins, which abounded, and afforded us excellent sport; though, when caught, they are no great delicacy even at sea, where fish is generally a treat.

Cocoa-nut trees grow in great abundance upon this coast, and are valuable property to the poorer natives, who obtain from them sundry necessaries, and sell the nuts at a good profit. This tree supplies them with toddy—an exudation of sap produced by making an incision in the trunk, from which many pints drop in the course of one night. It is sweet, and exceedingly agreeable when taken before sunrise; but after it has been allowed to ferment, a strong spirit is disengaged, which the poor natives drink in great quantities: it therefore finds a ready sale.

From the nut of this tree a very useful oil is extracted, which is used by the Hindoos for domestic purposes, for the services of their temples, and for anointing their bodies. It is now becoming in Europe an article of considerable domestic consumption, being employed with great success in the manufacture of soap and candles, as it is a purer and better material than tallow. The husk of the nut is manufactured into cables and smaller cordage, and has the peculiar property of being preserved in salt water.

The leaves of the cocoa-nut tree are employed for thatching houses, and the wood for sundry purposes. Upon the whole, this is the most useful production of the vegetable world in India, and it is frequently exposed to depredations from two animals as opposite in character as in size. The one is the elephant, which comes from the jungles and commits dreadful havoc among the plantations. Entering a cocoa-nut tope, it fixes on a tree which appears within the compass of its mighty strength, and seizing it with its trunk as high as it can reach, sways it to and fro with the nicest calculation of its resistance. If the tree does not readily yield, the wily animal tries another and another, until it meets with one which it can master. When the tree is so loosened as to be about to fall, the elephant places its foot upon the root, and lowers it gently with so calculating a sagacity, that one would almost think it had studied the laws of mechanical force.

The other formidable enemy of the cocoa-nut tree is a huge crab, or rather lobster, from twenty-four to thirty inches long, which abounds on the shores of those islands that form the Indian Archipelago. This creature having prodigious nippers, ascends the tree, to which it clings with great ease; and when it has reached the top, seizes the stem of the nut in its vast pincers, separates it from the cluster, and lets it drop upon the ground beneath. The lobster then descends, tears off the exterior coat with astonishing facility and quickness, cracks the nut, and sucks out the tender pulp. This lobster is a great delicacy.

On the sixth week after our departure from Cochin, we encountered a severe gale, which did us some damage, and our provisions were nearly exhausted. A duck curried was the only fresh food we tasted for several days, and a half-starved turkey was all that remained of our stock. Flying-fish were here happily abundant, many of which flew upon our deck, affording us on more than one occasion an unexpected luxury. We came at length to an anchor off Dagomar, a small town upon the Arabian coast, where we received a pilot on board to take us to Mascat.

On the second day after quitting Dagomar, about noon, we reached Mascat harbour, which is protected by stupendous rocks; between these is a narrow entrance of some danger, unless you have a skilful pilot. On the right of this strait is a curious conical rock, standing apart from the masses behind it, and quite surrounded by the sea, in which it appears to stand sentinel at the entrance of the harbour. At the base it has a cleft, resembling a mighty sabre-stroke, which seems to have thrown it slightly out of the perpendicular. It is a pic-

Drawn by W. Daniell, R.A.

Engraved by [illegible]

Printed by [illegible]

Near Muskat.

London, Published Oct 1, 1833, for the Proprietor, by Edward Churton, 26 Holles Street, Cavendish Square.

turesque object, but much increases the danger of approach to Mascat in stormy weather. Just as we came in sight of it, five boats bore down upon us, which, by their suspicious manœuvres, we had no doubt were Mahratta pirates. These boats are numerously manned. We showed them eight wooden guns, and flourished our fire-arms in such a way as to lead them to suspect that ours was an armed vessel,—which it seems they took it to be, for, finding we showed no disposition to run before them, they bore away towards the Malabar coast.

These pirate boats are long and narrow, generally carrying from fifty to sixty men, mostly Arabs. They hoist an immense latteen sail from a slight yard at least fifty feet long, and are fast sailers. Two of these boats might have taken us with ease; but our vicinity to Mascat was no doubt one strong reason, coupled with our bold appearance, for not attacking us. These pirates are much dreaded, and render a voyage up the Persian Gulf at all times dangerous. They are exceedingly ferocious, sometimes committing atrocious cruelties upon those who are so unfortunate as to fall into their power. The celebrated Angria, so formidable in the latter part of the seventeenth century, was the first who rendered the Mahratta piracies worthy of a place in history. Of him and his successors a short account may not be unwelcome to the reader.

CHAPTER XIV.

THE ANGRIAS.

About the middle of the seventeenth century, Canojee Angria was made Governor of Severndroog. He was originally a private Mahratta soldier, and had raised himself to the highest offices by his valour and conduct. He served under the Rajah both as admiral and general. When he became Governor of Severndroog, he assumed the authority of an independent sovereign, and upon the first opportunity seizing several of the vessels which he had formerly commanded, officered them with persons whom he had attached to his cause, and began to commit acts of piracy. He at first confined himself to the neighbourhood of the island under his dominion, until, by repeated successes, he had rendered himself sufficiently formidable to extend his depredations. He then soon possessed himself of nearly the whole of the Mahratta fleet.

Alarmed at the successes of this daring advènturer, the Mahrattas built three forts upon the main land, within point-blank shot of his little territory, a small rocky island, well fortified and difficult of access. He, however, baffled all their precautions and continued his depredations, making himself master of a large portion of their territory, in which were several commodious harbours, where he built fortresses, and established himself so securely that they were unable to dislodge him. He fortified the passes and defiles; and by taking into his service every desperate fellow who could obtain no employment elsewhere, his name became a terror to the whole country within the influence of his arms. He was at length so powerful at sea, that his vessels took the Darley East-Indiaman, with a hundred and fifty men, and the Restoration, an armed ship of twenty guns, fitted out purposely against them. They captured, also, from the French a ship of forty guns, having on board four hundred slaves; and had the audacity to attack Commodore Lisle, who commanded a small fleet, among which was a ship of sixty guns, another of fifty, besides several frigates and smaller vessels. From this time the family became independent princes, and for near a century were the terror of these seas. Their successes rendered them formidable even to the British and Dutch governments.

In 1754 the reigning prince, Tullagee Angria, having captured several of their vessels and treated his captives with extreme rigour, it was determined by the Bombay government to attack him in his stronghold; which determination was hastened by the pirate's success against three Dutch ships—one of fifty, another of thirty-six, and a third of eighteen guns—burning the former two, and capturing the latter. Upon this he grew so insolent, that he boasted he should eventually be master of the Indian seas, and commenced building two large vessels, one of which was to carry forty guns. In obedience to the determination of the Bombay government, Commodore James, then commander of the British marine force in India, sailed for the pirate's retreat with only four ships,—the Protector of forty-four guns, the Swallow of sixteen, and two bomb-vessels,—being the whole force then available.

The morning after the English Commodore had set sail, he fell in with seven of Angria's grabs and eleven gallivats, and gave them chase. The day following he was joined by the Mahratta fleet, consisting likewise of seven grabs and eleven gallivats, which united with him against the common enemy. These, however, shortly quitted the commodore, and anchored in Commoro Bay, where their crews landed and trifled away thirty hours; being prohibited by their religion from eating on board their ships, and being also enjoined a number of ablutions, and certain religious rites to be performed on shore.

Next day, while the Mahratta crews were on land performing their customary devotions, Commodore James received intelligence that the enemy's fleet was anchored in the harbour of Severndroog. After some delay, the English commander collected his dilatory allies, and proceeded forthwith to the pirate's stronghold. As soon as Angria's admiral saw them approaching in such force, he ordered that his ships should slip their cables and run out to sea, the gallivats towing the larger vessels. This gave them a manifest advantage over our ships, as there was almost a dead calm, and they could consequently make but little way. The chase continued the whole day; but so backward were the Mahrattas to engage their formidable foe apart from the English commodore, that although, from the light structure of their boats, which carried a single sail of immense dimensions, that turned readily to the wind, thus catching every breath of the breeze, they had, during the several preceding days, considerably outsailed our vessels, yet now, when the opportunity presented itself of showing their skill and spirit against an enemy from whom they had received such grievous injury, instead of embracing it with that alacrity which the impulse of retribution would naturally dictate, they kept far astern, while the pirates showed a perseverance and dexterity in their flight as surprising as it was successful. They threw out from their vessels everything that tended in the slightest degree to perplex or interrupt their course; and as there was scarcely any wind, they not only crowded all their canvass upon the yards, but fastened to the flag-staffs rugs, jackets, turbans, and anything that could tend in the slightest degree to accelerate their progress. By these means they baffled all the exertions of the English commander, and drew him so far from his station that he was obliged to relinquish the pursuit and return to Severndroog.

This fortress was situated on an island within a quarter of a mile from the main land; but the water within the frith was so shallow, that no ship above three hundred tons' burthen could pass through it. The fort was strongly, but not regularly fortified. Like that at Gibraltar, a great part of the works were hewn out of the solid rock with immense labour; and the other portions, where masonry was employed, were constructed of massy cubes of stone, from ten to twelve feet long, fastened with a cement which gave them the stability of one unbroken mass. The bastions were mounted with fifty-four guns. The largest fort on the main land belonging to Angria was called Fort Goa. It was built precisely in the same manner as that on the island, equally strong, and presenting a formidable battery of forty guns.

It seems strange that this dreaded pirate should have been allowed to carry on his depredations with impunity for such a length of time. The Bombay government, indeed, had long determined to suppress them, but nothing effectual had ever been done; for though several expeditions were undertaken, they had hitherto all failed. Commodore Mathews, with his squadron and a small army of Portuguese, had joined the Bombay sea and land forces in an enterprise against one of Angria's forts, but was defeated by the treachery of his allies, the Portuguese, who, dreading the enemy's power, thought it prudent to make peace with the pirate, and leave their associates, thus weakened, to the decreased chance of success. The expedition failed in consequence; and the ships and troops returned to Bombay, except the Shoreham man-of-war, which struck upon the rocks and was wrecked.

It being now evident that no final advantages were to be expected against this daring marauder, who had by this time become the terror of the Indian seas, unless the co-operation of the Mahrattas was first obtained, a treaty was entered into with that power, their sovereign agreeing to unite his forces with those of the British government, so soon as a feasible plan should be resolved upon for the reduction of Angria's forts. It was during this alliance that Commodore James proceeded against the Governor of Severndroog, as already stated. Disgusted at the base pusillanimity of his Mahratta allies, he determined to attack the pirate's principal fort with his own small squadron: consequently, on the day after the chase of his grabs and gallivats, he commenced a smart cannonading at break of day. The bombardment, though brisk, made little or no impression upon the walls, which were here nearly twenty feet thick and fifty-four feet high: the commodore therefore shifted his station, so as to bring Fort Goa within the range of his lower guns, while he directed those of the upper tier against Severndroog. The defence on this side being weaker, after some hours' cannonading he succeeded in destroying one of the bastions, and part of the parapet with which it was connected.

About noon, a shell happening to fall upon one of the houses within the fort, set it on fire, and the wind being strong, the flames soon communicated extensively to the neighbouring houses: these the garrison were prevented from saving by the severity of the cannonading, which was continued with undiminished energy. The fire spread with great rapidity, and after some time communicated with one of the magazines, which exploded, producing a tremendous confusion, and, very shortly after, a general conflagration. The consternation was beyond control,—men, women, and children rushed from their houses, ran to the farther side of the island, and embarked in boats, in hopes of reaching the main land in safety; but the Swallow, of sixteen guns, intercepted their flight, and made the greater part of them prisoners. Some few escaped, though only to carry terror among their friends.

The British commander now directed all his fire against Fort Goa, which was surrendered after a stubborn resistance; but immediately upon suspension of the fire from the commodore's ship, the governor crossed the strait, with a few chosen men, to the island of Severndroog, which had been entirely evacuated upon the blowing up of their second and chief magazine, that laid the town in ruins.

Though the island had suffered extremely from the fire of the British ship and the blowing up of the magazines, the natural defences were still remarkably strong, and the governor determined to hold out until he should receive succours, which he hourly expected. The commodore was now in possession of the three forts upon the main land, whilst the enemy retained only possession of that upon the island: against this latter the cannonading was continued, and a summons sent to the governor to surrender. He, however, refusing to capitulate, a number of seamen were landed, under cover of the fire from our ships and the batteries on shore, who, resolutely assaulting the gates with their axes, cut open the gate of the sallyport, and procured an entrance with very little loss.

Thus easily was possession obtained of a place which had bid defiance to all the governments of Europe and Asia for nearly half a century. The ships

Drawn by W. Daniell, R.A. | Engraved by J. C. Armytage

The Forts of Jellali & Merani, Muskat.

of Angria had swept the Indian seas with impunity, and frequently extended their captures to the Persian Gulf: Mascat was only protected by the natural strength of its position and the security of its harbour.

The harbour of Mascat is large, and one of the securest known. It is protected by a range of high rocks in the form of a horseshoe, there being a narrow entrance for small boats only, whilst larger vessels are obliged to go round the rocky ridge and enter at the main opening on the north side. The town lies on the western side, on the shore of a deep basin, where ships may anchor, secured from every wind that blows. There is a fort on the same side, near the entrance of the harbour, called Fort Jellali, built by the Portuguese when they had possession of Mascat. It stands upon a large, lofty rock behind the town, and, seen seaward, is extremely imposing. The fortifications are strong, and of fine stonework. From the beauty of the masonry, it is clear that Hindoo workmen were employed, as the fortifications have all the characteristics of their strong and compact mode of building, though the plan and aspect of the fort is decidedly European. The bastions and towers are of great strength, and during the time they were in possession of the Portuguese, were mounted with formidable batteries, served by a numerous and efficient garrison.

The fort is now occupied by the Arabs, and no longer formidable, presenting only a few brass cannon, and having been suffered to go into a sad state of decay. In the first Angria's time, though the

Portuguese were no longer masters of Mascat,—as it fell about this period into the hands of the Arabs,—yet he considered it too strong for him to attempt its reduction, and being so far distant from his territories, he no doubt thought it would be a useless acquisition.

After the surrender of Severndroog, the piratical chieftain could no longer make head against the British and Mahratta confederation. Immediately upon the capture of Angria's stronghold, the English commodore anchored off Bancoote, the most northern town of the pirate's dominions, which capitulated at the first summons. This place, which has an excellent harbour, is now added to the East India Company's possessions. The country around it abounds with excellent cattle, and supplies the presidency with superior sheep and oxen, extremely cheap. The best beef, perhaps, in India is obtained in this neighbourhood. The place, after its capitulation, was ceded by treaty to the Bombay government; but all other places on the coast which Angria had occupied were given up to the Mahrattas, and the British flag, hoisted on the several forts that had lately capitulated to the English commander, was struck, and replaced by the Mahratta colours. Nothing further was attempted after the fall of Bancoote, the season being too far advanced to render it prudent to continue longer at sea; Commodore James, therefore, returned to Bombay, where he received the highest acknowledgments for his signal services.

After the breaking up of the succeeding monsoon, Rear-Admiral Watson put into the harbour of Bombay with his squadron. While the ships were cleaning and repairing, Commodore James was despatched with a small fleet to sound the depths of the water at the entrance of the harbour of Fort Geriah, the capital of Angria's dominions. This service he performed; and having reconnoitred the fort, returned to Bombay with so favourable an account of the practicability of an attack, that this was finally determined on. Meanwhile Admiral Watson despatched a frigate and sloop, and several of the Company's armed vessels, with orders to cruise off Fort Geriah. These were shortly after joined by Commodore James in the Protector, accompanied by the Guardian frigate. He remained on this station about a fortnight, until the admiral arrived and joined the two squadrons, on the 11th of February 1806.

Upon the arrival of the English fleet, Angria became alarmed: he had never for a moment imagined that so large a force could be collected against him. Seeing, therefore, the formidable array which they presented, when united with the ships and armed vessels which had preceded them, he was so overcome by his apprehensions, that, with a pusillanimity hitherto supposed to have been foreign to his nature, he instantly abandoned the fort. This precipitation destroyed the confidence of his adherents. The Mahrattas, hoping to take advantage of his terrors,—for he had made overtures of peace to them apart from their allies,—sought to possess themselves of his wealth before the British admiral should be apprised of the real posture of affairs. Seizing the promising opportunity while Angria was labouring under anxious perturbation of mind, they insisted upon his sending an order to his brother, who was left in command, to put them in possession of the fort. This political duplicity is always a leading principle in Mahratta policy, it being a maxim with them, that anything is honourable which is done for the advantage of a state. With all their cunning, however, they could not elude the vigilance of Admiral Watson, who, finding that the fort had been abandoned by Angria, and left under the command of his brother, sent to the latter a peremptory summons to surrender. His summons not being attended to, the admiral divided his fleet into two lines, one composed of the King's ships, the other of those belonging to the East India Company. Weighing anchor early in the morning after Angria's flight from his capital, he stood in for the harbour in two divisions, the first being led by his own ship, followed by five others,—the second consisting of five frigates and four bomb-ketches. A smart fire was kept up from the enemy's batteries, and from their grabs, which flanked the fort. When the united squadrons, under the command of the British admiral, were brought into position, they opened a tremendous fire upon the fort and grabs, which soon silenced both.

In the course of the cannonading, a bomb was thrown into an armed ship taken by Angria from the East India Company, which blew up with a dreadful explosion, setting on fire the vessels in her immediate neighbourhood; and so rapid was the communication, that in a short time the whole of the pirate's fleet was destroyed. During the night the British admiral landed all his troops, under the command of

Colonel Clive, in order to frustrate the admission of the Mahrattas, which he had learned from a deserter was the intention of the besieged, as the governor had received orders from his brother upon no account to admit the English within the walls.

All the troops being landed, and prepared to act as circumstances might require, Admiral Watson sent a peremptory message to the commandant of the fort, declaring that if it were not delivered up to him within an hour from the time of his communication, the attack should be renewed, and no quarter extended to the garrison. The governor desired that there might be a cessation of hostilities until he could have his brother's determination upon the English admiral's message; stating that as his brother, when he left him in command, strictly forbade a capitulation, he could not comply with the terms of the summons until he heard from him who alone could give an answer.

Plausible as this pretence appeared, it was evidently only a feint to cover the sinister design of giving the place into possession of the Mahrattas, with whom the pirate was anxious to secure a peace. His wily efforts to gain time were of no avail; for Admiral Watson, seeing through the flimsy disguise, on receiving the commandant's reply, opened again upon the fort a severe fire, which, within half an hour, induced Angria to hoist a flag of truce. It was now, of course, expected that the enemy's colours would be hauled down and our troops admitted; but as this was delayed under the shallowest pretences, the cannonading from our ships was renewed with so terrific an energy that the garrison soon capitulated unconditionally. Colonel Clive then marched into the fort and took possession.

The garrison had suffered little loss, nor, on our side, was it at all severe. Upon entering Geriah, Colonel Clive was surprised to see what trifling mischief the works had sustained, notwithstanding the tremendous fire which had been directed against them. So great was the height and so extraordinary the thickness of their walls, that the garrison found an indestructible shelter behind them. All the ramparts not hewn out of the solid rock, as at Severndroog, were built of huge masses of stone, so prodigiously ponderous that no weight of metal could make an impression upon them. A year's cannonading would not have effected a practicable breach; yet such was the vigour of the fire poured from the British ships against these impregnable ramparts that it terrified the garrison into a surrender, in spite of the solidity of their battlements.

The treasure found within this town was not great. The money and effects were valued at about a hundred and twenty thousand pounds. Besides this, there were on the batteries two hundred guns, in good condition, six brass mortars, and a large quantity of ammunition of every description. The grabs which were burnt, consisted of eight ketches and one armed vessel. Upon the stocks were two large ships, in great forwardness, one of which was to carry forty guns, and the other twenty-six. Besides these, there was a large number of gallivats — small vessels that attend on the armed ships, to tow them when necessary, and are likewise used for boarding.

Colonel Clive, having obtained possession of Geriah, took care to prevent the Mahrattas from holding any intercourse with the garrison, whom they would have bribed to put them in possession. This intention was obviated by the vigilance of Colonel Clive, who did not permit them to approach the British lines. They made an offer of fifty thousand rupees to Captain Buchanan and Captain Forbes to be allowed to pass their guard; but the offer was rejected with indignation; and the Mahrattas, who boast of their wily policy, were surprised to find that our officers were inaccessible to a bribe, however large, which an Eastern prince would not hold it beneath his dignity to accept as a full and adequate return for a similar benefaction.

With the surrender of Geriah the power of Angria was completely broken, and his adherents dispersed. By degrees he was dispossessed of the whole of his forts; and he who had been a terror to all the native powers within the influence of his arms soon lost his ascendency; though the descendants of this family, up to the latter part of the eighteenth century, committed their piratical depredations under the once dreaded name of Angria.

CHAPTER XV.

MASCAT.—THE GOVERNOR.—THE HARBOUR.

A FEW hours after we saw the Mahratta pirate-boats, we were towed into Mascat harbour, the wind having subsided to a complete calm. We passed a frigate belonging to the King of Omar, which we saluted, and the compliment was returned. On the following day we paid a visit to the Governor and his son, who treated us with great courtesy, entertaining us with fruit and sherbet. The house, which was near the water, was rather a mean building; nor was his Highness's suite either numerous or splendid. Some eight or ten Arabs, equipped in a shabby military costume, stood at the entrance of the veranda, forming a sort of guard, and marshalled in military order, to pay us the customary honours as we passed over the Governor's threshold.

The Imaum of Mascat bears the title of King among the people under his domination, which is mild and equitable. His capital is a town of some importance. Immediately behind it there is an extensive ridge of naked rocks, rising to a vast height from the surface of the strait; and the whole aspect of the surrounding country is that of almost complete sterility. Date-trees, which will grow in very desolate places, are the only vegetable productions that can be said in any degree to abound. A few almond and tamarind trees are occasionally seen; but nothing can well exceed the repulsive feature of desolation which strikes the traveller upon the failure of rain, and this happened to be the case at the period of our visit. We were told that there had not been a day's rain for four years, and certainly the scantiness of vegetation seemed a sufficient voucher for the truth of this assurance. The inhabitants were suffering severe distress, in consequence of the scarcity of water; and the hot winds during the whole of our stay were so oppressive as to be at times almost intolerable.

We found provisions at Mascat reasonable, and the meat, poultry, and vegetables, remarkably good; this probably struck us the more forcibly, as the day before our arrival we had been reduced to our last turkey, which was all but starved to death when its throat was cut to make us a curry. For more than a week it had been kept alive by being crammed with stale fish and mouldy biscuit, the only aliment with which it could be supplied; and as we had scarcely any fresh water, the miserable creature was all but dead when it was killed. Had we continued at sea a couple of days longer, we should have been in a wretched condition, as the whole of our provisions were exhausted.

The harbour of Mascat, which is of great extent, is deep enough to float the largest vessels; and even in the cove, immediately before the town, several ships of war were at anchor while we were there. It is protected by several forts; but the principal are the two represented in the engraving, Jellali and Merani,* both built by the Portuguese. About the middle of the seventeenth century, they were dispossessed by the Arabs, who have retained them ever since. The two engravings exhibit different views of the same forts, which are both striking objects as seen from the sea and harbour. Since the Arabs have been masters of them, they have fallen into decay. Here the calm grey water, upon which the sun's rays seemed to dance as if they loved to sport and sparkle on its placid bosom, recalled to my mind the beautiful image of a Hindoo bard: †

> "Behold awhile the beauties of this lake,
> Where, on its slender stem, the lotus trembles,
> Brush'd by the passing swan, as on he sails,
> Singing his passion."

The city of Mascat is so fortified by nature, that if these fortresses were kept up, they would present insuperable difficulties to an invader. Arrian calls it Mosca, and speaks of it as being, even in his time, a considerable emporium of the trade of Arabia, Persia, and India. Mascat has always enjoyed this advantage, and even now possesses an extensive trade, being the great mart of the Persian Gulf. The two churches built by the Portuguese during the time that the town was in their possession are now desecrated to very different purposes than those of religion, one of them being converted into a magazine and the other into the residence of some of the government function-

* See Frontispiece. † Bhavabhuti.

aries. During the domination of the Portuguese, Mascat was in a flourishing condition, though they were never upon terms of amity with the Arabs, who sought every opportunity to dispossess them; and this they finally accomplished, through the treachery of a Banyan merchant. This person enabled them to make themselves masters of the city, in consequence of the abduction of his daughter by the governor. The Arabs have continued to hold possession of it ever since that period.

The Banyans are still numerous here, living under the protection of the Arabs, with whom they dwell in perfect harmony. They are allowed to follow their own modes of worship, and to be governed by their own laws. They set up their idols within their own houses, and are permitted to burn their dead upon the shore. The police is so admirably conducted, that there is not the slightest danger in walking the streets during any part of the night. The laws are rigidly enforced. Extensive theft is punished with death; slighter thefts are visited with mutilation,—generally with the loss of a hand: thieving, therefore, is so uncommon, that merchants leave their property in the streets without the slightest scruple.

A few days after our arrival, we made an excursion to Muttra, a small town about two miles distant, and paid a visit to an English officer who commanded an Arab ship of war. The crew seemed to be under perfect control, and to place absolute confidence in him. They appeared well acquainted with European naval tactics; but there was a want of smartness and ready alacrity in their manner of handling the ropes and performing the various duties of the ship that showed at once their great natural inferiority to British seamen. On our way to Muttra we found the scenery new, and, I may add, even interesting. The rugged peaks, upon which no marks of vegetation could be traced, and the barren aspect of the coast, gave an air of desolate grandeur to the whole scene remarkably imposing. The sight was the more striking from being unusual, and its natural repulsiveness was abundantly countervailed by the severe sublimity by which it was singularly characterized.

There is a something indescribably grand in that wild and stern desolation which Nature sometimes displays, as the traveller traces the almost endless variety of feature which she presents in different regions of the world. Whatever asperity those features may exhibit, they are never positively repulsive. There is a visible symmetry amid the superficial ruggedness, and a blended harmony of arrangement that cannot fail to arrest the eye wherever it turns, and to elevate the mind with an impressiveness that causes it to "look through Nature," even in her harshest aspect of desolation, and trace there the marvellous workings of an Omnipotent hand. View her how you will, the associations which crowd upon the mind are never painful; —they may provoke a grave and solemn tone of thought, but it is always such as produces a pleasing reaction upon the heart, which takes an impression through the mind, softened by its reflection, and strengthened by its own quick and fervid impulses.

I never yet looked upon any of those fearful lineaments in nature, the sight of which causes the blood to creep through the frame with a sluggish flow, or to rush onward with an almost painful revulsion, that I have not felt my soul working with those lofty aspirations which elevate it from the common contemplation of things into a sublime purity of sentiment at once edifying and entrancing. The least attractive flower contains its honey as well as the most beautiful.

On our return from Muttra, I was particularly impressed with the poverty of vegetation everywhere visible. The monotony of the prospect was nevertheless occasionally relieved by several picturesque castles, standing upon the very peaks of the rocks, and frowning over the precipices beneath them with a solitary solemnity that addressed a mute but intelligible sentiment to every bosom. The rugged outline of the mountain-scenery opening upon our sight in an endless variety of form, as we gradually advanced, and breaking in perpetually changing configurations upon the clear blue sky, which brought it into prominent relief, forcibly struck us, from its singular and impressive novelty. The peculiar shape, too, of the vessels which here and there dotted the clear expanse of the gulf, as we moved leisurely upon its placid waters, contrasted beautifully with the grim and lifeless sterility of the general scene.

Some of these boats, which are called buggolas, are of singular construction. They are ordinary trading-vessels of the Arabs between Mascat and the Malabar coast, where they are generally built, and chiefly, I believe, at Cochin. These boats are sometimes upwards of two hundred tons' burthen, having high sterns, with a sort of small poop; under this is the principal cabin, inclining towards the bow, which is low and pointed. The cabins, as in the budgerows, are lighted by Venetian sashes.

The buggola is rigged something like a lugger, and carries two immense latteen sails. The larger boats hoist a jib, when the weather requires a press of canvass. They are usually commanded by a lazy Arab. He resigns the whole management of the vessel to a subordinate, who never even consults him, but leaves him to the enjoyment of his siesta and the luxuries of eating, drinking, and smoking. The sailors look upon him as a father, and treat him with an affectionate familiarity which, according to our notions of subordination, would be subversive of all discipline. This is far from the case with them; for, whenever he exercises his authority, he meets with implicit and willing obedience. The attachment between these commanders and their men is much the same as that which used to exist in Scotland between the head of a clan and his inferior clansmen; nor is it ever to be shaken, except by positive tyranny.

Shortly after our return to Mascat, we were informed that despatches had arrived over land from England, and were ready to be forwarded to the Bombay government; but in consequence of the weather, which was now rather threatening, none of the buggola boats would undertake to carry them. We were in consequence applied to; and as it was our ultimate intention to proceed to Bombay, though we should have otherwise prolonged our stay at Mascat, still, there being nothing attractive to detain us further, we consented to take charge of the despatches, and proceed without delay towards our destination.

The Yong Vrouw Jacomina, otherwise the Cornwallis, was immediately got in readiness for the voyage. At this period the heat in the cove was so excessive that we could not remain on board the vessel without suffering great inconvenience. The thermometer stood at a hundred and ten degrees in our cabin. The reflection of the sun from the sheer uncovered rocks that towered on all sides above the harbour, was a chief cause of the heat being so intense. Two days before we sailed, an American vessel entered the port; on the following morning we met the captain, who invited us to go on board, and entertained us very hospitably. He assured us that, upon reaching Mascat, his ship was so overrun with bugs that it was a perfect purgatory, but in one night after he had anchored, the whole of them had been cleared by the cockroaches, which then swarmed as numerously as the bugs had previously done; he, however, found the former the lesser evil. This frequently happens in India: a ship swarming with bugs no sooner puts into port than she is boarded by myriads of cockroaches, which devour the whole of them in a few hours; thus verifying the Hindoo proverb—"Little things should not be despised: many straws united may bind an elephant."

When our vessel was ready we weighed anchor, and moved slowly out of Mascat harbour, with despatches on board for the Bombay government. The heat continued so great that we were anxious to get beyond the immediate influence of the reflected sunbeams, which, slanting from the rocks, were cast into the cove in a focus that rendered the atmosphere positively intolerable. Our progress was at first retarded by a dead calm; and when we cleared the port we were obliged to creep along the coast for several days, the breezes were so light.

Being soon short of water, and unable to obtain any from the land, happening to fall in with several country boats, we purchased a large portion of their stock, paying them five rupees for each half leaguer, the leaguer measuring about twenty gallons. Our progress was painfully slow while we continued in smooth water; and what rendered this the more distressing was, the apprehension which continually arose, that our stock of provisions would be exhausted before we could get to the end of our voyage, and that we might have no opportunity of replenishing.

The breeze now freshening, we got into a rougher sea, and bent our course direct for Bombay. The weather shortly became foul, and our vessel proved leaky. After labouring a good deal for some hours, we found that she had three feet water in the hold, and that it was fast increasing. All hands were summoned to the pumps, and the carpenter reported, upon examining her seams, that it would be necessary to return into smooth water in order that her sides might be caulked; as the intense heat of the sun in Mascat harbour had caused the pitch to run. Greatly to our annoyance, we put back and sent a boat on shore to obtain some dammar, a sort of resin used in this country for the purpose of covering the bottoms of boats. Having procured the necessary supply, we anchored in a small creek, where the seams were well covered with the dammar, and we were soon in a condition to put to sea. There was little to interest us on our course. Our chief amusement was fishing; and one morning we caught a small shark nine feet long, in the stomach of which, when it was cut open, we found a large piece of a coir cable, which had actually begun to digest. The fish gave us a good deal of trouble, as our Lascars were not very skilful in securing it. Its plunges upon the deck were not a little dangerous until it received a gash in the tail from a hatchet, which effectually prevented mischief. Our monotonous voyage at length terminated, and we cast anchor in Bombay harbour, by the side of an Indiaman.

> The gentle spring that but salutes us here,
> Inhabits there, and courts them all the year.

Happening to know one of the officers, I went on board the next day, and saw my young friend in a sad condition. A few nights previously, it being extremely hot, he had slept with the port open, which admitted a draught through his cabin. While he slept, the insidious land wind blew upon him, and he awoke with his lower extremities paralyzed. When I saw him, he could move his hands only; and apprehensions were entertained by the surgeon of the ship that he would never recover the use of his limbs. These apprehensions were sadly verified in the issue, for he died a complete cripple within two years from this period.

We delivered our despatches and were honoured with an invitation to dine at Government-house. As the weather was oppressively hot, and within the fort at Bombay is by no means the coolest part of the island, we pitched our tents upon the esplanade, which at this season had the appearance of an irregular encampment, all the military men and many of the junior civilians living under tents for the benefit of a cooler air.

A day or two after our arrival at Bombay I was strolling about sunset on the beach of Colaba,—a small island separated from Bombay, only when the tide rises, by a narrow creek, the passage being perfectly dry at low water,—when my attention was arrested by a singular object. A man approached me in the common costume of the lowest orders, having only a cloth wrapped round his loins. I could not help being forcibly attracted by his appearance. His skin was perfectly white, as white as chalk; and when he came near me I perceived that it seemed glazed, as if it had been seared with a hot iron. His hair, for he wore no turban, was precisely the colour of his skin, and hung in long strips upon his lean and withered shoulders. His eyes, excepting only the pupils, were of a dull, murky red, and he directed them perpetually towards the ground as if the light was painful to him, which, upon inquiry, I discovered to be the case. His gait was slow and tottering, and his limbs were shrunk to a state of attenuation quite ghastly. His ribs were so prominent that they might be counted at a distance of several yards, and the whole anatomical development was so singularly conspicuous, that he seemed to stand before me a living skeleton. He did not at first venture to approach within several yards of me. I advanced, but he gently retreated, beseeching me to give a miserable man a few pice to save him from death, as he was an object of universal scorn, and an outcast from his tribe. His supplication was piteously imploring. He bid me not come near him, as he was a polluted creature, against whom the hand of every one was raised, and for whom there was no pity. By speaking kindly to him, I in a short time obtained his confidence when he stood still and allowed me to stand close beside him. I asked him the reason of his extraordinary appearance. He told me that he had been for years a martyr to the leprosy, which, though at length cured, had left upon him the brand of irremediable pollution. The very hue of his skin had changed from a deep brown to a cadaverous and sickly white, and no one could mistake that he had been a leper.

In India lepers are held to be accursed of the Deity; they are in consequence universally shunned, and many yearly die in an abject state of destitution truly deplorable, from the universal abandonment to which their dreadful visitation exposes them. Though this poor man was of the lowest caste, none of the members of his tribe would hold intercourse with him, and he was cast forth a wanderer, where he could find none but such as were labouring under a similar infliction who felt any sympathy in his wretchedness.

Nothing can be more melancholy than the thought

of a human creature so situated. Not only an outcast from general society, but shunned even by the most degraded of his tribe, he has no home but such as he makes for himself apart from the haunts of men, who frequently drive him into the jungles, where he becomes the prey of wild beasts; or when he refuses to withdraw himself beyond the remotest neighbourhood of human habitation, in violation of every law both human and divine, the members of his own family will frequently put the wretched creature to a cruel death.

So attached are the Hindoos to life generally, which they consider upon any terms the greatest boon of Heaven, that they seldom relinquish it by a voluntary death, except when fanaticism, which with them is a positive frenzy, urges them to some deed of self-immolation, in order to obtain the immediate possession of an immortality of bliss. But although these acts of frantic devotion are not uncommon, yet the circumstance of Hindoos putting themselves to death merely to get rid of the burthen of a sorrowful existence, is comparatively rare. The leper will bear about with him the curse of his leprosy, with all its attendant miseries, and pour forth his complaints to the unconscious winds; yet, even in the midst of privations and bodily sufferings which it is appalling to contemplate, he will endure his load of misery, and cling to life with a pertinacity scarcely to be conceived.

In order to show the summary mode of proceeding against these poor afflicted creatures, a quotation from Ward's Preface to his View of the History, Literature, and Mythology of the Hindoos, may suffice:— "Mr. W. Cary, of Cutwa, in Bengal, was once present at the burning alive of a poor leper. The friends of this wretched man had dug a deep pit, and had kindled a large fire at the bottom, when the leper, unable to walk, rolled himself over and over until he fell into the pit; but as soon as he felt the power of the flames his screams were dreadful, and he used every possible effort to rise and extricate himself, calling upon his relations, who stood around, to help him. Upon these relations, however, he called in vain; for, instead of affording the help he claimed in accents that might have softened a tiger, they pushed him back into the fire, where he struggled for a while, and then perished."

Knowing the wretched condition of the unfortunate leper in India, I could not but pity from my heart the miserable object before me: but pity was to him no boon; I therefore gave him all the money I had, and turned homeward, while his blessing came upon my ear with a deep and thrilling tenderness.

CHAPTER XVI.

BOMBAY.—THE FORT.—PARSEES.

Bombay was originally composed of a cluster of small islands, with numerous back-waters, producing a rank vegetation—at one time dry, and at another overflowed by the sea. So unwholesome was it formerly considered, that no person settled at this presidency was supposed to have a chance of living more than three years. This is not the case now; though still within the fort, and especially during the rains, it is very unwholesome.

The island of Bombay is at present the principal British settlement on the west coast of India: it is seven miles long and three broad, and forms, with the neighbouring islands of Colabah, Salsette, Butcher's Island, Caranjah, and Elephanta, one of the finest harbours in the Indian seas. Upon the first of these islands stands a lighthouse, which rises from the sea to the height of a hundred and fifty feet, and the light at its summit is seen at a distance of seven leagues. The capital of this island is about a mile long and two furlongs broad, and surrounded by strong fortifications. What is called the modern town is built in a low unwholesome spot, the ground being so flat that many of its houses are on a level with high-water mark;

Bombay

many are below, and very few above it, at the spring-tides.

During the monsoons it is necessary to go from house to house in boats; and for several months the unwholesome effects of these inundations are felt by the inhabitants. Formerly, the whole of that part of Bombay which at present forms the esplanade was covered with cocoa-nut trees; but now the whole space is cleared from the higher extremity of the island to Dungaree, a large town solely inhabited by the native population.

The accompanying view is taken from the back of the island, behind the fort, which is seen on the promontory; and Colabah lighthouse appears in the distance on the right. The castle presents a regular quadrangle, with numerous works, especially towards the harbour. The fortifications of Bombay are considered extremely strong, except on the land side, where they would offer but a feeble resistance to an enemy once landed and capable of making regular approaches. The town within the fort was begun by the Portuguese, but has been finished by the British: the houses, however, which have at different times been erected, are built much upon the same construction as those raised by the Portuguese; so that the town has still a mean appearance, compared with the presidencies of Calcutta and Madras. The sea washes the walls of the fort on three sides; on the fourth is the esplanade.

The town on the north side is inhabited principally by Parsees, who, though a highly enlightened race of people, are generally so filthy in their houses, that it is quite disagreeable to pass through the streets in which they live. Bombay is a barren rock, and therefore holds out no prospects to the agriculturist; but in a commercial point of view it is a place of importance. It has the finest docks of any settlement in India, from which many ships of war of the first class have been launched, and many large Indiamen. All these have been built solely by Parsees, who rent the docks from the Company, and possess an exclusive monopoly in this department, all the repairs of whatever ships put into Bombay to refit being done by them. They are decidedly the best shipwrights in India. The Jumsetjee family were, and I believe still are, the head builders on the island, to whom great wealth has accrued from their success in this lucrative business.

From the year 1810 to 1820 they built twelve ships of war, four of which carried seventy-four guns; besides a great number of merchant-ships, from a thousand to six hundred tons' burthen.

The teak forests, from which the supply of timber is derived, cover the western side of the ghaut mountains in the province of Arungabad, the numerous rivers which descend from those hills affording a ready conveyance for the timber.

The ships constructed of teak are far more durable than any others, but in general they sail more heavily. Those launched from the docks of Bombay have the reputation of being the best ever built out of Europe; they are therefore more highly valued than those launched from any other oriental port. The great staple exported from this island is cotton, which is sent yearly to China in large quantities. A screw is employed in packing the cotton, by which fifteen hundred pounds' weight is reduced to the measurement of one ton. The screw is worked by a capstan which has eight bars, and to each bar there are thirty men.

In the year 1816, the population of Bombay, including natives and all the different foreign races, amounted to nearly a hundred and sixty-two thousand souls, thirteen thousand of which were Parsees. In addition to the above aggregate, it is computed that from sixty to seventy thousand persons resort to this island for commercial purposes, where they take up their temporary abode; and that it is therefore never without a floating population averaging the sum of those two amounts.

Some of the wealthy natives live in great splendour, having large establishments, and houses so capacious as to afford habitations to the families of several married children at the same time.

There is only one English church in Bombay, and that is within the fort; but there are several Portuguese and Arminian churches, both within and without the walls; besides which, there are three or four small synagogues, the Jewish inhabitants amounting to about a thousand. The largest pagoda, a building of no very striking beauty, is in the black town, and dedicated to Momba Devi.

The Arminians here form a respectable though not a numerous body of Christians. They differ both from the Greek and Latin churches, and have, under the severest oppressions, like the still more primitive members of the alpine churches of Piedmont, maintained inviolable the tenets and institutions of their ancestors. They are subject to a prelatical hierarchy.

The Parsees possess a considerable portion of the island, many among them being persons of great wealth and engaged in extensive commerce. In almost every European house there is a Parsee partner, who supplies the principal portion of the capital. These people are a quiet, inoffensive community, admirable men of business, universally shrewd and intelligent, and partial to the society of Europeans. They are a fine race, with handsome features, black, lively eyes, bushy beards, which they shave, except on the upper lip, light brown complexions, and remarkably expressive countenances. Their women, when young, are pretty; but they soon grow coarse, and their habits in general are filthy: there are indeed exceptions, but such are comparatively rare.

These people worship the elements, especially fire; and numbers of them may be seen every morning at sunrise on the esplanade prostrating themselves before the great prototype of fire as he rises from the ocean, in the fresh and genial glory of his brightness, to fructify and gladden the earth. The women are never seen among them during their devotions, in which they are not allowed to participate.

The Parsees adhere rigidly to their ancient customs. Their mode of burial is peculiar. Near Malabar point, and close by the shore, is their chief cemetery, a circular, uncovered building, from fifty to sixty feet in diameter, and near thirty feet high.

It is built up within, leaving a parapet about a yard and a half high, the interior space sloping in a gentle convexity to the cĕntre, where there is a well five yards broad. Immediately round this well are grooves, in which the bodies of the dead are deposited, and left expŏsed to the vultures. As soon as those voracious birds have stripped the bones, the surviving relatives return to the cemetery and cast them into the well, whence they are removed at certain periods, by means of subterraneous passages, and flung into the sea.

There is a story current that the person who has charge of the cemetery watches every body deposited within it, to observe which eye the vultures or crows first pluck out; if it be the left, the doom of the deceased is evil; if the right, happy. The public burial-places of the Parsees at Bombay are five in number; but the more wealthy generally build one for themselves and families.

This island owes its original importance to the Portuguese, to whom it was ceded in 1530. They retained possession for upwards of a century, when Charles the Second of England claimed it as a part of his queen's portion. During the Portuguese government it was a comparative desert; but almost from the moment it fell under British domination it became a flourishing settlement. It was finally transferred from the crown to the East India Company, the 27th of March 1668, upon payment of an annual rent of ten pounds in gold on the 30th of September of every successive year. In 1691 this island was visited by the plague, which, when its ravages ceased, left only three civil servants alive. In 1702 it was again devastated by this dreadful scourge, and the garrison reduced to seventy-six men.

From its position, Bombay commands an extensive traffic with those countries which lie upon the shores of the Persian and Arabian gulfs, with both the western and eastern coasts of India as well as with China, where it exports vast quantities of cotton-wool. The other chief exports are sandal-wood, pearls, gums, and drugs, from Arabia, Abyssinia, and Persia; pepper from the Malabar coast; birds' nests and other produce from the Maldives, Lackadives, and eastern islands, and elephants' teeth from Cambay. The China ships generally arrive at Canton towards the end of June or beginning of July, and lie there idle, except delivering and receiving their return cargoes, until the month of December or January.

In 1808 the quantity of cotton brought to Bombay for exportation was eighty-five thousand bales of seven hundred and thirty-five pounds, making a total of sixty-two million four hundred and seventy-five thousand pounds' weight.

This settlement likewise carries on a considerable commerce with Europe and with different parts of America, though their most extensive trade is to China. The imports from Europe are principally articles of the finer manufacture, such as cottons and other piece goods, wine, beer, and articles for domestic consumption.

Here are excellent rope-walks, equal to any in Great Britain, except in the King's yard at Portsmouth. The dockyard is very capacious, and admirably contrived, being well supplied with naval stores of all kinds, and fitted up with every convenience for ship-building and repairs of vessels; for which purposes a large stock of timber is kept up. The new dock constructed by Major Cooper is a noble work, scarcely inferior to the finest docks in Europe.

A court of judicature is held at Bombay by a single judge, with the title of Recorder, the authority and practice of this court being altogether conformable to those of the Supreme Court of Calcutta. The law practitioners are three barristers and eight attornies. That few crimes of magnitude occur at Bombay is proved by a public statement made by Sir James Macintosh, the Recorder, in May 1810, that for six years prior to that period he never had occasion to condemn any criminal to death. Petty crimes, however, are of frequent occurrence, the number of persons convicted between the 10th of June 1812, and the 24th of January 1814, amounting to no less than eight hundred and seven; of whom eighty-six were for wounding, beating, and assaulting; four hundred and seven for theft, and a hundred and ninety-one for vagrancy. The police magistrate in his report on this occasion, describes Bombay as the resort of the vagrants and unprincipled of every province from the mouth of the Indus to Goa, who are mere sojourners for the purposes of thieving, and immediately withdraw to the continent to realize their plunder and convert it into money. In 1813, the famine which prevailed throughout Ajmeer, Guzerat, and Cutch, had caused an increased influx of vice, profligacy, and poverty from these regions.* The travelling distance from Bombay to Calcutta is thirteen hundred miles, and to Madras seven hundred and seventy.

The scene upon the esplanade during our stay was usually animated, and frequently reminded us of a far distant, but far dearer land. The cadets, who lived in a small enclosed encampment without the fort, used to play at cricket every afternoon towards sunset, and the game was often contested with great spirit and skill. One morning a Jew ventured within the enclosure occupied by these young men, and offered for sale some bottles of atar of roses. He had already presented himself at the door of my tent, showing me his perfume as an extraordinary bargain; and I had purchased a small bottle from him, for which I paid him a rupee, a very trifling sum considering the value of the perfume. He, however, stated, that having obtained it from an Arab ship wrecked near Cochin, he was enabled to sell it for a mere trifle. I had not the slightest suspicion that I was not purchasing genuine atar, though I was dealing with a Jew. Shortly after he left me I opened the bottle and found in it nothing but cocoa-nut oil, the cork having been scented to disguise the imposture.

The Jews at Bombay are just as practised in deceptions of this kind and in the art of chaffering as their brethren of Rosemary-lane or Monmouth-street in the other hemisphere. In the present instance, the im-

* Vide Hamilton; also Public Documents passim.

poster did not escape with impunity; for the moment he had sold one bottle within the cadet encampment, it was opened, and the deception detected. A hue and cry was instantly raised, and the Jew seized by a dozen strong young men just fresh from Europe. He was tried upon the spot by a sort of drum-head court-martial, and unanimously sentenced to be tossed in a blanket. He petitioned loudly to be released, fell upon his knees, shed tears, poked his broad forehead into the palm of his hand, and supplicated with abject entreaties that he might be allowed to depart. When asked to return the money for his counterfeit perfume, he solemnly swore he was the most ill-used man in the world, as the Sahibs had taken his oil but forgotten to pay him for it. He would rather have parted with his heart's blood than with the rupees.

No blanket being at hand, as such a thing is not commonly used in that warm country, a carpet was taken up from one of the tents, the Jew tumbled into it neck over heels, and the next moment he was tossed as if from a bull's horns by the hearty exertions of eighteen youths, who felt they were administering summary justice upon a scoundrel who had been guilty of a daring and audacious fraud. It was ridiculous to see the unhappy Jew darting into the air, sometimes with his head uppermost, at others with his feet,—now describing a broken arch, then so many crooked lines, and roaring all the while like a gored ox. This well-deserved punishment was continued for about five minutes; he was then rolled out of the carpet, without having sustained the slightest injury. No sooner did he feel the ground, than he was on his legs in an instant, and darted from the scene of his disgrace with the agility of a greyhound.

On the night of this amusing incident a circumstance occurred which led to very different consequences. Among the cadets then encamped upon the esplanade was a fine young man, whom I had known a sprightly, promising boy in England. I was spending the evening with him in his tent, where he had invited two or three friends. Some time after our meeting, he engaged in a game of backgammon with one of his guests, who had but a few months before obtained his ensign's commission. The latter was an Irishman of mild and gentlemanly manners; my friend, on the contrary, being a person readily and exceedingly excitable. It unfortunately happened that the run of luck was altogether on the side of the Irishman, who occasionally bantered his irritable opponent upon his ill play, but with the greatest good-humour. The latter at first looked grave and vexed, bit his lip, and dashed the dice upon the backgammon-board with an energy as unnecessary as it was ungentle. This was several times repeated, but without any more direct manifestation of temper;—the game at length terminated.

Mortified at having been beaten several times in succession, the vanquished youth urged his successful opponent to another trial of skill: the latter would have declined, but my young friend was urgent, and they again seated themselves at the table, and began to play. Success still continued to follow the more deliberate Irishman, who, moreover, played with a temper and coolness which gave him an additional advantage over his intemperate adversary. I was watching the game with some interest, when the rash youth, excited to a sudden paroxysm of rage at a merry remark by his gay competitor, in consequence of the former having made an injudicious move, dashed the dice-box into his face, at the same time stamping and swearing like a maniac.

The injured party instantly quitted the tent without uttering a word; and I endeavoured, but in vain, to persuade his aggressor to follow and apologise for the unwarrantable provocation he had offered him. Nothing could appease his vehemence; he said he was determined to brave all consequences, and urged, in justification of his violence, that he had been impudently sneered at. I foresaw at once the consequences, but not the extreme consequences, of this reckless folly. As, however, my suggestions appeared to give umbrage, I soon ceased to urge them, and quitted the unhappy youth with certain forebodings, the worst of which were too soon realized.

Early the following morning I entered his tent. He was absent; but I had not been long within it, when I saw him brought home to die. I assisted the very person whom he had so grievously insulted the preceding evening to bear him from his palenkeen and place him on his bed. He was soon stripped, and the wound examined by a surgeon who had been hastily summoned. Its appearance was to my mind anything but promising; it was small, the orifice appearing scarcely larger than sufficient to admit a pea, and a thin stream of blood trickled tardily from it. The ball had passed into his body between the ribs. Minute as the wound appeared, it nevertheless had a certain aspect of fatality which I cannot describe. This was probably the effect of association à priori, the immediate effect produced heightening and aggravating the cause.

From the first moment I saw the unhappy young man borne helpless from his palenkeen, and heard that his extremities were paralysed from a shot through the body, I had no hope. When the surgeon quitted his tent, he confirmed this impression, stating that the patient could not live forty-eight hours. I looked upon the prostrate man as he lay panting upon his bed, and my heart rose to my throat with such a fierce and indomitable impulse of emotion, that I thought I must have choked: I was relieved by a flood of tears. Suppressing my distress, I approached the couch. The wounded youth grasped my hand firmly, and said—"My friend, I am dying; I feel that the streams of life are cut off from the fountain, which must soon cease to flow. I already seem to be more than half dead; for I have no feeling below my heart. My sensations are too ominous to be mistaken: it is time my peace were made with Heaven, where I am shortly to appear; but with what result! Well, I have brought this upon myself; it is the just penalty of my rashness." Such were his expressions, as near as I can recollect them; and though many years have elapsed since they were uttered, they nevertheless seem to rise as vividly to my memory as if they had been pronounced but yesterday. This was one of those events which never quit the mind, but cling to the recollection like a wild untractable creeper to the forest-tree.

From this time my unhappy friend was never easy unless the person who had shot him was at his bed-side. He expressed towards him the most kindly feeling, exonerating him from all blame, and taking the whole odium upon himself. The young Irishman scarcely quitted him for a moment, but with a pale countenance, and his eyes frequently suffused with tears, that eloquently told the depth of his emotion, administered all his medicines to the dying man; though every pang which he witnessed thrilled through his own frame with a sympathetic agony so fierce and prostrating, that he could scarcely maintain his spirit amid the frequent repetitions of the shock: I never witnessed grief more intense.

On the second evening, I learned from the survivor in this fatal encounter, that immediately upon reaching his tent on the night he had been struck, he sent a challenge to his aggressor, who met him the next morning on the beach about sunrise, when three shots were exchanged, at the desire solely of the offending party, the third of which proved fatal.

To the surprise of the medical attendant, the wounded man lingered for six days. I was with him during his last moments. It was a sad sight; and when my thoughts recur to it, the recollection shakes me even now. He had not for one instant entertained the slightest hope of recovery, and there was at first rather a stern than a calm confiding resignation to his fate; but this subsided after a while, and was succeeded by a patient submission to the determination of Providence. The last day of his life he gave me his keys, desired I would take charge of his papers, and having dictated a will, which I wrote and attested, resigned himself meekly and calmly to death. He spoke with confidence of the Divine mercy: it was true, he said, that he had been sadly remiss in his religious duties, but this had happened more from thoughtlessness than irreverence. I was surprised to see this perfectly quiet acquiescence in the decision of an immutable will, with which he looked forward to the moment that comes to all, but comes to few without exciting emotions of doubt, if not of alarming apprehension. The tone of his conversation was solemn, but firm. He occasionally shed tears; but through those tears the clear light of hope beamed, which imparted to them a brightness and a glory not to be described. They dried upon his cheek, yet left not there the hue of sorrow nor the stain of remorse: he had made his peace with Heaven, and spoke with a holy confidence of a welcome into God's joy.

He remained calm until evening, when his senses began to wander. This wandering increased rapidly and to a painful excess, until, about midnight, it had attained to a perfect paroxysm of madness. Such was his strength, that, although the whole of his body from the fifth rib downward was paralysed, it required the efforts of three persons to keep him down. His exertions were prodigious, and his outcries appalling. After a desperate struggle, he died at two o'clock in the morning.

He had no relative near him; this was a sad and bitter reflection. As I looked upon the fair and beautiful corpse — for he was a remarkably handsome youth, and finely formed — I could not but read a lesson that will be remembered to the end of my days. The young Irishman was deeply affected: he assisted me to lay him out. Though he died after a severe paroxysm, his countenance nevertheless had subsided into an expression of placid repose.

Next morning three young surgeons came for the purpose of ascertaining where the ball was lodged, which they had in vain endeavoured to extract. I was present during this painful scene, and saw the body mangled and hacked as if it had been the carcass of a hog. I forbear to enter into the details of the revolting process of dissection — for such it was — and the cold, callous indifference with which these young medical practitioners tried their clumsy skill upon the remains of my poor young friend. The ball was at length found, lodged in the lumbar region on the right side. It had passed through the backbone, and of course ruptured the spinal marrow: when found, it was flattened and jagged.

On the same day, early in the afternoon, I attended the body to its last receptacle, accompanied by all the brother officers of the deceased, who followed with silent and solemn sympathy; and when the sublime service for the dead was concluded, three volleys were fired over the grave that received his mangled remains. As I stood in the gloomy churchyard and listened to the solemn service for the dead, I could not forbear recalling the beautiful lines of Youn :—

"What is the world itself? thy world?—a grave!
Where is the dust that has not been alive?
The spade, the plough, disturb our ancestors;
From human mould we reap our daily bread.
The globe around earth's hollow surface shakes,
And is the ceiling of her sleeping sons.
O'er devastation we blind revels keep;
Whole buried towns support the dancer's heel.
The moist of human frame the sun exhales;
Winds scatter through the mighty void, the dry.
Earth repossesses part of what she gave,
And the freed spirit mounts on wings of fire.
Each element partakes our scatter'd spoils,
As nature wide our ruins spread: man's death
Inhabits all things but the thought of man."*

* Night 9th.

CHAPTER XVII.

THE GUEBRE PRIEST.

During my stay at Bombay, a story of a Parsee was related to me, which I think will not be considered by the reader out of place in these pages. It was said to have happened about the beginning of the last century. Jumsajee Merjee was a priest who had got into bad odour with his tribe by his licentious conduct and neglect of the duties of his holy office. In consequence of having allowed the sacred fire to become extinguished, he was expelled from the community to which he belonged. Provoked at his degradation, he quitted Bombay, securing a passage for himself and an only daughter in a ship bound to Calcutta, proceeded up the Ganges, and finally took up his abode among the ruins of old Delhi.

These ruins are still splendid in their decay, and scattered over a surface of twenty square miles. Some of the tombs of Patan chieftains are in a high state of preservation; and the one represented in the engraving, which overlooks, though at a distance, the comparatively modern city of Shahjehanabad, is even now almost entire, and a few years ago only showed slight marks of the dilapidations of time. It stands upon an eminence, surrounded by the splendid remains of palaces, temples, and mausoleums, pointing, in the triumph of its own decaying grandeur, to the pageantries of earlier times, when kings and courtiers thronged those halls which are become the refuge of reptiles or form the lairs of wild beasts. Although this once magnificent city was the greatest in Hindostan before the Mahomedan invasion, it now presents nothing but a scene of sublime desolation. The soil around it is arid and unproductive, and during the dry season the river is not navigable but for boats of the lightest burthen.

Hither the exiled Parsee proceeded with his only daughter, a beautiful girl of sixteen, who voluntarily accompanied her father in his melancholy exile, and beguiled his hours of bitter dejection. Conceiving that he had been deeply wronged, he determined to throw off all respect for the laws that govern society, and signalize his sense of personal injustice by retaliating wrong where none had been received. To his daughter he did not communicate his intentions; but, arriving at the place which he had determined upon for his future abode, told her that there she must henceforward make up her mind to fix her home. She acquiesced with buoyant readiness, being always eager to give her parent pleasure by implicit submission to his wishes. They were alone: two bullocks bore their little property, which consisted of nothing more than a few household necessaries, their wearing apparel, and two hundred rupees in gold.

The bullocks were driven by the Parsee, his daughter occupying the back of one; and he finally halted at the entrance of the Patan's tomb already mentioned.

Drawn by W. Daniell R.A. — Engraved by R. Brandard

Tomb of a Patan chief, Delhi.

It was an octagonal building of considerable size, rising into a regular and graceful dome. The architectural ornaments, though few, were in good preservation. Placed upon an elevation, it commanded the surrounding plain, and afforded at the same time a beautiful view of the modern city. There was a small entrance, under a richly embellished pediment on the river side of the tomb. The door had been broken down, and the walls were a good deal defaced.

Upon reaching this spot the Parsee entered, in order to ascertain whether it might be converted into a practicable dwelling, his daughter meanwhile remaining outside with the bullocks. The passage was of some length, and a good deal encumbered with rubbish. He proceeded, nevertheless, without much difficulty until his progress was arrested by an unexpected impediment. Having reached the end of the entrance passage, terminated by two alleys, branching off circularly to the right and left, he was about to enter the one at the right, when he found his neck and chest encircled by something which gradually increased its tension, until he felt the pangs of suffocation. His arms were kept down to his sides, so that he could not move them; and this was accompanied with such a frightful constriction, that he began to imagine the unquiet spirit of some great criminal had assaulted him for invading the solemn depository of the dead. He heard no sound—this, no doubt, his own loud gaspings might have prevented; and at length such was his agony, that, uttering a loud cry of distress, and at the same time exerting all his strength, he pressed forward, and reaching a doorway entered a large octagonal chamber, lighted by several apertures in the roof, where, overcome by terror and bodily suffering, he fell upon the pavement. The consciousness of his guilt now rushed for the first time upon his heart, filling it with a thousand vague terrors. The visitation of the Omnipotent had, as he thought, fallen upon him. He fancied himself doomed to a death as mysterious as it was dreadful; and, though he struggled with all his might, his efforts were unavailing, and he gave himself up for a lost man. As he could not describe, neither shall I attempt to depict, the horror of his feelings at that fearful moment.

His daughter, hearing from without a sharp piercing cry, immediately entered the passage. She had been unloading the oxen, and as some of the packages were bound with strong cords, she was obliged to cut them; — a large knife therefore was in her hand when she rushed into the tomb. The darkness for a moment embarrassed her; but guided by the loud breathings of one whom her quick ear instantly satisfied her was in jeopardy, she sprang fearlessly over the rubbish. Arrived at the termination of the passage, she was soon guided by the sound to the apartment in which her father was lying. When she entered, the immediate change from almost total darkness to light, which fell directly upon the object of her search, who was lying under one of the apertures in the roof, prevented her for the moment from ascertaining the danger to which he was exposed. He was unable to speak, and only answered her questions by a loud guttural gasp, which sounded like the cry of one in the immediate agony of strangulation. In an instant, the instinct of filial tenderness suggested to her the extent of her parent's danger. She rushed to the side of the prostrate man, and at once the mystery was resolved. A large snake was coiled round him, with its head opposite to his face, and gradually tightening its folds in order to crush him to death. The daughter, roused to an unwonted spirit of energy by her father's peril, raised the knife, which she still held, and striking with all her force upon the monster's body, severed the spine. The snake instantly uncoiled from its victim, and writhed with agonized contortions about the apartment. It did not attempt to renew the attack; and the Parsee, by this time having recovered his breath, seeing the condition of his enemy, took the knife from his daughter's hand, and attacking the powerful reptile, quickly despatched it. It proved to be a young boa constrictor, about eighteen feet long—a fortunate circumstance for Jumsajee Merjee, for had it been a full-grown snake of that species it would certainly have destroyed him.

As soon as he had killed the boa, as a precaution against any similar attack,—a circumstance by no means probable, as those creatures are almost invariably found single,—he kindled a fire in the principal apartment of the tomb, and lighting a torch, proceeded to examine the different recesses, in order to clear them from any unwelcome occupants to which time and neglect had given an undisturbed possession. He found a number of large bats clinging to the walls, which dropped upon the ground when his torch came in contact with their deformed bodies, some of them measuring three feet from the extremity of one wing to that of the other, and showing their teeth with a determination to resent further aggression the moment he placed his fingers within two inches of their noses. With deliberate prudence, he knocked about a dozen or two of these creatures on the head, and flung their carcasses to the vultures. He destroyed, besides, a number of snakes, frogs, lizards, scorpions; and when, after several hours of minute search, he fancied he had sufficiently cleared the place of its noxious inmates, he prepared to make it the temporary dwelling of himself and daughter, until a more commodious asylum could be found; and being a disgraced man, he thought that such an asylum suited best with his condition.

The next day, he drove his bullocks to a village at some distance, where he disposed of them for a few rupees, and returned to the tomb. Here he dwelt for some time in perfect security; and after a while was joined by three other Parsees, who had been likewise degraded from their community, and were glad to associate with one under a similar interdiction. They were all men of reckless daring, as is generally the case with those upon whom society has fixed the brand of alienation. Among these men without characters, and alike indifferent to the opinion of their tribe and to the consequences of their misdeeds, the lovely daughter of Jumsajee lived intact, like a jewel surrounded by common earth, the brightness of which is no longer obscured than while the crust of the mine is around it;—the lustre is still within.

"What words shall picture what those looks conveyed—
The lore of love those lotus eyes revealed!
What firmness could resist the honest warmth
Of Nature's mute expressiveness, nor fall
Before those orbs, that now, like opening buds,
Beneath the creeper of the tremulous brow
Expansive bloomed, and, now retiring, shrunk
But half averted from the answering gaze,
Then dropped the veiling lashes o'er their brightness!"

Like most Eastern women of her tribe, she calmly acquiesced in whatever line of conduct her parent might think fit to pursue, without presuming to question either the propriety or prudence of his determination. She performed the necessary domestic duties of his household in silence; and if she did not acquiesce in, she never attempted to oppose, what was done by him, to whom she had been taught from infancy to consider absolute obedience an imperative and religious obligation.

Not long after his union with the three desperadoes of his own tribe, there were certain indications of a lawless course of life, which did not tend to render the tomb either a desirable or a happy home to the fair daughter of Jumsajee Merjee. It was soon evident to her that her father had become a freebooter, which she could not but think, in the silence of her sombre dissatisfaction, a vocation ill becoming a priest of the Guebres, the ancient worshippers of fire, and the only true votaries, as she imagined, of the most primitive religion. She frequently witnessed scenes which caused her heart to loathe her home; yet she uttered not a word of complaint, though it was evident, from the restless motion of her eye and the hurried vacillation of her step, that she was under the influence of a perturbed spirit.

Her father could not be unobservant of this change in his daughter, from the buoyancy of youthful confidence to the feverish aspect of continual apprehension: yet he chose not to notice it. He flattered himself that if she sympathised in his disgrace, as a child ought to do, according to his notions of filial obligation, she would soon become reconciled to what only now shocked her tender sensibility because it was new to her inexperience, and she had yet to learn how to appreciate the true demarcation between real good and evil.

Such was the shallow sophistry of his reflections, which he rather desired than believed; but his conclusion to these reflections always was, that whatever direction his daughter's feelings might ultimately take, he should, nevertheless, force them to succumb to his paternal influence. He had, however, yet to learn how impossible it sometimes is to warp the human heart against its natural bias. It may acquiesce in silence and in agony; but it will never be really subdued by tyranny, though it may be silenced, racked, and broken. The heart that turns to virtue, like steel to the magnet, though it may be violently torn from the object to which it clings, will not therefore relinquish its tendency. The impediment once removed, it will leap with the accelerated force of vehement reaction to the good which it adores, and unite with it the closer for the temporary restraint. Oppression may crush the most energetic spirit, but can never enslave it, when it has once attained that high moral elevation which stamps upon our frail humanity the impress of God's image. A spirit may indeed be extinguished, but cannot be subdued.

It could no longer remain a secret from the daughter that Jumsajee had united himself to a band of desert robbers. He was visibly amassing treasure from his depredations. He was in the habit of absenting himself for days together; he would then return with his companions, laden with booty, which was always secretly deposited in some dark recess of the tomb. The four Parsees, having been alienated from their tribe, ceased to observe those forms to which all true Guebres adhere with rigid scrupulosity. They extinguished fire with indifference; they saw the sun rise without making a single prostration; they beheld the moon and stars, but not one thought was directed to Him who has so beautifully spangled the heavens, and written upon the broad page of the sky the grandest record of his omnipotence; they had, in fact, abjured their faith, and Zerdusht was no longer to them either an oracle or an object of veneration. Caring not with whom they associated, so long as such association procured them advantages, they became companions of the lowest among the Hindoo outcasts.

In the course of time the name of Jumsajee was notorious as chief of a formidable gang of robbers; but as he took care that the scene of his predatory exploits should be at a distance from the tomb which he had made his dwelling, he thought himself secure from all chance of discovery. He now occasionally absented himself, with his three companions, for several weeks, leaving his daughter with the wife of the only one of them who was married. Such fellowship by no means tended to soothe the harassed spirits of this unhappy girl, as her companion, so far from seeing anything base in the practices of her husband and his associates, advocated the propriety of robbing, especially under the circumstances in which they were placed, deeming anything justifiable from which individual benefit might accrue. The poor girl, instead of being released during the absence of her father from having the fruits of vice continually forced upon her view, was constrained to hear its perpetual vindication, which rendered her home such a scene of mental conflict, that she would have preferred a life of rigid asceticism to that which she was now obliged to lead.

Upon one occasion, in following his predal avocation, the Parsee nearly lost his life. The party, of which he was head, had committed a robbery in the territory of Napaul upon a wealthy traveller, whose money they had secured, and having done this had separated, to obviate the risk of detection. Meanwhile Jumsajee, who had not quitted the spot, observed two horsemen making towards him at full speed, and well armed, accompanied by the person who had been plundered. It was clear that the Parsee was the object of their speed; and as there appeared little probability of being able to make a successful resistance, his only chance was in immediate flight.

He rode a small dark roan Arab, of great strength and fleetness, upon which he knew he could rely. The moment was critical, the horsemen were fast approaching; he therefore dashed his heels into the flanks of his steed, which bounded off like an antelope, and was in a few moments at the top of its speed. Every object lost all definite outline to the eye of the rider as he was carried forward with a sort of winged swiftness that rendered him almost breathless. He urged his horse up a steep ascent, which the hardy little animal seemed to climb with a dexterity equal to its fleetness.

The horsemen, though left far behind, continued the pursuit with unabated perseverance, so that he trusted his chance of escape entirely to his horse. The mettled Arab bounded up the steep, panting and straining; but it was evident that such exertion could not last long, as the Parsee was a heavy man,—moreover, the horses of his pursuers being much stouter, and their riders lighter, the probability of escape seemed every moment to lessen. They now gained rapidly upon him, and the certainty of capture seemed inevitable, in consequence of the Arab stumbling upon a fallen tree and throwing Jumsajee with violence over his head. For a moment he was stunned; but rising, he remounted with admirable agility, urging his steed furiously towards the brink of a precipice.

The armed horsemen were by this time close at his heels, and his ear caught the gasping eagerness with which they sought to capture him. He heard the pant, the strain, and the suppressed snort, so common when exertion has almost reached its climax, and exhaustion is fast succeeding to the failing efforts of the overwrought muscular energies. Looking behind him, he perceived that he had not a moment to lose, and with that desperation which calculates upon no choice between a voluntary and inflicted death but the former alternative, he spurred his faithful Arab towards the ravine. With one mighty bound, it sprang forward at the prick of the spur; stood a moment with inflated nostril, dilated eye, and projected ears, over the terrific void; then plunged desperately down the gulf with a spring that carried it several yards beyond the brink. One of his pursuers was at the moment close behind him, and, not being aware of the precipice, he had not time to check his horse, which leaped likewise over the brink. It, however, first made an effort to turn, which was ineffectual, then followed the Parsee's Arab so close that there was only a few seconds between the leaps.

Jumsajee's horse had taken so tremendous a spring as entirely to clear every projection of the precipice, and pitched upon the thick underwood which grew densely in the ravine below. This broke its fall, and probably saved the life of its rider; though the horse was killed upon the spot, and Jumsajee escaped with a broken arm and leg. The other horseman was not so fortunate. The struggle which his horse had made before taking the fatal plunge prevented it from springing beyond the uneven surface of the mountain; it consequently struck upon a large piece of rock that projected midway, which was torn from its bed with the force of the shock, and came, together with the horse and rider, to the ground, where it rolled over them and crushed them to death. Amidst all his sufferings, Jumsajee had sufficient cause for congratulation, as he had escaped certain destruction with the fracture of two of his limbs, and his enemy lay dead at his side. Unable to stand, he crawled from the thicket into which he had been thrown, and with extreme difficulty reached an opening in the jungle where a narrow path had been cut through the underwood, which gave him some hope of assistance in his present miserable plight. His hope was not long disappointed, for he had not been there many hours when a solitary Pariah passing through the wood saw him, and readily offered that assistance which he so much needed. The Pariah had a miserable hovel upon the borders of the jungle, surrounded by beasts of prey and infested by noxious vermin, into which he bore the wounded man upon his shoulders, and laid him upon the coarse, tattered rug that formed his own bed.

This poor Pariah was a despised outcast, who dwelt apart from his race, owing his daily subsistence to the uncertain produce of the forest. He dwelt in utter solitude, yet his human sympathies were not crushed, but full of robust life. He attended upon his suffering guest with unremitting attention for six weeks. Jumsajee, through the natural soundness of his constitution, had recovered from his injuries in this time. He now took leave of his host, to whom, in the overflowing of his heart, he gave all the money he happened to have about him; which was a fortune to the needy Pariah, who received it with such acknowledgments as sufficiently showed the completeness of his destitution. The Parsee, upon his recovery, quitted the jungle, and at length reached his home, after an absence of two months, his daughter having already began to mourn for him as for one dead.

CHAPTER XVIII.

THE GUEBRE PRIEST.

ALTHOUGH Jumsajee Merjee had prudently adhered to his first plan of committing his depredations at a distance from his home, his fame as a robber had nevertheless spread far and wide; he therefore thought that he should be more secure if he quitted the lonely tomb which he had hitherto made his abode, and fixed his future dwelling among the less solitary but more sequestered buildings upon the same plain. There was such a choice of places, that the difficulty of selection was not great; and after examining several edifices still in a sufficient state of preservation to afford him and his family a commodious abode, he chose an elegant mausoleum among a cluster of several which, though dilapidated within, were perfectly entire without, and promised a securer asylum, as he thought, than the one he had lately occupied. This latter, being placed upon an eminence, and commanding a striking view of modern Delhi, was occasionally visited by stragglers for the mere beauty of the prospect, and his privacy was in consequence disagreeably invaded. The circumstance of its being inhabited created no surprise, as nothing can be more common in India than to see ruins taken pos-

Tombs of Patan chiefs, Old Delhi.

session of by those who have not the means of erecting dwellings for themselves.

The Parsee's new residence was a small mausoleum between two of still great magnificence, the beautiful domes of which rose grandly from a flat roof that covered the whole space occupied by the building. The walls were surmounted by delicate minarets, which formed a marked contrast with the general solidity of the structure. Jumsajee had selected the smaller edifice, as less likely to attract observation, there being nothing in its external appearance to invite the scrutiny of the inquisitive traveller. His daughter was quite a passive party in this change: she acquiesced in her father's determination; but the very motive which dictated the change was to her a sufficient reason for regretting it. The same process was adopted in the new dwelling which had been pursued in the old one to get rid of the bats and reptiles, until the whole were ejected by the fiery ordeal.

Shortly after this removal, an incident occurred which gave an unexpected direction to the monotonous course of events that had hitherto marked the life of the Parsee's daughter. As she was one day returning from the river with her brass pitcher upon her head, she was pursued by a buffalo that appeared excited to the extremest pitch of fury. She had no means of escape, and, knowing the impossibility of avoiding the infuriated beast, she turned and calmly awaited its approach. She looked on the threatened destruction of herself with calm self-possession, nor did she for one moment blench as the peril approached.

When the buffalo was within a few yards of her, a youth suddenly sprang past the beautiful girl from behind, and stood before her enemy. The excited animal instantly made a plunge towards him, but he adroitly avoided the intended mischief by a vigorous spring. The buffalo, not to be thus easily foiled, turned shortly upon him, and when it was just in the act of raising him upon its horns and hurling him into the air, he made a desperate leap forward upon the animal's back, and with the quickness of thought, taking a second spring, alighted on the ground upon his feet; he now suddenly seized the buffalo by the tail, and began to twist it, to the terror of the enraged brute, which, after turning furiously round in two or three unavailing attempts to reach its punisher, darted forward across the plain, and was quickly out of sight.

The poor girl, who had stood perfectly calm and collected during the whole period of her own peril, was so agitated at witnessing that of the stranger, that, overcome by the strong reaction of her feelings, as soon as there was no longer cause for apprehension, she fainted upon the pathway. Her preserver, taking a small quantity of the water still remaining in the vessel which had fallen from her head, threw it into her face, and she quickly revived. Distressed at finding herself in the arms of a stranger, and too evidently one of a people with whom she had never yet held communion, she felt painfully embarrassed. Her brave rescuer, who proved to be a young Englishman, seeing her uneasiness, and being aware of the unconquerable reluctance of Parsee women to have any intercourse with persons not members of their own tribe, retired from her immediate vicinity, at the same time showing her the most tender and delicate attention. She was evidently touched by the subdued courtesy of his manner; and while she offered him her acknowledgments for the generous interposition by which her life had been saved, there was a tremulous hesitation in her speech which showed that she said less than she felt. Observing this, he presumed that she was only deterred from inviting him to her home by the conventional restrictions of her tribe; he therefore followed her at a respectful distance, until she reached her sepulchral habitation.

Her father was not a little surprised to see her accompanied by an Englishman; but she soon made him acquainted with the cause, by stating, with eloquent simplicity, the peril from which the young stranger had just rescued her. The father listened with anxious interest, and warmly recognised the deliverer of his child, whom, in spite of his occasional harshness, he really loved with earnest affection, as one to whom he was bound by the strongest ties of gratitude.

Inviting him into a part of the tomb to which his daughter had not access, Jumsajee entertained his guest with English wines and sherbet; after which the latter related to him that he had been dismissed from the British army, for having challenged a superior officer; that he had in consequence quitted the neighbourhood, in order to seek employment in the Mahratta service, being determined not to depart from India a disgraced man.

The Parsee was interested in the young stranger's narrative, who had travelled from Cawnpoor to the plains of Delhi, without anything but the clothes he then wore, except a small bag containing five hundred rupees. The trifling similarity between the young Englishman's position and his own kindled a sympathy in the breast of the Guebre priest; and he pressed him, at least for the moment, to take up his abode in some of the ruins around him, as he could be there secure from being apprehended by the British authorities, in case his hostile intentions should have transpired. This suggestion was not at all opposed to the latter's feelings, which were actuated by the consciousness that he should be within the immediate vicinity of the Parsee's daughter: he had seen her but for a short period, yet the peculiar circumstance which caused their meeting had thrown over it a colouring and a glow not to be effaced from his memory.

There happened to be a compartment in the tomb occupied by Jumsajee and his family of which they made no use; here, after having applied a torch to the walls and crevices, as a hint of banishment to all reptile occupants, the Englishman determined to take up his temporary quarters. This was a singular association; perhaps it had never before occurred that a European had dwelt under the same roof with a Guebre; but the fact was, that Jumsajee had nearly repudiated all the prejudices of his tribe, and become very little nice in his choice of associates. He had not made any excursion from the tomb since his accident, though his companions occasionally exercised their skill in a small way; still the English stranger was utterly unconscious that he was abiding with common plunderers, and they did not think there could be the slightest necessity for making him wiser upon so delicate a point.

The new guest seemed entirely to have forgotten his original intention of offering his services to the Mahrattas, but continued, day after day and week after week, to occupy the recess in the tomb. The Parsee now began to absent himself, as formerly, upon plundering excursions, and thus the Englishman had occasional opportunities of seeing and conversing with the daughter. At first she manifested a suppressed repugnance to meet him; but by degrees this abated, and she finally met him without embarrassment. The woman who had been her only female companion since her parent's banishment from the home of his fathers was not a person whom she could either confide in or respect; it was therefore a relief to her sometimes to converse with one who seemed to entertain a silent sympathy with her solitary state, and to whom her society was evidently more than a common gratification.

The consciousness of being appreciated was a feeling to which she had been hitherto unaccustomed; and in proportion as it was new and enjoyed, so did its novelty and freshness diffuse a charm over her naturally buoyant but now subdued spirit, of which she anxiously encouraged the endurance. It opened a new world to her unsophisticated view; or, if it did not open a new world, it at least suggested new trains and objects of speculation which to her were delightful, because they raised her spirit from the depression of undefined apprehension, and from the torpid monotony of seclusion to the awakened liberty of thought; while hope presented a prism through which she saw the wide field of existence tinged with the most brilliant hues, and diversified with the most beautiful objects.

These frequent interviews between the lovely Parsee and the young Englishman ripened by degrees into a warmth of attachment that finally broke down the barrier of social prejudices, and opened a familiar intercourse: it was reciprocal, and alike dear to both. There existed the warmest affection between them, which was mutually recognised and acknowledged. In proportion to her innocence was the unmingled confidence which the Parsee girl reposed in the man who had won the affections of her young and guileless heart.

> She loves, but knows not whom she loves—
>   Nor what his race, nor whence he came :
> Like one who meets in Indian groves
>   Some beauteous bird without a name,
> Brought by the last ambrosial breeze
> From isles in undiscover'd seas
> To show his plumage for a day
> To wondering eyes, and wing away.
> Will he thus fly—her nameless lover?
> Allah forbid!

His feelings were no less ardent; and though in the object of his earnest attachment he saw a being whose mind was darkened by the absurdities of a Sabean creed, yet he distinguished such a clear central light of moral purity amid the spiritual darkness in which her quick perceptions were shrouded, that the incidental deformity was completely merged in the positive intellectual beauty. Amid the deep absorption of his thoughts, the question would frequently rise to his lips, though they did not utter it—if she is so pure as a heathen, what would she be as a Christian? Time ripened the attachment, which was only not perceived by the father because he was so much from home. The stranger declared his affection to the lovely Parsee girl, and with all the artlessness of her free and sanguine nature she confessed how deeply it was returned. She now, for the first time, disclosed to him the occupation of her parent, which, though he had been so long under the same roof with the Guebre, but apart from his family, he had not yet perceived, attributing all he saw to the peculiarity of Oriental habits. He was a good deal disquieted at the disclosure; and the beautiful girl, who in the quick scrutiny of her love perceived his emotion, did not hesitate to express her abhorrence of a mode of life which had long been to her a source of intense misery.

The Englishman looked upon her with that sort of thrilling commiseration which invariably draws the heart closer to the object; and in the romantic ardour of his passion, its fervent sophistry rising to his mind as the sober dictate of truth, he persuaded himself that he was influenced by a holy impulse to snatch her from the moral contagion to which she was perpetually exposed, and place her in a more elevated position among her species, where she might have the full opportunity of embracing that good which was evidently the object of her natural predilection. He was young and enthusiastic, and had been withheld from entering into the service of the Mahrattas by the attractions of this interesting heathen, to whom he had now declared the state of his heart.

Looking forward to the probable direction of his future life, it was not very evident to him how his attachment to the Parsee girl could be consistent with his future prospects. His family were well connected in England, but not wealthy; and the circumstance of his having been dismissed from the service in which they had fancied him ultimately provided for, left him little hope of any future provision from them. The difficulties appeared so many, when he directed his views onward, that he soon ceased to allow them to disturb his mind, but, occupying himself with the present, was the happiest of human beings. He possessed the devoted affections of a lovely girl, whose whole sum of happiness was in his custody, and the result was such as could scarcely fail to follow from an attachment so fervent between two persons by whom the restrictions imposed by society upon the actions of its members had not been practically felt, and who were, therefore, not likely to be governed by laws which, in their present position, they did not fancy themselves called upon to recognise.

After a while, it became too evident to be matter of speculation that the interesting daughter of Jumsajee Merjee was soon to become a mother. The father's anger at this discovery knew no bounds; he struck the poor girl to the earth, and forced her paramour to quit the tomb. He immediately held a consultation with the three Parsees as to what punishment should be inflicted, when they came to the unanimous conclusion that she ought to die. Her alliance with a Christian was, in the estimation of these heathen robbers, a deadly sin. The father had some struggles to overcome before he could bring his mind to so fearful a determination. He at length, however, vanquished his paternal scruples, and determined to take the right of punishment into his own hand.

After balancing for some time what sort of death she should die, he decided upon cremation; and it was likewise resolved that the author of her shame should expiate his offence by undergoing the same sentence. The young Englishman, though banished from the tomb, nevertheless did not quit the neighbourhood, resolving not to abandon the object of his attachment to the heartless tyranny of a parent, who, as he had never consulted her happiness, could have no just right of control over her actions—at least, not according to her lover's code of equity. When he heard that Jumsajee seriously thought of putting her to death for an offence of which she was perhaps the least culpable party, his heart sickened within him; and he made up his mind, whatever might be the consequences, to leave no means untried to rescue her from so dreadful a doom. He cared not for his own life if he could only be the means of saving hers, and therefore determined to brave all consequences.

Full of his purpose, he sought the presence of the exasperated and inexorable father, and implored a reversal of the sentence which the Parsee had passed upon his fond and guiltless child. He besought him, in terms of earnest supplication, to relax from the fierce severity of his determination, promising to repair immediately to the presidency with his daughter, and give her a lawful and inalienable claim to his protection by making her his wife. The parent heard him with a grim smile, and, instead of answering, desired his companions to seize and bind him; at the same time protesting that he should not only visit his daughter with the punishment of death, but that her seducer should partake of her doom. Expostulation was useless; the unhappy lover was in the power of his enemy, and incapable of resistance.

His arms were now secured by strong cords; he was thrust into that compartment of the tomb which he had lately occupied, and the next day was fixed upon for the execution of the unhappy lovers.

The morning was dull and overcast, and the time appointed for the awful sacrifice to the indignation of an inexorable parent was just before the sun should descend behind the distant horizon. Towards the afternoon, fitful gusts announced the approach of a tempest.

> "Bright Indra's bow appears: the genial rains
> From the full clouds descend and drench the plains.
> Quick lightnings flash along the troubled sky,
> Pierce the fresh moistened earth and parch it dry.
> Like curling dust the distant showers appear,
> And the swan flies before the watery year."*

The thunder muttered, and there were occasional showers: still, the necessary preparations for the exe-

* Specimens of Hindoo Poetry.

cution were not interrupted. A quantity of dry wood had been conveyed into the tomb during the morning, and immediately behind the building a stout stake was driven into the earth, about the size of a man's leg, and just five feet high: it was a dry bamboo; and to this the victims were to be attached, in order that they might consume together. The preparations were at length completed. When this was announced to the Parsee's daughter, she exhibited no emotion, and did not utter a word. She feared not to die; and to her there was a consolation in the thought that she was about to be accompanied in her journey to another world with him in whom all her affections were absorbed. The natural romance of her nature was roused into unusual action by the awful position in which she was placed: this kindled her enthusiasm, and she hailed death as the removal of an eternal barrier between her and the object of her adoration. She supposed that he was no less reconciled than herself to that stern adjudication, which would remove two affectionate hearts beyond the reach of mortal tyranny.

Her lover, though neither so calm nor so full of anticipation, was still tolerably resigned to the fate that awaited him—the absorbing passion of his soul quickening his resolution, and flinging a sort of halo round the dismal preparations of death. There was, nevertheless, an occasional wavering of mind as it dwelt involuntarily upon the change he was about to undergo, the fearful question arising whether his separation from the object of his love might not be eternal. His firmness was rather the result of temperament, and of those stimulating feelings which his peculiar situation excited, than a settled habit of soul, induced by the fervour of religion, and of hopes engendered in the bosom of such as love it for its own sake, and follow it because obedience to God is with them, not a slavery, but an acceptable service.

Towards the afternoon the rain had entirely subsided; still, peals of thunder were heard at intervals, while the flashes that succeeded were distinct and vivid. These threatenings of the heavens did not retard the preparations for the sacrifice which the victims of a father's wrath were about to undergo. Large logs of wood were piled immediately round the stake, just allowing room for the criminals to stand, side by side, within a circle of three feet diameter. Under the logs was placed a quantity of light fuel, and the whole covered with a profusion of ghee, to accelerate combustion.

About a quarter of an hour before sunset the victims were led forth, and bound to the fatal pyre. They were not allowed to approach each other until they reached the stake. By this time the thunder had become awfully loud, and the lightning fearfully menacing; this, however, did not divert the purpose of Jumsajee Merjee. His victims were led to the stake, and being placed within the circle, were both tied together to the bamboo with strong silken cords. An awful silence prevailed; nothing was heard save the perpetual crashing of the thunder. The lips of the poor girl became white, and trembled with emotion, as she looked upon the object of her affection at her side, and thought of the sufferings she should be doomed to witness. Her emotion sustained him, and he cheered her in a calm tone, first breaking the silence, which had not before been interrupted by a human voice since they had been led from the tomb to the place of execution. They had occasionally conversed upon the vast superiority of the Christian over the heathen faith; she had therefore imbibed from her lover some notions of a Redeemer, although those notions were imperfect. She felt, however, a holy confidence that both were about to undergo a change for the better, and was therefore comparatively insensible to the terrors of death.

When all was prepared for the consummation of this awful judgment, the lovely girl tenderly begged her father to embrace her:—he silenced her affecting appeal with a solemn, but obdurate malediction. Her head drooped as the curse issued deliberately from his lips, and a tear suffused her eye as she turned it slowly upon her companion. His was fixed upon her with a glance that quickly recalled her to a sense of the position in which she was at that moment standing, and her face kindled with a lofty expression of resignation that seemed to bid defiance to the terrible array of death.

A lighted torch was now placed within her grasp and that of the young Englishman; but just as they were about to apply it to the fuel, a flash of lightning struck the stake to which they were both tied and shivered it in pieces. Two of the Parsees were struck dead; and the father fell upon his knees in consternation, imagining that the Guebres' God had, in his wrath, elanced a stream of sacred fire from heaven and destroyed two of his companions, for their having ceased to reverence that holy element. The intended victims were released—the Deity was supposed to have interfered in their behalf. The daughter was restored to her father's favour, who henceforward eschewed robbery, and accompanied his child and the young Englishman to Calcutta. Here the two latter were immediately married according to the rites of the Christian church, and eventually inheriting the father's wealth, proceeded to England, where the wife became a Christian; and the husband never found cause to regret that he had espoused the daughter of a Parsee.

On the Island of Elephanta

CHAPTER XIX.

ELEPHANTA.—A GECKO.—A CATTI.

One of our first excursions after our arrival at Bombay was to Elephanta, a small island situated within the harbour, and called by the natives Garapori. It is about five miles and a half from the Mahratta shore, appearing something like a long hill split in two, there being a low, narrow valley running between two abrupt eminences which skirt it on either side. The island is rather more than six miles in circumference, and uninhabited, except occasionally by a few miserable outcasts, who resort thither when they can find no more commodious shelter—such, at least, was the case when we visited it. About a furlong from the beach there used to stand a huge misshaped figure of an elephant, rudely carved from an immense mass of black rock, and from which the island received its modern name of Elephanta, given to it by the Portuguese. This figure has now fallen. The engraving represents it just as it stood previously to 1814, when the head and neck dropped off; it is, I believe, the only representation that has ever been given. This colossal sculpture, when I last saw it, was surrounded with so thick a growth of underwood that I had some difficulty in making my way to it. While I was passing under its body, I heard a sharp, modulated sound, so unusual that it caused me to start, and on turning suddenly round, I saw a large green lizard, nearly a foot long, which crawled into the grass, and I lost all further sight of it. I made some inquiries about the existence of such an animal on this island, for it struck me that it must have been a species of the Gecko, so well known in Egypt as a poisonous lizard; but I could not obtain any satisfactory information upon the subject, for no one seemed to be conscious of the existence of such an animal. I nevertheless felt satisfied in my own mind that I had seen one of those venemous reptiles. The Egyptian Gecko is a creature of so singular a character that a description from the work of an eminent naturalist will not, I apprehend, be unwelcome to the reader.

"Of all the oviparous quadrupeds," says the Count de la Cépède, "this is the first which contains a deadly poison. Nature, in this instance, appears to act against herself. In a lizard, whose species is but too prolific, she exalts a corrosive liquor to such a degree as to carry corruption and dissolution among all animals into which this active humour may penetrate: one might say, she prepares in the Gecko only death and annihilation. This deadly lizard, which deserves all our attention on account of its dangerous properties, has some resemblance to the cameleon; its head, almost triangular, is large in comparison with its body; the eyes are very large; the tongue flat, covered with small scales, and the end is rounded. The teeth are sharp, and so strong, that, according to Bontius, they are able to make impressions on the hardest substances—even on steel. The Gecko is almost entirely covered with little warts, more or less rising; the under part of the thighs is furnished with a row of tubercles, raised and grooved; the feet are remarkable for oval scales, more or less hollowed in the middle, as large as the under surface of the toes themselves, and regularly disposed one over another, like the slates on the roof of a house. The tail of the Gecko is commonly rather longer than the body, though sometimes not so long; it is round, thin, and covered with rings or circular bands, formed of several rows of very small scales. The colour of the Gecko is a clear green, spotted with brilliant red. The name Gecko imitates the cry of this animal, which is heard especially before rain. It is found in Egypt, in India, at Amboyna, and the Moluccas. It inhabits by choice the crevices of half-rotten trees, as well as humid places. It is sometimes met with in houses, where it occasions great alarm, and where every exertion is used to destroy it speedily. Bontius writes that its bite is so venemous that, if the part bitten is not cut away or burned, death ensues in a few hours."

The following is the account of Bontius:—"This creature, which is not only found in Brazil, but also in the isle of Java, belonging to the East Indies, and which by our people is called Gekko, from its constant cry, is properly an Indian salamander. It is about a foot long; its skin is of a pale or sea-green colour, with red spots. The head is not unlike that of a tortoise, with a straight mouth. The eyes are very large, starting out of the head, with long and small eye-apples.* The tail is distinguished by several white rings. Its teeth are so sharp as to make an impression even on steel. Each of its four legs has crooked claws, armed at the ends with nails. Its gait is very slow; but wherever it fastens it is not easily removed. It dwells commonly upon rotten trees, or among the ruins of old houses and churches. It oftentimes settles near the bedsteads, which makes the Moors sometimes pull down their huts. Its constant cry is gekko; but before it begins, it makes a kind of hissing noise. The sting† of this creature is so venemous that the wound proves mortal, unless it be immediately burnt with a red-hot iron or cut off. The blood is of a palish colour, resembling poison itself.

"The Javanese used to dip their arrows into the blood of this creature; and those who deal in poison among them,—an art much esteemed in Java by both sexes,—hang it up, with a string tied to the tail, on the ceiling; by which means, it being exasperated to the highest pitch, sends forth a yellow liquor out of its mouth, which they gather in small pots set underneath, and afterwards coagulate into a body in the sun. This they continue for several months together, by giving daily food to the creature. It is unquestionably the strongest poison in the world. The urine of this animal is of so corrosive a quality, that it not only raises blisters wherever it touches the skin, but turns the flesh black and causes a gangrene."‡ The

* Eye-balls.

† It has no sting, but bites.

‡ A rather singular circumstance occurred whilst I was upon a journey from Bombay to Poonah. Having slept under a tent at

inhabitants of the East Indies say that the best remedy against this poison is the curcumie root. Such a Gekko had got within the body of the wall of the church in the Receif, which obliged us to have a great hole made in the said wall to dislodge it from thence."*

After rain, the Gecko quits its retreat; its walk is not very quick; it catches ants and worms. The eggs of this creature are oval, and commonly as large as a hazel-nut. The female covers them carefully with a slight shelter of earth, and the heat of the sun hatches them. The Jesuit mathematicians sent into the East Indies by Louis the Fourteenth have described a lizard in the kingdom of Siam, named Tokaie, which is evidently the same as the Gecko. That which they examined exceeded one foot in length to the end of the tail. The name Tokaie, like that of Gecko, is an imitation of sounds made by the creature.

Hasselquist writes thus concerning the Gecko. "It is very common at Cairo, as well in the houses as without. The venom of this animal has a singularity, in that it issues from the balls of its toes. It seeks all places and things where salt has been employed; and where it has walked over them, this dangerous venom marks the track. In the month of July 1750,

Panwell—a low, swampy station, a few miles from the presidency—upon rising in the morning I discovered a black spot upon my forehead, the size of a sixpence. It appeared exactly as if the skin had been seared, and was rather tender, though not so much so as to cause me any inconvenience. It continued for nearly a month, during which period a new skin formed over the spot. What had produced it I never could ascertain.

* See Churchill's voyages, vol. ii. p. 12.

I saw two women and a girl at Cairo who narrowly escaped death from having eaten cheese upon which this animal had shed its venom. I had another occasion at Cairo of being convinced of the sharpness of its venom, as it ran off the hand of a man who was endeavouring to catch it; his hand was instantly covered with red inflamed pustules, attended by a sensation like that which is caused by the stinging of a nettle. It croaks at night almost like a frog."

This reptile yields in malignity to no serpent whatever. Foskall, the Danish naturalist, says of it,—"The Gecko is called in Egypt, Abu Burs, 'Father of Leprosy,' that is, extremely leprous: at Aleppo, simply Burs, 'Leprosy.' It is frequent in the houses at Cairo; wanders about in summer weather; has much the same squeak as a weasel; is not much seen in winter, but hides itself in the roofs of houses, and reappears in the middle of March. If the tail be separated from the living animal, it will give signs of life and motion half an hour afterwards. They say this lizard hunts and lives on poultry. Its name is said to be derived from its properties; for if it drops any of its spittle on salt intended for the table, it would produce a leprosy on any man who should partake of it; for this reason they carefully put away salt, or keep an onion by it, which the lizard cannot bear. Others think its name is taken from the resemblance of its colour to that of a leper."

It is remarkable that, notwithstanding the ample account furnished of this reptile, there is no evidence whether it has the fang-teeth of venemous serpents, or whether, being imbued with venom throughout, it

Drawn by W. Daniell R.A. Engraved by John Pye.

Entrance to the Caves of Elephanta

poisons by its touch, its exudations, and its saliva, and no otherwise. Bontius speaks of its bite or sting. It has recently been ascertained that the Ornithorinchus paradoxus of New Holland possesses a venom, emitted from the spurs with which Nature has furnished it.*

Upon quitting the stone elephant, we ascended the hill in our palenkeens by a steep path, and about midday came to the first cave, which is merely a small unfinished chamber, supported by two pillars. It possesses no feature to engage the traveller's attention. About a third further up the hill, the principal cavern opens upon the view, as you ascend a narrow path thickly wooded on either side. The entrance of this excavation is less imposing, when first seen, than might be expected, and generally disappoints the traveller. It is low, and the face of the rock from which it is hewn is so broken as entirely to destroy all beauty of proportion; but when you are sufficiently near to look into the temple, the sight is truly imposing. You see a vast chamber cut out of the solid rock, the roof supported by rows of beautiful columns, the capitals of each forming a cushion, so admirably cut as to appear as if yielding to the weight of the superincumbent mountain. The principal temple is surrounded by handsome colonnades, the pillars of which are carved with great delicacy. It is a square apartment, and every side is covered with groups of figures in alto-relief. At the bottom, facing the vestibule, in a recess about the centre, is a colossal bust with three faces, which are upwards of five feet in length; the whole

* See Calmet's Dictionary of the Bible, 4to. Fragments. Vol. iv.

statue being six yards high. It is supposed to represent the Hindoo triad—Brahma, Vishnu, and Siva. This, however, has been questioned by some modern inquirers, who, I think, appear to have left the matter precisely as they found it.

The area of the temple is a hundred and thirty feet long by one hundred and twenty-three broad, the roof being originally supported by twenty-six pillars and sixteen pilasters: of the former, eight are broken and several others much mutilated. The height of the chamber varies from fifteen to eighteen feet. The walls are covered with gigantic figures in alto-relief, many of which exhibit great nicety of proportion and no mean skill of execution. The groups have all a reference to the mythology of the Brahmins; while the caverns of Kenneri and Carli, in the neighbourhood, are decidedly Buddhist temples. All the Hindoo deities have peculiar symbols belonging exclusively to each, by which they may be recognised as readily as ancient families in Europe by their armorial bearings. "This temple," says Mr. Moore, "may be called a complete Pantheon; for among the hundreds—I may say thousands, of figures there sculptured, every principal deity is found. Many deified heroes in the more modern mythological romances, contained in some of the Puranas and Tantras, will have been exalted since the excavation of this wonderful cavern; but I strongly believe that all the gods of the Vedas, or, if I may so term them, all the legitimate Hindoo deities, will be found in its different compartments, if not indeed too much defaced for recognition."*

* Hindoo Pantheon, p. 241.

There is one piece of sculpture in a recess of this temple remarkable for the spirit and beauty of its execution; it is a colossal figure, fourteen feet high, representing the Siva Vindex of the Hindoo Pantheon. It has been much mutilated by the Portuguese, the whole of the lower extremities having been completely broken away; nevertheless sufficient remains to give a just idea of this fine sculpture. The expression of the countenance is admirable, exhibiting an unrelenting ferocity, characteristic of the divinity which it pourtrays, yet blending with that ferocity a certain majesty that seems to elevate it above the vulgar brutality of human passion. It originally had eight arms, several of which are now broken, and is marked with the awful insignia of an avenging deity. There are many other statues of equal size, but I think none of equal beauty as a work of art.

When Bishop Heber visited this cavern, he confesses that his expectations, though highly raised, were much exceeded by the reality. "Both the dimensions, the proportions, and the sculptures," says he, "seemed to me to be of a more noble character and a more elegant execution than I had been led to suppose. Even the statues are executed with great spirit, and are some of them of no common beauty, considering their dilapidated condition and the coarseness of their material." Here full justice is done to this extraordinary excavation; but with an unaccountable departure from his general mild and gentle caution, that amiable and really great man comes to the hasty and unauthorised conclusion that the temple caves at Elephanta are not of extreme antiquity. The following are among his chief reasons for such a decision.

"The rock out of which the temple is carved is by no means calculated to resist, for any great length of time, the ravages of the weather. It evidently suffers much from the annual rains; a great number of the pillars, nearly one-third of the whole, have been undermined by the accumulation of water in the cavern; and the capitals of some, and part of the shafts of others, remain suspended from the tops like huge stalactites, the bases having completely mouldered away. The ravages are said to have greatly increased in the memory of persons now resident in Bombay, though for many years back the cave has been protected from wanton dilapidation, and though the sculptures, rather than the pillars, would probably have suffered from that vulgar love of knick-knacks and specimens which prevails among the English more than most nations of the world."

After stating a few other reasons of much less weight, the amiable and learned bishop comes to the following conclusion:—"On the whole, in the perfect absence of any inscription or tradition which might guide us, we may assign to Elephanta any date we please. It may be as old as the Parthenon, or it may be as modern as Henry the Seventh's chapel; but though the truth, probably, lies between the two—I am certainly not disposed to assign to it any great degree of antiquity."

It may be worth while to examine these corollaries, and the premises from which they are drawn. In the first place, the assertion, that "the rock out of which the temple is carved is by no means calculated to resist for any great length of time the ravages of the weather," is altogether gratuitous. Nothing appears in the cavern itself to establish this fact; for the dilapidated state of the pillars and statues does not proceed, as Bishop Heber supposed, from the gradual process of decay, but from external violence. It is a well known fact, that the first settlers among the Portuguese, in their blind zeal against idolatry, defaced many of these Hindoo temples, exercising upon them the rage of intemperate bigotry. In the caves of Elephanta and Salsette, they kindled fires at the bases of the columns, and when these were in a state of red heat, suddenly threw water upon them, by which process they subverted a great number and mutilated many more. Instead, therefore, of the columns having mouldered away to their capitals, they have been rudely thrown down by physical agency, and some of those which remain are at this moment so perfect as entirely to overthrow the bishop's conclusion; since, if the progress of decay has been so rapid as to have greatly increased in the memory of many living men, and some of the pillars have been so strongly acted upon as to have entirely mouldered away, it cannot be likely that any one pillar in the cavern should have escaped the operation of its own inherent principle of decay. Supposing, for a moment, that this cavern is not of greater antiquity than Bishop Heber imagines,—say fifteen hundred years,—still, if the mouldering is so rapid as to be perceptible by persons now living, the whole structure would have been one heap of ruins long before the lapse of half the number of ages which the learned prelate admits it most probably to have existed. I confess I am among those who lean to the arguments which have been advanced in favour of the extreme antiquity of these excavations, and am inclined to assign to them as remote a date as those which have been so long celebrated in Upper Egypt.

The great temple at Elephanta is no longer employed as a sanctuary of devotion by the Hindoos, which is to my mind an additional presumption that it is not comparatively a modern structure; as such structures would be much less likely to be deserted than those of which the origin is cast back into the remotest antiquity, when the world was still in its youth, and consequently the habits and manners of men, by comparison, in a state of infancy.

We spent an entire day in this interesting cavern, not returning to Bombay until after sunset. Another party besides ours had visited the island, whom we had joined, and passed quite a convivial day together. Among the latter was an officer, with an attendant, who happened to have great personal attachment towards him, in consequence, as I understood, of some service which the former had rendered him under circumstances of peculiar embarrassment. This man was altogether a remarkable person; he was a Catti, a tribe of which Captain Macmurdo has given the following characteristic account:—"The Catti differs in some respects from the Rajpoot; he is more cruel in his disposition, but far exceeds him in the virtue of bravery; and a character possessed of more bravery than a Catti does not exist. His size is considerably larger than common,—often exceeding six feet. He is sometimes seen with light hair and blue-coloured eyes. His frame is athletic and bony, and particularly well adapted to his mode of life. His countenance is expressive, but of the worst kind; being harsh, and often destitute of a single mild feature."

This description perfectly agreed with the man to whom I have alluded, with the exception only of the expression of his countenance, which was handsome, and betokened nothing either harsh or unfeeling; on the contrary, his whole demeanour, though indicating extreme decision of character, was gentle and courteous. The officer whom he attended mentioned his extraordinary dexterity in the use of his weapons; as a proof of which, he engaged that the Catti, armed only with a stout bamboo, should defend himself against the united attack of any four natives, armed with swords, or whatever weapons they might choose to select, except firearms and missiles.

The man readily agreed to undertake so unequal a contest, when four of our followers were selected, and armed with heavy sabres. A square place was marked out as the lists, in which the combatants were to display their dexterity. The conflict was short and decisive. In a few seconds, the Catti, having prostrated two of the swordsmen, the two others declined any further trial of skill. His dexterity, strength, and quickness were amazing; he baffled his antagonists at every turn, displaying uncommon adroitness in the exercise of his bloodless bamboo. His opponents seemed astounded at his prowess, and were glad to relinquish the contest.

We did not reach Bombay until some time after sunset.

CHAPTER XX.

SALSETTE.—ELEPHANT HUNT.

Our next excursion was to Salsette, an island eighteen miles long and thirteen broad, united to Bombay by a causeway built while Mr. Duncan was governor of the presidency. The island of Salsette was formerly a place of great sanctity, having numerous rock temples hollowed out of its hills, two or three of which are of great splendour. About the centre of the island is an artillery station, beyond which the country, before dull and uninteresting, becomes more picturesque. The greater part of the land is covered with a thick jungle, from which numerous hills arise, chiefly composed of granite, without order or uniformity, and imparting an agreeable variety to the otherwise monotonous prospect. The forests abound with tigers and other beasts of prey, so much so that solitary travelling in this island is at all times dangerous. In consequence of the valleys being narrow, enclosed by lofty hills, and covered with a thick forest, Salsette is very unhealthy. It was here that the seeds of that fatal malady were received which deprived Jacquemont, the French naturalist, of his life, and science of a valuable labourer.

The hamlets are chiefly composed of a few miserable huts, scarcely deserving the name of villages, and inhabited by the destitute among the poorest Hindoos. Tanna, the capital, is a considerable town, populous, and with an aspect of prosperity that renders it a cheerful residence to about a hundred European soldiers who have retired from the service and settled there with their families. The entire population of Salsette is estimated at fifty thousand souls; and the inhabitants generally, though the large majority of them are destitute to the last degree, are so peaceable, that in the year 1813, it was stated by the magistrate, that for upwards of two years no native of the island had been committed for trial. The dialect of the people is a strange jargon, being a mixture of several native dialects combined often with a barbarous English, which renders them altogether unintelligible to a stranger.

Our halt for the night was in a small valley entirely surrounded by hills. It was a romantic spot, partially cleared from the jungle, and in the centre grew a small but vigorous banyan tree. Beneath its shade our followers quietly took up their quarters, having first prepared their curries, and refreshed themselves after a hot and painful march.

A party of Nautch girls, on their way to Tanna, entertained our party with the native dance and song. As I gazed on the really merry scene I could not help feeling with the Arabian poet,*

> " But ah ! thou know'st not in what youthful play,
> Our nights, beguil'd with pleasure, pass'd away ;

* Lebid.

Gay songs and cheerful tales deceiv'd the time,
And circling goblets made a tuneful chime;
Sweet was the draught, and sweet the blooming maid,
Who touch'd her lyre beneath the fragrant shade.
We sipp'd till morning purpled every plain,
The damsels slumber'd, but we sipp'd again:
The waking birds that sang on every tree,
Their early notes, were not so blithe as we."

On the following morning we proceeded to the mountain in which the celebrated caves are excavated; these are so numerous, that the principal hill is literally perforated like a honeycomb. The road was so rugged and narrow as to render the progress of our palenkeen-bearers slow and difficult.

Although obliged to proceed singly all the way, we were amply repaid in the issue for the difficulties and toil of our journey. The excavations in this hill are not only numerous, but likewise remarkable for their rich and elaborate decorations. One of the caves, a large chamber nearly square, and covered with magnificent carving, is called the durbar;—no doubt from its appropriation to certain purposes of state during the time that this island was under the Mahomedan domination.

The principal temple in the series is really a splendid thing of its kind, and was converted by the Portuguese into a place of Christian worship. You ascend to the entrance by a few steps, when you advance into a lofty portico bounded externally by a richly carved parapet. On one side is a high pillar surmounted by three lions rudely carved, but still in good preservation. The main props of the roof of the vestibule are two square thin columns, the shafts of

Entrance to the large cave at Salsette

which are not distinguished by the slightest ornament. Upon entering the temple you are struck by the extreme exuberance of the sculpture. It is larger than the Elephanta cavern, and much more lofty. A splendid colonnade of octagonal pillars decorates three sides of the area, which forms a parallelogram. Some of these pillars are elaborately wrought, others are comparatively plain, though none are without ornament.

The roof is vaulted, there being circular ribs of teak wood corresponding with the arch, and extending nearly to the capitals of the columns on either side. For what purpose they were placed there does not appear, though Bishop Heber takes them to be an argument against the remote antiquity of the cavern; but this is about as conclusive an argument as to say that Windsor Chapel was not built before the reign of Charles the Second, because some of the ornaments of the choir were carved by Gibbon, who was born during the reign of that monarch. The teak ribs may have been added since the temple was excavated; or if they have existed without showing signs of decay for sixteen or eighteen hundred years, the latest probable date assigned even by Bishop Heber himself to these excavations, there surely can be nothing to obviate the inference that their existence may not have doubled that period.

In this beautiful chamber we passed the night; and by way of affording the reader some entertainment while he supposes us to be taking our rest, I will give a description of an elephant hunt, just communicated to me by Mr. Benjamin Torin, at which a friend of his, Mr. Nathaniel Kindersley, was present, and of which he sent him the account. I give it pretty nearly in Mr. Kindersley's own words.

Here I am again at Periacolum; and now that I have ample leisure I shall give you a minute account of an elephant hunt, at which I was present. It is one of the most magnificent spectacles that can be imagined. I arrived at the pits just as the day broke on the ninth of the present month, and having desired that none of my establishment should accompany me, orders were immediately issued for drawing the elephants up. I ran to the summit of a hill forming one side of the entrance into the enclosure prepared to receive the herd, and a finer scene I never witnessed. The sun had not yet risen; and there lay a valley before us extending several miles, enclosed on either side by a wall of hills, like those of Courtallum, the whole covered with heavy forest jungle.

I stood upon an elevation which commanded a complete view of the scene. There was a line of fires more than a mile in extent, kept up by upwards of three thousand people, by which the herd of elephants was surrounded, being gradually urged towards the enclosure by the fiery circle narrowing upon them, from which they retreated in terror. What little wind there was blew from the north, and the light feathery smoke lay upon the tops of the trees like a thin mist, overspreading the whole southern part of the valley, but leaving the enclosure perfectly clear.

The summits of the hills were covered as usual with those morning vapours which in this country produce that nameless singularity of effect when the slanting beams of the rising sun penetrate their unsubstantial bosoms, and become refracted in ten thousand varying hues over the smiling landscape. Everything was so still that, but for the operations of the men in the valley, who formed the line of which I have spoken, Nature might be said to be not yet roused from her repose. The general calm opposed a striking contrast to the close array of hunters actively employed in accelerating the motions of those gigantic creatures which were about to be entrapped. Groups of armed men were warming themselves over the expiring embers of watch-fires that had been kindled in different passes of the hills, where they had been placed as guards lest any of the herd should attempt those passes. Their position was picturesque; and while their arms occasionally reflected a sudden blaze of the dying fires excited by their breath, the dim outline of their figures, robed in white tunics, placed in direct relief against the dark clothing of the hills, would have furnished a fit subject for the pencil of the sublime and terrible Neapolitan.*

Not an elephant was yet to be seen, but an occasional roar from the jungle announced that the herd was gradually approaching the snare. As soon as the order for driving them forward reached the line, there was a general and busy stir. The fires brightened, and the important business of cooking for the multitude commenced previously to opening the grand act of the drama,—that of securing the elephants within the enclosure. This was a large space, surrounded by a deep ditch, except at the entrance,

* Salvator Rosa.

nearly two yards broad, and several feet deep. Within this ditch was a low railing of strong pointed stakes, rising full eighteen inches from the surface of the ground. At the lower end of the enclosure were a number of deep pits not more than two feet apart, and covered with light materials, but so skilfully as to resemble the ground. The jungle within the railed area was extremely thick, and preserved with great care, in order to divert the animals' attention, as they advanced towards the snare into which they were hastening; for their perception of danger is so acute that it is a difficult matter to baffle it; and even under circumstances similar to those which I am now detailing, I imagine it would be next to impossible to entrap them, if they were not thrown off their guard by their terrors.

The driving commenced at nine o'clock in the morning, the sun pouring a clear broad flood of light upon the scene, tinging the hollows of the mountains, and clothing in one broad mass of radiance their tall but well wooded summits. Tomtoms, horns, shouts, muskets, and rockets were employed to urge forward the refractory herd, which had become exceedingly excited by the close proximity of the fires. The prodigious roaring of these huge creatures, uniting with the din raised by the hunters, produced such a hurly-burly that I was nearly stunned. I now changed my situation, placing myself upon an elevation above the opposite angle of the entrance towards which the elephants were rapidly but reluctantly progressing.

After some time the herd crossed a vista of the forest, where a rude road had been cut. They passed in battalions. In the first division I counted twenty-five. This was succeeded by a second and a third, the whole amounting at least to seventy elephants. You may imagine what a fine sight it was to behold so many of those stupendous creatures in a state of nature, varying in height from two to fourteen feet. At length a huge male stalked majestically from the jungle, bringing up the rear and occasionally turning round upon its pursuers with a most menacing aspect; but its contemplated aggression was repelled by the line of fires. Nothing, however, could induce it to advance beyond the vista. There it made a sudden pause, and sounding an alarm with that shrill note peculiar to the elephant, and which is called trumpeting, the whole herd instantly faced about, set up a terrible roar, and vigorously charged the line; the larger leading the charge in single file, and the smaller following with all speed, the jungle crashing before them, and their determination appearing so fierce that I trembled for the men opposed to this tremendous array of strength and desperation.

The beaters redoubled the din of their tomtoms, horns, and other clamorous instruments, while the musketeers tried to check the career of the elephants by smart volleys; still nothing could stop them until they were brought up by the line of fires. This was repeated three times, but the desperate creatures were as often driven back, until they grew weary of such ineffectual efforts, and remained still, as if determined calmly to await the issue. At length it was announced that four large and three small elephants had entered the snare; but as it would have been impossible to close the entrance upon them without excluding their companions, and thus giving them a chance of escape, we determined, as the most prudent course, to despatch them forthwith. In less than a quarter of an hour three were shot dead. The young ones fell into the pits, but one of the four old ones made its escape through the entrance with six or eight balls in its head.

The driving was tried again towards evening, and there is no doubt we should have secured them all in the course of the night, had not a fire unfortunately broke out which threatened the entrance of the enclosure. This was, nevertheless, prevented, though it burned with great rapidity and fierceness. Extraordinary exertions were used, but nothing could arrest its progress north and east, quite down to the edge of the enclosure, where it was stopped by the ditch. It was not got under until past midnight; thus many hours were lost, for there was no chance of being able to urge the elephants forward in the face of such an awful conflagration. Quiet, however, being at length restored, we anxiously looked forward to the morrow with hopes of more confirmed success. As you may suppose, we passed an anxious night. The least shift of the wind would have at once rendered all future efforts fruitless, and thus have baffled our anxious expectations. With the dawn it was discovered that a large male bison had fallen into one of the pits, and a noble creature it was. Its pugnacious appearance, combining ponderous strength with extreme activity, its clear dark brown coat as glossy as that of a sleek Arabian charger, its ample and majestic horns rising from its forehead like a glory, the round, bright, full eye glowing with noble ferocity, and seeming to beam with a glance of ardent indignation at being thus entrapped in a pit, and thereby rendered unable to show its desperate powers of retaliation, altogether impressed me with a feeling amounting to respect for the bovine species—of which this animal may certainly be considered the monarch —such as I had never before entertained.

I forgot to mention, that the day before, about noon, a single elephant rushed into the enclosure. It was quite frantic, threatening to charge the fence, which there was reason to apprehend it would break down, as this happened to be weak in that spot before which the creature stood with a fearful aspect of mischief. We were all instantly upon the alert; and I, being the most active, was the first to get a shot at the enraged animal, and dropped it headlong into the ditch, quite dead, with a single ball. It was not above five yards from me when I fired, and being so large a mark I could not well miss taking a fatal aim; there was, however, something awful in such a gigantic creature all rage and strength, in one instant converted from a stupendous exemplar of the living principle, into a mere huge mass of inanimate flesh, bones, and sinews.

In the evening of the 10th the whole herd, with the exception of the large male already spoken of, and one or two others, crossed the vista, where their retreat was immediately cut off by a line of fires. Thus hemmed in, they had no alternative but to try the pass, and about sunset the first elephant went through. A more interesting moment cannot be imagined. I am unable to tell you my feelings; the mental excitement —the feverish glow of spirits—the rush and bounding of the blood from the heart to the very extremities, palpably felt, and impelling action by an irresistible physical impulse, all beyond the power of description. Everything was now secure. The beaters, pressing on the herd, hurried them forward with tremendous outcries, and, in the course of twenty minutes, sixty-four elephants were securely lodged within the snare. The scene was truly awful; the whole number enclosed rushed simultaneously towards the stakes, bellowing, roaring, shrieking, and manifesting every symptom of violent fury. The foremost being checked in their precipitate career, gave the shrill scream of alarm, and endeavoured to retreat, but it was too late. They had advanced into the toil, and there was no chance of escape. Blue-lights, rockets, muskets, and fire, were severally seen through the dusk, creating a confusion and uproar not to be described.

Several young elephants had been rolled into the pits at the first rush. As it was now too late to proceed further in accomplishing the objects of the hunt, arrangements were made for securing the prisoners during the night. In order the better to effect this, the whole enclosure was surrounded by natives, fires were lighted, and a constant watch was kept. Scarcely a minute elapsed without some attempt being made by the captives to effect their escape; and three separate charges were tried by the whole body upon the entrance of the snare, but they were successfully repelled by the fires and musketeers, placed behind the fence to guard this important pass. We were sleeping, or, I should rather say, supposed to be sleeping, in our clothes, and ready for action, within ten yards of all this mighty turmoil. In the morning, we found that the whole of the jungle, which nearly covered their prison, had been cleared during the night by the elephants, save only some large trees, that defied both their strength and sagacity.

The work of destruction commenced at a few minutes after six o'clock, and by eleven the whole of the larger elephants were killed. It was a frightful scene of carnage. The number destroyed was sixty, and thirteen only were saved. We were all glad when it was over, for the slaughter had at last become truly horrible. The ground was strewed with gigantic carcases, and never did I see so frightful an array of death. The resistance was now confined to one or two of the larger elephants, which were speedily despatched. After this monstrous carnage, nothing remained but to secure the younger prisoners, which was readily accomplished by driving them into the pits, and having fastened a rope to the neck and hind-leg of each, these pits were gradually filled with bundles of straw, allowing the captives by degrees to step higher and higher towards the surface, until they were able to walk out of their prisons. They were then made fast to trees, and we began to try a more familiar acquaintance with them by giving them water-plantains and sugar-cane; by these and similar means some of them were rendered comparatively docile in a few hours, whilst others continued refractory for several days. The most refractory, however, were easily tamed.

As the bodies of the first day's victims were becoming very offensive, we changed our quarters, moving off to a place about five miles' distance from the pits. I started from Madura that night, rejoiced to quit a scene which had fatigued me exceedingly, and produced a painful excess of excitement which I was glad to have the opportunity of abating by repose.

The only accidents that had occurred during this formidable hunt were two, at least of a serious nature. One poor fellow had his leg fractured by an elephant, which charged him in the plain before the herd was secured within the snare; and a palenkeen-bearer's arm was broken by a musket-ball. It is really astonishing that so few accidents happened, when the number of people employed is considered—not less in the whole than four thousand, and that for twelve days—together with the nature of the sport, and the extreme hazard to which every individual employed is necessarily exposed. You will probably recollect my reading to you part of a newspaper account of the destruction of an elephant at Exeter Change, when some fifty persons, and amongst them a file of soldiers, took a whole day to despatch it. Now we, in an enclosure not more than two hundred yards in diameter, destroyed fifty elephants in about five hours, and certainly forty-five of them were killed by five persons. I send you the tail of a large elephant, that fell instantly dead to a two-ounce shot of mine at a distance of seventy yards. It had been previously knocked down twice, but rose again. We counted seventeen balls in the front and on one side of its skull after it was dead; allowing four only for the side on which it lay, it had received twenty-one balls in its head before it finally fell to rise no more.

I dare say you have now had quite enough of the hunt, and so have I, nor shall I ever feel any desire to see another; at the same time, I would not have missed this, as an opportunity may probably never again occur of witnessing so grand a one.

CHAPTER XXI.

CAVERN TEMPLES AT SALSETTE.

THE following morning I took my gun, with a determination to try the jungle for game, but previously amused myself with examining some of the smaller excavations. I found that these abounded to an extent scarcely credible, but all that I entered were, in every respect, vastly inferior to the large cavern already described. The sculptures were fewer, and of a much meaner order, though occasionally there were some striking groups to be seen—illustrating the mysteries of Buddhism, to which these caves were, by universal consent, originally dedicated.

From the portico of one of the caverns the prospect is singularly striking. A long ledge, of several feet in width, supported at either end by the solid rock from which it is cut, protects the spectator from the influence of the sun, and allows him to enjoy without inconvenience the beauties of a scene remarkable for its peculiarity and grandeur. The portico is terminated towards the body of the building by a row of tall, massive columns, gracefully proportioned, and with no ornament, except on the bases and capitals. With the superincumbent ledge, which they support, they form a vestibule of great elegance. Under its

The upper caves, Salsette

grateful shade I stood for some minutes, contemplating the splendour of the view around me, beholding everywhere a mighty record of God's omnipotence. It is hardly possible to imagine how frequently this conviction is forced upon the mind while travelling in this magnificent country—for here the prodigies of Art bear a sort of collateral testimony to the wonders of Nature; but yet, how does the vast and stately grandeur of the mountain, crowned with everlasting snow, rising in solemn dignity from the plain, with all its accompaniments of animal, vegetable, and mineral production, and projecting its lofty crest into the clouds, as if to hold communion with beings of a higher world—how does it bring down to the lowest extreme of comparative insignificance the mightiest productions of human labour! It is clear that Nature has everywhere furnished the elements of Art; the one is an accessory to the other; and consequently, wherever Art prevails in its greater dignity and success, the glories of Nature are heightened to the contemplations of the philosopher, and even to the commonest admirer of the Creator's works!

In no country upon earth, not even excepting Upper Egypt, have the prodigious powers of the human mind been displayed to a greater extent than in India; and I confess I never entertained so exalted an idea of human capability as it deserves until I had witnessed those stupendous productions of man's ingenuity, so frequently presented to the traveller's eye on the peninsula of Hindostan.

Struck by the scene before me, I sat myself down upon a stone under the rocky porch of the cavern.

Before me gushed a narrow but deep stream, which tumbled down the mountain in a broken line, appearing at the distance like a narrow stripe of silver lace upon a green velvet mantle, but, upon a nearer approach, bounding and hissing over opposing rocks with the force and energy of "a thing of life." Just before it reached the place where I had seated myself, its waters gurgled and fried over a bed of rocks, which formed a considerable slope in the hill, and produced a cascade that sung one of Nature's lullabies with a far more sublime, if with a less harmonious, cadence than babbling brooks. As I sat in this romantic shade, I felt

> "The freshness of the breeze that sweeps the blossoms
> And wafts around the champaka's perfume,
> Breathing melodious with the buzz of bees
> That cluster in the buds, and with the song
> The köil warbles thick and hurried forth,
> As on the mangoe's flowery top he sits,
> And, all inebriate with its nectar, sings."

On the right of this picturesque waterfall was a deep glen, in which the growth was so close that there the tiger roamed undisturbed and made his lair, without fear of intrusion from a human foe. Across the stream was an abrupt conical hill, in the bosom of which a small cave-temple had been hollowed. It had a low square portico, supported upon three plain pillars. There was nothing in the interior, which I afterwards examined, to attract attention. Its appearance was sufficiently striking from the opposite portico, under which I was sitting. Some of our party had taken their station near the summit of the hill, in order to enjoy with less interruption the surrounding prospect. Our attendants were dispersed hither and thither; a group of them standing before the entrance of the smaller excavation, some sleeping under the shade in the natural recesses of the hill, and others threading the jungle in pursuit of game.

After I had received all the enjoyment from my reflections which they were capable of affording, I descended the mount, and entered a thicket in the valley below, which led me into an almost impassable forest. Here and there, however, were comparatively clear patches, and occasionally spots under cultivation, where I had the common sport of partridge and quail shooting, and contrived to kill a couple of hares. Having shot as much game as I thought would be useful, I desired the attendant who accompanied me to take it to the cavern; whilst I proceeded further into the jungle; but I was careful not to lose sight of certain localities, which indicated my situation and the way by which I was to return.

I had a double-barrel gun made by Mortimer, one barrel of which was charged with shot and the other with ball;—a practice I invariably observed, lest a deer or some large game should cross my path upon which small shot could make no effectual impression. The growth was so thick in some places, that I could scarcely advance, and I at length grew so tired of the little progress I made, in proportion to the labour employed, that I resolved to return. I had advanced but a short way towards the entrance of the wood, when, to my surprise, I saw a tiger leisurely crossing the path, within ten yards of the spot upon which I was standing. My uneasiness was considerable at seeing myself within reach of a creature whose powers of mischief are so formidable, and whose method of destruction is so summary. I was quite alone, but my gun was, at least, a probable protection. To my great gratification, the tiger passed on its way without attempting to molest me.

The jungle through which it advanced was comparatively thin, so that I did not lose sight of the beautiful beast when it entered the thicket. The moment it crossed my path all sense of danger appeared to subside within me, and impelled by an impulse, as unaccountable as it was irresistible, I levelled my gun and fired. The ball told upon the tiger's hind-leg, which I could instantly perceive was broken; but the enraged animal, uttering an appalling yell, rushed from the thicket, and came bounding before me upon three legs with a restrained and unnatural motion, yet evincing a determination of revenge as difficult to avoid as it was imminent and menacing. I had no power of destroying my angry foe, as I had but one barrel loaded, and that was with common shot. There was no time to lose, for the creature was within a few yards of me; I therefore raised the gun to my shoulder, and knowing the tiger could not spring, allowed it to approach within six yards from where I stood, when I fired at its head, in the hope of blinding it. My fire made a signal impression, for the agonized beast rolled upon its back, yelling as if in dreadful agony. Meanwhile, seeing that it was still full of sturdy life, I threw my gun upon the ground near me, and climbing a tree, awaited the issue of my imprudent aggression. After the lapse of about a minute, the tiger rose and shook its head, still continuing to yell with frightful vehemence. I could perceive that its face was dreadfully lacerated by the shot; nevertheless it soon became evident that the wounded animal had not been totally blinded, for with a sudden sharp roar it shuffled towards the tree, the wounded leg dangling behind it perfectly useless.

When it reached the tree which I had ascended, to my consternation it attempted to scramble up the trunk; and as this was low and its branches numerous, I began to fear that I had calculated upon my security too soon. The ferocious brute was already upon the lower boughs, and I was beginning to think of some effectual mode of frustrating its savage design against me, when I perceived a charcoal-burner advancing armed with the instrument of his vocation. Reaching the spot where the tiger was still struggling to propel its ponderous body between the thick branches of the tree, on which I was already beginning to tremble for my life, he planted a well-directed stroke upon the creature's hind-leg that had not been wounded, and dividing the tendons, my enemy dropped powerless before him. With a deliberation that showed he was no novice at this sanguinary work, he despatched the now impotent animal by giving it one or two desperate gashes on the throat, which severed the windpipe, and soon laid it lifeless at his feet.

At my request he skinned it, and carried it behind me to the cavern, where I was greeted by the earnest congratulations of my friends, when they had heard the account of my escape; and giving the poor Hindoo a gold mohur,* he departed, so well satisfied that he declared he desired no better fortune than to encounter a tiger every day with a broken leg, if the reward of despatching it should be equal to that which he had just received.

We now prepared for our departure from this interesting island. It was still early, and the sun was very powerful, especially in the valleys, where its rays were caught and reflected by the bare face of the mountain; still, as a great part of our route lay through narrow paths, thickly overshadowed by the almost undisturbed growth of centuries, we were not much incommoded. Some of our party amused themselves with shooting, but I was not among the number, having already had sufficient sport for one day, and not having recovered from the excitement produced by the morning's peril.

We halted a day at Tanna, where there were some European officers, who received us with great hospitality; and when they heard of my encounter with the tiger, related several escapes still more narrow, thus completely blunting the edge of my adventure, which to me had been one of much alarm notwithstanding. Here we passed the night, and on the following morning returned to Bombay.

As the period of the monsoon was now near, I determined to take the opportunity of exploring this island and its immediate dependencies before the rains

* The value of the Bombay gold mohur is about thirty-five shillings.

should set in. I did not, however, see much worth recording. Beyond the city within the fort, and the fort itself, there is little to engage a traveller's attention. The black town is large and populous, but the streets are narrow, the houses low, mean, and filthy; in short, its whole aspect excites impressions of great wretchedness and destitution among the larger proportion of its population, though this is really not the case: for there is a good deal of wealth, even amongst those whose dwellings present to the eye not only the absence of all comfort but the presence of much actual privation. The monotonous features which this town exhibits are somewhat relieved by a few European buildings, there being several Portuguese chapels and one or two Armenian churches.

The most conspicuous edifice is the jail. Here I saw a culprit condemned to death for murder. The man's aspect was sullen and ferocious. He was confined in a small cell, which opened into a narrow court, where he was allowed to walk by day, being locked up at night. He was eating his rice with an appetite and apparent relish that rather surprised me, hearing he was to be executed the following morning. I did not interrupt his meal, which he despatched with amazing promptitude. I then entered into conversation with him upon the nature of his crime, and endeavoured to ascertain his ideas of a state of future retribution. He was very morose, and unwilling to give any explanation of his feelings. When I urged him, he said, looking at me with a grim smile, "Can you furnish me with anything that will remove the bitters of death? My cup is prepared, and I must drink it!"

"No, indeed," said I, "I have no power to render your doom a welcome one, which would be the case if I could remove its bitters: but perhaps I might be able to impart some consolation to a wretched spirit."

"Those are idle words; such are the officious bablings of fools. What consolation can you impart who are in a far worse condition than I am? My time is come; what then remains for me but to die?"

"Do you not feel sorrow for the dreadful deed which has brought you into such a sad situation?"

"Why should I feel sorrow? He deserved the death I inflicted upon him. It was to be his doom, and I was to be the instrument of bringing it upon him. I am not to blame. It was my destiny, and I must die for it. What then? I shall but fulfil the conditions of my mortality."

His notions of predestination were so stubborn and rooted that I could not stir them; and he at length became exceedingly impatient. I left him to fortify himself for death, which, as I afterwards learned, he met on the following morning with sullen indifference, eating a large plate of rice immediately under the gallows, as he said scoffingly, to prepare him for his long journey.

Such is generally the brutal apathy with which Hindoo criminals expiate with their lives any capital violation of the laws. Though their love of life is extreme, and they will adopt every possible means to avoid the sad issue of humanity until Nature sends forth her summons, they nevertheless meet it when it unexpectedly comes upon them, with a factitious hardihood induced by those notions of absolute necessity which renders them stubborn predestinarians. This, however, is by no means universal among them; but, when the notion is entertained, it is inveterate, and almost invariably the belief of the profligate among their communities.

After quitting the murderer I was introduced by the keeper of the prison to a young officer confined for debt. It still wanted a full hour of noon; but he had evidently been indulging in "potations deep," as his speech was thick and his gait unsteady. He was quite a young man, as it struck me, about two-and-twenty. His face was flushed, his cheeks bloated, his eyes red and bloodshot, his dress disordered, his hair thick and uncombed, and his whole appearance bore visible notations of the burning brand of early debauchery. He invited me into his apartment, in which were two fractured chairs, a broken teak table, and a small camp bed. The floor was strewed with various articles of dress. Upon the table lay two or three fractured glasses, some cigars, a common native hookah without a mouthpiece;—in fact, every thing before me was a melancholy token of the worst habits,

> "And seemed to speak variety of wretchedness."

The young epicurean did not appear conscious that there was anything like misery in the world. His mirth was boisterous, his laugh incessant, his conversation voluble, and yet, amidst it all, there was a morbid indifference that seemed to have overlaid his youthful and elastic spirit like a cold wintry blight upon the opening primrose. I could find no room for mirth, though my companion assumed a gaiety foreign to his condition. He told me that his motto was " a short life and a merry one ;" that he had given and received fifteen shots within the last six months without a scratch on either side ; that it was, therefore, evident he was not to be the victim of gun-powder.

" I bear a charmed life !" said he, flourishing his clenched fist over his head ; and when this ebullition had subsided, with puffed cheeks that were one uniform tinge of deep crimson, his eye the while rolling dull and languid beneath the lid, he gulped a deep draught of arrack, slightly diluted with water.

Habits of intemperance were so confirmed in this unhappy youth, that he was never sober beyond three or four hours in the morning. The characters of death were already written legibly in his pursed and flaccid forehead. The worm was evidently at the root, but he seemed not to heed it, or, if he did, it gave him no concern. It was useless talking to such a man ; I therefore quitted him with a painful emotion of sorrow at the blight which had so sadly fallen upon him. Within a month from the time I saw him he was in his grave.

The most remarkable place in Bombay is Malabar Point, a conspicuous promontory, in which there is a large rift in the cliff. This is considered a sacred spot by pilgrims and other Hindoo visionaries who resort thither for the purposes of spiritual expurgation. By passing through this aperture they imagine that they obtain remission of their sins, and as it is rather narrow, the exility of the half-starved devotee renders that comparatively little laborious to him which is really a matter of difficulty to the more bulky sybarite. This act of devotion is attended with some danger during the monsoons, for the cliff being at a great elevation above the beach, and among rocks at no time easy of access, the lashing of the surge at their base, when the sea dashes over them, sometimes almost to the brow of the cliff, renders the footing of the penitentiary frequently precarious, and requires much caution to perform this act of silly superstition.

Near this spot is an agreeable village almost entirely inhabited by Brahmins, where there is a fine large tank, walled all round with beautiful masonry, with a descent to the water by a broad flight of stone steps. Here these holy men—holy at least by profession, if not by nature—pass their lives in indolent enjoyment, which for the most part consists in indulging, without stint, the suggestions of appetite. Some of them are said never to pass beyond the immediate neighbourhood of their homes, yet the spot is so healthy that they generally attain to a good old age.

Not far from Malabar Point stood the house formerly occupied by Mrs. Draper, the celebrated Maria of Sterne. This circumstance has consecrated it to a certain extent in the eyes of many persons; but there is nothing else to signalize it, and probably by this time it no longer exists, though when I left Bombay, it was still in a very habitable state, occupied by a subaltern officer and his family.

There is a large village at Bombay called Mazagong, entirely inhabited by Portuguese. Here the finest mangoes in India are produced. So much esteemed are they that they are sent to all the southern parts of the peninsula sufficiently near to obtain them in good preservation. The Portuguese have been exceedingly successful in cultivating this fruit, as the mango of Goa, a Portuguese settlement on the Malabar coast, next to that of Mazagong, is the most highly prized. It is said that those mangoes produced in the neighbourhood of this village had attained such celebrity during the reign of the Emperor Shah Jehan, as to be regularly sent to Delhi for the imperial table.

There are two plain but not inelegant Roman Catholic churches at Mazagong, and a convenient dock for vessels of small burthen. About eight miles from the capital, at the extremity of the island, is a small fort called Sion, built upon an elevation, which rises abruptly from the plain, something like a depressed sugar-loaf. This fort commands the frith between Bombay and Salsette, across which a causeway was built under the direction of Mr. Duncan, when governor, with a drawbridge in the centre, but too narrow for carriages to pass except in fine weather.

There is another small native town on this island called Mehim, situated on the northern side; it is chiefly distinguished by a Portuguese college for Roman Catholic priests, though nothing can be more contemptible as a seat of learning. This town and the adjacent villages contain a population of near sixteen thousand souls.

As the season had now advanced we engaged a

house on the beach, struck our tents, and took possession of our more substantial residence, where we remained with very little to vary the monotony of an in-door life during the period of the monsoon.

I have now brought the first series of this work to a close, and, as the two first volumes have obtained a popularity beyond what I had ever anticipated, I am anxious to contradict a report which has prevailed to my prejudice respecting the right of authorship. It has been rumoured that in this work I have merely arranged the materials supplied by my brother, the Reverend Richard Macdonald Caunter. Now, in order to check the tendency of such a rumour, I take this public opportunity of most unequivocally contradicting it, and declare that Mr. R. M. Caunter, so far from having furnished a single hint, did not even know of the existence of the Oriental Annual until the first volume was printed. The report, however originating, is a mischievous calumny; and I trust that those persons who have heard and believed it will receive this public assurance, that the whole of the volumes, quotations of course excepted, were exclusively written by me; and I entreat them further to believe that I am incapable of putting my name to a book which I did not write.

THE END.